PANORA

of Cities in the United States and Canada

PANORAMIC MAPS
of Cities in the United States and Canada

A Checklist of Maps
in the Collections of
the Library of Congress,
Geography and Map
Division

Second Edition
Compiled by
John R. Hébert;
revised by
Patrick E. Dempsey

Library of Congress
Washington 1984

Library of Congress Cataloging in Publication Data

Library of Congress. Geography and Map Division.
   Panoramic maps of cities in the United States and Canada.
   First ed. published in 1974 under
   title: Panoramic maps of Anglo-American
   cities.
   Bibliography: p.
   Includes index.
   Supt. of Docs. no.: LC 5.2:P19
   1. Cities and towns—United States—Maps—Bibliog-
raphy—Catalogs. 2. Cities and towns—Canada—Maps—
Bibliography—Catalogs. 3. Library of Congress.
Geography and Map Division—Catalogs. I. Hébert,
John R. II. Dempsey, Patrick E. (Patrick Eugene),
1949-   . III. Title.
Z6027.U5L5   1983   [HT122]   016.912'7   82-600316
ISBN 0-8444-0413-6

For sale by the Superintendent of Documents,
U. S. Government Printing Office, Washington, D. C.
20402.

Contents

Preface to the Second Edition

This checklist records 1,726 panoramic maps of U.S. and Canadian cities in the collections of the Library of Congress, Geography and Map Division. This revised list identifies manuscript and printed maps of cities in forty-seven states, the District of Columbia, and nine Canadian provinces, including photocopies of originals in other repositories. Interest in the study of panoramic maps has increased substantially since John R. Hébert's list first appeared in 1974. His descriptive essay on the panoramic map industry in Victorian America, slightly revised to reflect new information generated by the addition of 609 maps, precedes the entries. The general index to city names, artists, publishers, and lithographers/printers enhances the usefulness of the checklist.

The Library of Congress has a large, although not complete, collection of panoramic maps. The nucleus of the collection consists of maps received by copyright deposit, but the files have also been enriched by transfers from other federal agencies, purchases, gifts, and photoreproductions of originals in other libraries and archives. Most of the Library's panoramic maps, including those in this checklist, are in the Geography and Map Division, although 120 duplicate panoramic maps are preserved in the Prints and Photographs Division.

Form of Entry

The columns in the checklist include, respectively: (1) entry number, (2) city name and date, (3) Library of Congress classification number, (4) artists, (5) publishers and, if noted on the map, place of publication, or in the case of facsimiles, names of persons or firms responsible for reproductions, (6) lithographer or printer, with location if noted, and (7) map size. The 609 new entries in the second edition have been interfiled with the 1,117 original entries by means of a decimal system in order to keep all the entries in correct alphabetical and chronological order. This system helps the user who may still need to refer to the first edition and will also allow for the addition of new entries to any possible future editions. Users are advised to consult the index to locate all maps of a particular city because maps are listed by the name in the title and the titles of several entries include multiple city names. Side views or insets to the main map are not always indicated in the list, although all are indexed, and no differentiation has been made between colored and non-colored views. Names of artists, publishers, and lithographers are given as they appear on the maps, except that the words "and" and "Company" are consistently abbreviated "&" and "Co." All items recorded are printed maps unless otherwise noted in the map size column with such descriptive terms as "facsimile," "manuscript," "negative photostat," "positive photostat," "film negative," or "photograph." The map size is given in inches with the vertical dimension given first.

How to Order

Black-and-white photoreproductions of most of the original maps cited in this checklist may be purchased from the Photoduplication Service, Library of Congress, Washington, D.C. 20540. The 16 by 20 inch matte finish photographic prints are recommended for decorative purposes, and 8 by 10 inch glossy prints are best suited for use in publications. In a few instances, it will be necessary to order multiple overlapping photographic prints or photostatic copies because maps larger than 37 by 48 inches cannot be reproduced on a single film negative. Requests for cost estimates or purchase orders should refer to the maps by city, date, and entry numbers. While it is not possible to supply reproductions of panoramic maps for which the Library has only photocopies, names and addresses of libraries holding originals of these items or commercial firms which may sell facsimile reproductions of them will, if known, be supplied upon request.

The Geography and Map Division is interested in securing originals or photocopies of panoramic maps not already in its collections and will welcome information which may lead to such acquisitions.

Acknowledgement

The Geography and Map Division gratefully acknowledges the generosity of its greatest benefactor of panoramic maps, Mr. James R. Warren, Sr. Mr. Warren developed a fascination with panoramic maps when in 1930 he first saw a view of his hometown, New Brighton, Pennsylvania, drawn by Thaddeus Mortimer Fowler. His long-term interest in recording biographical data about Fowler, Albert Ruger, and the Bailey brothers has helped to generate a renaissance of interest in this lost art.

James R. Warren's contact with Thaddeus M. Fowler's daughter-in-law, in addition to other Fowler descendants, convinced Roxana Fowler that her famous father-in-law's works should be preserved in the Library of Congress. Due to Mr. Warren's persistence and devotion to the study and search for panoramic maps, scores of panoramic maps by Fowler and others have been deposited in the Geography and Map Division.

Patrick E. Dempsey
Geography and Map Division

Introduction

A popular cartographic form used to depict U.S. and Canadian cities and towns during the late nineteenth and early twentieth centuries was the panoramic map. Known also as bird's-eye views, perspective maps, panoramas, and aero views, panoramic maps are nonphotographic representations of cities, portrayed as if viewed from above at an oblique angle. Although not generally drawn to scale, they show street patterns, individual buildings, and major landscape features in perspective.

Preparation of panoramic maps involved a vast amount of painstakingly detailed labor. For each project a frame or projection was developed, showing in perspective the pattern of streets. The artist then walked in the street, sketching buildings, trees, and other features to present a complete and accurate landscape as though seen from an elevation of 2,000 to 3,000 feet.[1] These data were entered on the frame in his workroom.

Perspective mapping was not unique to the United States and Canada or to the Victorian period. Mathias Merian, George Braun, Franz Hogenberg, and others produced perspective maps of European cities in the late sixteenth and early seventeenth centuries. These early European town plans, most often portraying major political or marketing centers, were small in size and were generally incorporated in atlases or geographical books. The perspective was usually at a low oblique angle, and streets were seldom identified by name. In some instances, the views were hypothetical, and one pattern might be used to represent various European cities.

A modified version of the Renaissance city view was employed in the United States before the Civil War. Like their European predecessors, these perspectives, usually of large cities, were drawn at low oblique angles and at times even at ground level. Street patterns were often indistinct.

Also popular during this period were views of American cities drawn as though viewed from extremely great heights.

Victorian America's panoramic maps differ dramatically from the Renaissance city perspectives. The post-Civil War town views are more accurate and are drawn from a higher oblique angle. Small towns as well as major urban centers were portrayed. Panoramic mapping of urban centers was unique to North America in this era. Most panoramic maps were published independently, not as plates in an atlas or in a descriptive geographical book. Preparation and sale of nineteenth-century panoramas were motivated by civic pride and the desire of the city fathers to encourage commercial growth. Many views were prepared for and endorsed by chambers of commerce and other civic organizations and were used as advertisements of a city's commercial and residential potential.

Advances in lithography, photolithography, photoengraving, and chromolithography, which made possible inexpensive and multiple copies, along with prosperous communities willing to purchase prints, made panoramic maps popular wall hangings during America's Victorian Age. The citizen could view with pride his immediate environment and point out his own property to guests, since the map artist, for a suitable fee, obligingly included illustrations of private homes as insets to the main city plan.

Real estate agents and chambers of commerce used the maps to promote sales to prospective buyers of homes and business properties. Henry Wellge's 1892 panorama of Norfolk, Virginia, for example, was distributed with the compliments of Pollard Brothers Real Estate, and Thaddeus M. Fowler's 1893 view of Morrisville, Pennsylvania, was commissioned by realtor William G. Howell.[2]

Panoramic maps not only showed the existing city but sometimes also depicted areas planned for development. Fowler's 1890 map of Childress, Texas, and 1907 map of South Rocky Mount, North Carolina, are examples.

Panoramic maps graphically depict the vibrant life of a city. Harbors are shown choked with ships, often to the extent of constituting hazards to navigation. Trains speed along railroad tracks, at times on the same roadbed with locomotives and cars headed in the opposite direction. People and horsedrawn carriages fill the streets, and smoke belches from the stacks of industrial plants. Urban and industrial development in post-Civil War America is vividly portrayed in the maps.

As late as the 1920s, panoramic maps were still in vogue commercially. A view of Derby, Connecticut, by Hughes & Bailey, used on a letterhead of this period, includes a description of the various advantages the city could offer a new industry or a prospective home buyer. The promotional pitch concluded with the following observation:

The many Natural Advantages of Location, the Cheapness of Power, Varied Industries, Skilled Labor, Facilities for Transportation, Proximity to other Large Manufacturing Communities combine to make Derby Exceptionally Attractive to the Manufacturer and Home Seeker as a Commercial and an Industrial Center.[3]

Norris, Wellge & Co.'s 1885 view of Madison, Wisconsin, illustrates another use of panoramic maps. In addition to those sold for wall hangings, copies of the view were used by S. L. Sheldon to advertise his farm implement store. The map is framed by eighteen pictures of farm machines, including the Gasaday sulky plow, the J. I. Case agitator, the Buffalo Pitts coal or wood burning

traction engine, and Esterly's twine binding harvester. Sheldon sent copies of the panorama to his patrons, along with a request for their continued patronage. Similarly, Fowler's 1889 map of Hamburg, Pennsylvania, contains two advertisements below the neat line. One portrays W. William Appel's photographic studio, jewelry store, and residence, with a lithographic reproduction of the owner. The other, an advertisement for W. H. Grim, dealer in musical instruments and sewing machines, includes a view of his shop and a representation of a Miller organ, one of Grim's stock items.

There is little information about the number of prints usually published or the customary selling price. Obviously, more impressions were made of the maps of large cities than of those picturing small towns. An estimate from Meriden Gravure Company, Meriden, Connecticut, the printer of Hughes & Bailey and Hughes & Cinquin aero views in the 1910s and 1920s, noted that between one hundred and two hundred fifty copies of each view were generally printed.[4] However, Oakley H. Bailey, one of the bird's-eye view artists, stated in 1932 that he had made sketches of nearly six hundred different places and that total reproductions had exceeded a million copies. Simple arithmetic indicates that Bailey's estimate works out to approximately two thousand copies of each view.[5] Considering the scarcity of many views, it may be assumed that the average printing was probably in the neighborhood of five hundred impressions.

The cost of the individual bird's-eye view was very likely determined by the number of impressions and the buying capability of the

citizenry. The following note, appended to H. H. Bailey's 1872 view of Milwaukee, Wisconsin, gives some help:

Our birdseye view of Milwaukee (size 26×40 inches) is now ready and for sale by all the Booksellers and Stationers. . .Price $3.00. Our charges for mounting the same on plain frame and varnishing are. . .50 cts. For framing in 2½ inch polished Black Walnut Frame, (also mounted and varnished). . .$2.50
Holzapfel & Eskuche, publishers
443 East Water Street.[6]

This particular view, printed in several colors, was quite handsome. Smaller views and those in two tones did not command as high a price. (Money was not the only exchange medium for views. Thaddeus Fowler reportedly accepted quantities of flour and beans on occasion for his town views.[7]) We may assume that the price of panoramic city plans increased during the twentieth century, and therefore, the range in cost was probably from one to five dollars.

The most successful print publisher in the nineteenth century was the firm of Currier & Ives. Best remembered for their views of daily life in Victorian America, they also prepared bird's-eye views of New York City, Chicago, Boston, San Francisco, and Washington. However, they were not a leading panoramic mapmaking firm, and their distinctive views were primarily of large cities. Most post-Civil War panoramic maps were of parochial interest, highlighting small cities and towns, and were more detailed than the average Currier & Ives' city perspective.

Albert Ruger, Thaddeus Mortimer Fowler, Lucien R. Burleigh, Henry Wellge, and Oakley H. Bailey prepared more than 55 percent of the panoramic maps in the Library of Congress. Albert Ruger was the first to achieve success as a panoramic artist. The collections of the Library's Geography and Map Division contain 213 city maps drawn

Albert Ruger (1829-1899)

or published by Ruger or by Ruger & Stoner. The majority came from Ruger's personal collection, which the Library purchased in 1941 from John Ramsey of Canton, Ohio. Before this accession, there were only four Ruger city plans in the Geography and Map Division. Born in Prussia in 1829, Ruger emigrated to the United States and worked initially as a mason. While serving with the Ohio Volunteers during the Civil War, he drew views of Union campsites, among them Camp Chase in Ohio and Stephenson's Depot in Virginia. He continued to draw after the war, and his prints include a famous lithograph of Lincoln's funeral car passing the statehouse in Columbus, Ohio.[8]

By 1866 Ruger had settled in Battle Creek, Michigan, where he began his prolific panoramic mapping career by sketching Michigan cities. Full descriptions of many Ruger views of Michigan cities are contained in John Cumming's *A Preliminary Checklist of 19th Century Lithographs of Michigan Cities and Towns*. Towns in some twenty-two states and Canada, ranging from New Hampshire to Minnesota and south to Georgia and Alabama, were sketched by Ruger. He continued his activity into the 1890s, moving his business to Chicago, Madison, Wisconsin, and St. Louis as he sought new markets. In the late 1860s Ruger formed a partnership with J. J. Stoner of Madison, Wisconsin, and together they published numerous city panoramas. Ruger was particularly productive during the 1860s; in 1869 alone he produced more than sixty panoramic maps. In addition to city plans he drew views of university campuses, among them Notre Dame, Shurtleff College, and the University of Michigan. Albert Ruger died in Akron, Ohio, on November 12, 1899.

The name which appears on the greatest number of panoramic maps in the collections of the Library of Congress is that of Thaddeus Mortimer Fowler. He was born in Lowell, Massachusetts,

Thaddeus Mortimer Fowler (1842-1922)

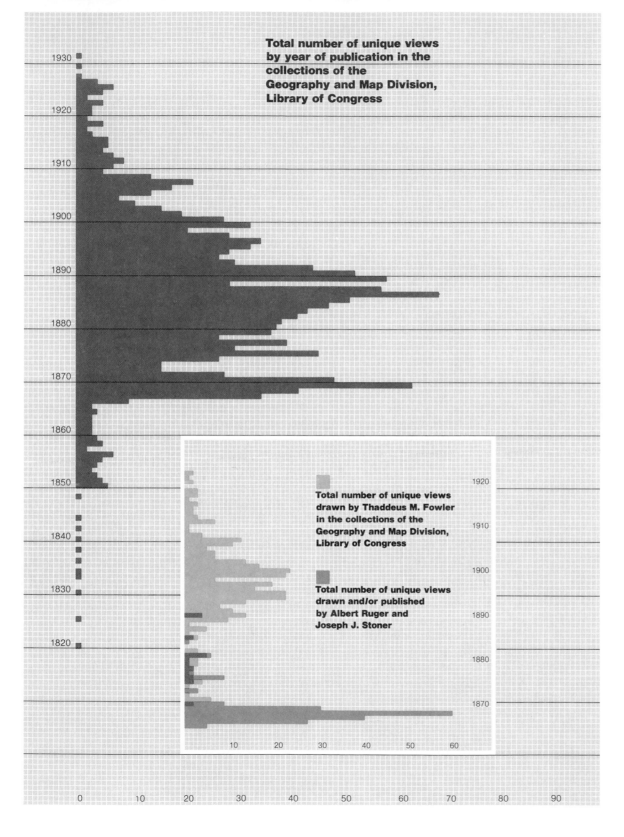

Total number of unique views
by year of publication in the
collections of the
Geography and Map Division,
Library of Congress

Total number of unique views
drawn by Thaddeus M. Fowler
in the collections of the
Geography and Map Division,
Library of Congress

Total number of unique views
drawn and/or published
by Albert Ruger and
Joseph J. Stoner

on December 21, 1842, and ran away from home at the age of fifteen. When the first call for military volunters for the Civil War was issued by President Lincoln, Fowler was in Buffalo, New York. Although initially rejected because he was underage, after some maneuvering Fowler was sworn into the 21st Regiment of the New York Volunteers at Elmira, New York, in May 1861. He received an ankle wound at the Second Battle of Bull Run and was honorably discharged at Boston in February 1863, leaving the hospital on crutches after refusing amputation. He then visited army camps where he made tintypes of soldiers. In 1864 Fowler migrated to Madison, Wisconsin, where he worked with his uncle J. M. Fowler, a photographer. He established his own panoramic map firm and in 1870 produced a view of Omro, Wisconsin. This was followed the next year by panoramas of Peshtigo, Sheboygan Falls, and Waupaca, Wisconsin.[9] The Boston Public Library has six views drawn and published by Fowler in the 1870s. During that decade, he was employed as an artist by J. J. Stoner. Fowler moved from Madison around 1880 to northern New Jersey, first to the Oranges and later to Asbury Park. A panoramic map of Stewart, Ohio, which appears in D. J. Lake's *Atlas of Athens Co., Ohio* is the earliest Fowler view in the Library of Congress's collections.[10] Between 1881 and 1885, Fowler was located successively in Lewisburg and Shamokin, Pennsylvania, and in Trenton, New Jersey. On April 1, 1885, he moved with his family to Morrisville, Pennsylvania, where he maintained his headquarters for twenty-five years. One of the inconveniences of his profession was the recurring need to find new territory for his artistry. In a 1913 request for an increase in his military pension, Fowler noted that "although claiming home where my family was located—I was on the road as Publisher and Canvasser ever since the war."[11]

Morrisville served as a convenient operating center as Fowler began to draw and publish views of Pennsylvania, West Virginia, and Ohio cities. His production of Pennsylvania panoramas was greater than that of any other artist for a particular state. In the Library of Congress's collections are 220 separate Fowler views of Pennsylvania, representing 199 different towns. There are, moreover, an additional 165 Fowler views of Pennsylvania towns in the Pennsylvania State Archives and at Pennsylvania State University. This is an outstanding production record.

At various periods during his career, Fowler was associated with other panoramic artists. The association with James B. Moyer, of Myerstown, Pennsylvania, from 1889 to 1902 was particularly extensive and productive. Some city maps were also published under the imprints Fowler & Kelly, Fowler & Albert E. Downs, and Fowler & Browning. After 1910 Fowler prepared panoramic maps of cities in Connecticut, Massachusetts, New Jersey, and New York for Oakley H. Bailey, who marketed his prints as aero views.[12]

Throughout his career, which extended over fifty-four years, Thaddeus Fowler never ceased to find pleasure in drawing and publishing panoramic maps. In a letter to his granddaughter written in 1920, he said that he felt "an unadulterated joy"[13] while sketching a view of Middletown, New York. This was the expression of a man who at that time had been working at his profession fifty years! In the same letter Fowler alluded to some of the problems viewmakers encountered. He was in Allentown, Pennsylvania, in 1918, he recalled, preparing an aero view of the city, probably in association with Oakley H. Bailey. Airplanes and a dirigible circling the city were included in the trademark of the aero view to give the impression that some of the information was derived from aerial reconnaissance, which, of course, was not true. Some Allentown citizens

noticed the view with the planes on the manuscript map. In the excitement engendered by World War I, Fowler was accused of being a German spy and was jailed. Members of his immediate family drove from Morrisville to identify their father, who suffered injury only to his pride in the incident. In the 1920 letter previously cited, Fowler also noted that Oakley H. Bailey had

taken up my job at Allentown where I left off. The Sec'y of the Chamber of Commerce was very much taken with the drawing as far as I had it done and promised to help. Mayor Gross was very gracious and also favored the idea very much. Quite a different reception Bailey had to mine. There's no doubt we will do well there.[14]

The Allentown panorama, the largest extant Fowler view, apparently was never published. The original drawing was presented to the Library in 1970 by his daughter-in-law, Mrs. T. B. (Roxana) Fowler. The magnificent pen-and-ink manuscript with grey wash, which measures 28 by 71 inches, engaged Thaddeus Fowler and Oakley H. Bailey for over four years. A feeling of the city's vitality was expressed by drawings of operating industrial plants, trains in motion, city thoroughfares filled with automobiles and pedestrians, and a group of fans watching a baseball game. The Allentown map was one of the last to which Fowler contributed. He died in March 1922 in his eightieth year, following a fall on icy streets incurred while preparing a panorama of Middletown, New York. Fowler's career spanned the entire period of panoramic map production, and only Oakley H. Bailey shares this distinction.

The views of Thaddeus Fowler include cities and towns in at least twenty-one states and Canada.[15] To date, 411 separate Fowler panoramas have

been identified. Of the 324 in the Library of Congress, the majority were acquired on copyright deposit. In 1943, 60 Fowler views of Pennsylvania and West Virginia were purchased from the Laurel Book Service, Hazleton, Pennsylvania, among which are 11 of the Library's 28 Fowler views of West Virginia. In 1970 and 1971 the artist's daughter-in-law Mrs. T. B. (Roxana) Fowler and her family presented to the Library a collection of over 100 of his maps, 46 of them not previously in the Library's collections. This group has been kept together by the Library as the Fowler Map Collection.

An analysis of Fowler views of Pennsylvania towns suggests that the panoramic artist concentrated on a specific geographical area in a given year, very likely to minimize transportation problems.[16] From 1889 to 1894, for example, he sketched cities in eastern Pennsylvania. In 1889 he focused on Schuykill County, from 1890 to 1892 he focused on the Scranton and Wilkes-Barre area, and in 1893 he mapped the area north of Philadelphia. He made views of cities between Morrisville and Chambersburg in 1894 and from 1895 to 1897 worked in the western part of the state, especially around Pittsburgh and in the northwest sector of Pennsylvania. In 1898 and 1899 Fowler sketched West Virginia towns and from 1900 to 1903 was back in western Pennsylvania. Subsequently he made trips to Maryland, Virginia, North Carolina, and Georgia to draw city plans and to investigate the possibility of expanding his trade into the South, which proved unsuccessful.

Fowler gained commissions for city plans by interesting citizens and civic groups in the idea of a panoramic map of their community. After one town had agreed to having a map made, he would seek to involve neighboring communities. By noting that he had already secured an agreement for a view from one town in the area, he would play on the pride, community spirit, and sense of competition of adjacent communities. By such promotional procedures he garnered commitments for panoramic maps from a limited geographical area, thus eliminating travel expenses. Similar methods were employed by Ruger, Stoner, and Burleigh.

Oakley H. Bailey, another outstanding panoramic map artist and publisher and a close friend of Thaddeus Fowler, was born of Quaker parents June 14, 1843, in Mahoning County, Ohio. He enrolled in Mount Union College, Alliance, Ohio, in 1862. His studies were disrupted temporarily in 1864, while he served with the 143d Ohio Volunteer Militia, Company F, but he returned to school after his service obligation and graduated from Mount Union in 1866. He taught briefly in the area school system, but in 1866 he left Ohio and entered business with his brother H. H. Bailey and edited a business directory of Ohio. His territory reached as far as Chicago, Indianapolis, and Minneapolis. In 1871 he turned to the profession of making panoramic maps. Bailey's career began in Madison, Wisconsin, but by 1874 he had moved to Boston. From headquarters there and in New York City, Bailey published panoramic maps of American cities until the late 1920s, first under the name bird's-eye views and later as aero views.[17] His brother H. H. Bailey, who also drew views, was Oakley's partner for many years.

There are 127 Bailey items in the Library of Congress, and the Boston Public Library has 242 views drawn or published by Bailey between 1874 and 1891. A Bailey drawing of Atlantic City, measuring over seven feet in length, shows five or six miles of the famous boardwalk, myriad hotels, other buildings, and the ocean front. His maps were issued under the imprints of Oakley H. Bailey, Oakley H. Bailey & Co., O. H. Bailey & J. C. Hazen, Bailey & Fowler, Bailey & Hughes,

Oakley Hoopes Bailey (1843-1947)

Howard Heston Bailey (1836-1878)

Bailey & Moyer, Fowler & Bailey, and Hughes & Bailey. In the 1920s the firm of Hughes & Cinquin produced panoramic maps under the sponsorship of Oakley H. Bailey, who had retired in 1927. Perhaps by that time Bailey's eyesight had become too weak to permit him to continue the tedious, close work required of a panoramic artist. He died on August 13, 1947, in Alliance, Ohio, at the age of 104.

When asked in 1932 why he had gone into the panoramic map business instead of farming, Bailey replied that at an early age he had realized that pastoral pursuits were filled with too many uncertainties. He chose instead the career of panoramic map publishing and remained active in it for fifty-five years, drawing and publishing maps of cities in some twenty northern states and Canada.[18] In a 1932 interview he further noted:

The business has been practically without competition as so few could give it the patience, care and skill essential to success. But now the airplane cameras are covering the territory and can put more towns on paper in a day than was possible in months by hand work formerly.[19]

Equally as prolific as Bailey in publishing maps of Northeastern U.S. cities was Lucien R. Burleigh of Troy, New York. During the 1880s Burleigh views of New York and New England were particularly popular. The Library of Congress has 163 Burleigh panoramic city plans. State and local archives in New York may contain even more of Burleigh's views. An 1883 Troy city directory listed Burleigh as a civil engineer. By 1886 he had become a lithographer and view publisher, publishing under the name Burleigh Lithographing Company. An advertisement in the 1886 city directory stated that the firm did fine work in all branches of engraving and printing, with "views of buildings and villages a specialty."[20] Burleigh published panoramic maps as late as 1892, but his most productive years

were from 1885 to 1890. Views were published under his personal name and under the imprint Burleigh Lithographing Company or Burleigh Lithographing Establishment.

Henry Wellge, like Albert Ruger, was a Midwestern panoramic map artist and publisher. He worked initially for J. J. Stoner but in the 1880s established his own company. His views of towns in twenty-four states were issued under several imprints—Henry Wellge & Co., Norris, Wellge & Co., and the American Publishing Co. Among other noteworthy panoramic map artists were Herman Brosius, Rene Cinquin, Albert E. Downs, Eli S. Glover, Augustus Koch, George E. Norris, and George H. Walker. Walker was also a successful publisher of atlases and maps.

The urban areas in the Midwest and Eastern United States were of primary interest to panoramic map artists. Several of the artists began their careers in the Midwest, particularly in Madison, Wisconsin, and during the 1860s and 1870s a large number of panoramic maps of Midwestern cities and towns appeared. By the late 1870s the Madison group had dispersed. Ruger and Stoner remained in that city, but Bailey and Fowler moved eastward to virgin territory. The latter two and Lucien Burleigh made the Middle Atlantic and New England states the chief production center for bird's-eye views during the 1880s and 1890s. It was in these areas, moreover, that the panoramic map business had its final flurry of activity in the 1920s.

During the 1860s and 1870s the major publishers and lithographers of panoramic maps were concentrated in the Chicago-Milwaukee area

because of the proximity to the artists' center of Madison. Beck & Pauli Lithographers (Milwaukee), Joseph J. Stoner (Madison), and Merchants Lithographers and Chicago Lithographers (Chicago) were responsible for a large percentage of the panoramas. Adam Beck and Clemens J. Pauli operated one of the most active lithographic firms in this area, producing views drawn in thirty states and Canada. Beck and Pauli printed views from 1878 to 1889, being most active during the mid-1880s. Clemens J. Pauli tried his own hand at drawing and printing views in 1889.

Another active producer was Charles Shober, whose panoramas appeared under several imprints, including Charles Shober & Co., Shober & Carqueville Lithographing Co., and the Chicago Lithographing Co. Joseph J. Stoner was the Madison publisher most identified with the Milwaukee-Chicago area panoramic map business. Every major view artist except Lucien R. Burleigh had works published at one time or another by Stoner. By the 1880s publishers and lithographers on the east coast of the United States rivaled the Midwestern companies.

In the Far West[21] and the South panoramic maps never attained the popularity they achieved in the area north of the Mason-Dixon line, between Maine and Minnesota. Attempts to extend the industry to the South and the West were not particularly successful, although panoramic maps of a few cities in Alabama, Arkansas, Montana, New Mexico, North Dakota, South Dakota, and Colorado were produced. Views of communities in the state of Washington were drawn by Eli S. Glover and Henry Wellge in a span of one or two years in the 1870s or 1880s. Wellge's views of the state, for example, were all drawn in 1884. The South was economically unable to support views of their cities during Reconstruction, and northern canvassers probably would not have been welcome. More significantly, perhaps, the focal point of life in the South was the farm or plantation, not the village or town as in the Midwest and the Northeastern states.

Similarly, the panoramic map business never gained in popularity in Canada. The Library's collections contain only 36 panoramic maps of Canadian cities. The Public Archives of Canada has 112 unique panoramic maps of which 48 are original views.

The Library's collection includes the largest panoramic map published, Camille N. Dry's 1875 *Pictorial St. Louis; The Great Metropolis of the Mississippi Valley,* which was dedicated to the famous Mississippi River bridgebuilder Capt. James B. Eads. It was produced on 110 plates, which when trimmed and assembled created a panorama of the city measuring about 9 by 24 feet. Dry issued the panoramic map in an atlas, the preface of which included the following notes regarding its preparation:

A careful perspective, which required a surface of three hundred square feet, was then erected from a correct survey of the city, extending northward from Arsenal Island to the Water Works, a distance of about ten miles, on the river front; and from the Insane Asylum on the southwest to the Cemeteries on the northwest. Every foot of the vast territory within these limits has been carefully examined and topographically drawn in perspective . . . and the faithfulness and accuracy with which this work has been done an examination of the pages will attest.

The St. Louis panorama evidently was prepared to show the city's progress at the United States Centennial celebration of 1876. The verso of each plate contains information on various aspects of St. Louis economic life, including businesses, professions, schools, churches, and governmental organizations. Every building in the area was drawn on the map, and 1,999 specific sites were identified by name. A note in the preface requests that any mistakes detected be looked upon with a lenient eye by an indulgent public "in view of the magnitude of the work, the originality of the idea, and the difficulties encountered in carrying it out." Dry's map of St. Louis is a magnificent extension of the normal single-sheet lithographic view and one of the crowning achievements of the art. Also impressive for their size and detail are the colored view of Washington (1883-84), which measures 4 by 5½ feet, and that of Baltimore (1869), measuring 5 × 11 feet, both published by the Sachses of Baltimore.

Although the separate print was the most common panoramic map format, views of cities and towns also appeared as illustrations in nineteenth-century state and county atlases. Credit was often not given to the artist in such publications, but some of the leading panoramic map artists probably prepared views for these atlases. Ruger, for example, prepared a landscape view for the title page of E. L. Hayes's 1877 atlas of the upper Ohio River and Valley. The town views in Andreas's 1875 Iowa atlas, although unsigned, also resemble Ruger's work.[22]

Surviving panoramic maps are very popular today and command premium prices from map and print dealers. Facsimile reproductions of panoramic maps are likewise in demand. Historic Urban Plans of Ithaca, New York, has published more than one hundred facsimiles of low and high oblique angle views of American cities.

Panoramic maps give a pictorial record of Anglo-America's cities during the post-Civil War period and for many localities provide the sole nineteenth-century map. No other graphic form of this era so effectively captured the vitality of America's urban centers.

Notes

1. "A 'Young' Old Timer," *Sebring (Ohio) Times,* 1932. The article is an interview with panoramic map artist Oakley H. Bailey. Our copy of the article is from Mrs. T. B. Fowler, Morrisville, Pennsylvania.
2. The information on the Fowler view is derived from an interview with his daughter-in-law, Mrs. T. B. (Roxana) Fowler of Aberdeen, Maryland, in November 1971.
3. From Hughes & Bailey's 1920 view of Derby, Connecticut, drawn by Thaddeus M. Fowler.
4. Letter from Harold Hugo, president, Meriden Gravure Company, Meriden, Connecticut, to John Hébert, February 1, 1972.
5. "A 'Young' Old Timer," *Sebring (Ohio) Times,* 1932.
6. View on file in the Geography and Map Division, Library of Congress.
7. From interview with Mrs. T. B. (Roxana) Fowler, November 1971.
8. John Cumming, comp., *A Preliminary Checklist of 19th Century Lithographs of Michigan Cities and Towns* (Mount Pleasant, Michigan: Clarke Historical Library, Central Michigan University, c1969), p. iii.
9. Five of the six Fowler views of Wisconsin (Oconomowoc 1870, Omro 1870, Peshtigo 1871, Sheboygan Falls 1871, and Waupaca 1871) are in the collections of the State Historical Society of Wisconsin, Madison, Wisconsin; the sixth Fowler view (Burlington 1871) is in the collections of the Burlington Historical Society, Burlington, Wisconsin.
10. The 1870 Fowler view of Oconomowoc, Wisconsin, included in the Library's list of panoramic maps predates the 1875 Ohio view. However, it is a positive photostatic reproduction of an original in the State Historical Society of Wisconsin, Madison.
11. From Thaddeus Fowler's military pension records, National Archives, Washington, D.C.
12. Information on Fowler from his military pension record, National Archives, and from an unpublished account of his life by his son, Thaddeus B. Fowler. A copy of the son's recollections was given to the author by James Raymond Warren, Sr. From that same source we learned that Fowler married Elizabeth Anna Dann in 1875 in Madison, Wisconsin. Five children came of this union.

For Further Reading

13. Fowler to Ruth Fowler, April 11, 1920. Ruth Fowler later became Mrs. Clarence Sinclair, Morrisville, Pennsylvania.

14. Ibid.

15. To our knowledge, his Canadian views include Windsor, Nova Scotia and Windsor, Ontario in 1878; Kentville, Nova Scotia in 1879; Winnipeg, Manitoba in 1880; Norwich, Simcoe and Tilsonburg, Ontario and Winnipeg, Manitoba, in 1881.

16. According to James R. Warren, an acknowledged expert on T. M. Fowler, at least fifty maps covering five states held in the collections of the Boston Public Library which are signed "O. H. Bailey & Co." are, in fact, maps drawn by Fowler in the early 1880s. Warren asserts that the maps were left unsigned because Fowler did not want his creditors to know his whereabouts and so had no fixed abode although he was moving from town to town in the provinces of Ontario, New Brunswick, and Nova Scotia. The maps contain many of Fowler's conventional artistic trademarks including the slanted lettering, the back slanted figures 1 and 7, and smoke emitting from steamships, railroads, and factories. Fowler would oftentimes include his own image in the views.

17. "A 'Young' Old Timer," *Sebring (Ohio) Times*, 1932.

18. Ibid.

19. Ibid.

20. *Troy, New York, Directory*. . .1886. (Sampson, Murdock & Co.), p. 558.

21. George Henry Goddard drew low oblique angle views of California towns in the 1850s. John W. Reps' *Cities of the American West* (Princeton, N.J.: Princeton University Press, c1979) cites over three dozen panoramic maps of California towns as well as many other towns in the Far West published between 1865 and 1900.

22. See E. L. Hayes, *Illustrated Atlas of the Upper Ohio River and Valley from Pittsburgh, Pa. to Cincinnati, Ohio. From United States official and special surveys*. . .(Philadelphia: Titus, Simmons & Titus, 1877), and Alfred T. Andreas, *A.T. Andreas' Illustrated Historical Atlas of the State of Iowa* (Chicago: Andreas Atlas Co., 1875).

Beckman, Thomas. *Milwaukee Illustrated: Panoramic and Bird's-Eye Views of a Midwestern Metropolis, 1844-1908.* Milwaukee: Milwaukee Art Center, 1978. Exhibition dates: April 14–June 18, 1978.

Canada. Public Archives. *Bird's-Eye Views of Canadian Cities: An Exhibition of Panoramic Maps (1865-1905), July to November 1976.* Ottawa: Public Archives of Canada, 1976.

Comstock, Jim, and Peter Wallace. *West Virginia Picture Book.* Richwood, W.Va.: Jim Comstock, 1978. West Virginia Heritage Encyclopedia, vol. 51.

Cummings, John W., comp. *A Preliminary Checklist of 19th Century Lithographs of Michigan Cities and Towns.* Mount Pleasant, Mich.: Clarke Historical Library, Central Michigan University, 1969.

"Early Views of Midwestern American Cities." Chicago Historical Society *Bulletin*, 2d series, II, March 1936, pp. 7-24.

Fornwalt, Russell J. "Bird's-Eye Views of America Collected by Virginia Hobbyist." *The Collector*, Heyworth, Ill., August 1981 issue, p. 3. Copy is also available in the Geography and Map Division Pamphlet File.

Hansen, Judith W., comp. *Pennsylvania Prints: From the Collection of John C. O'Connor and Ralph M. Yeager: Lithographs, Engravings, Aquatints, and Watercolors from "The Tavern Restaurant."* University Park, Pa.: Museum of Art, The Pennsylvania State University, 1980. Exhibition dates: January 13-March 30, 1980.

Hébert, John R. "Panoramic Maps of American Cities," *Special Libraries*, Vol. 63, No. 12, December 1972, pp. 554-562.

———. "Western City Panoramic Maps." 1975. Unpublished article available in the Geography and Map Division Pamphlet File.

Holzer, Harold. "Bird's-Eye Maps: Regional Chauvinism in Lithographs." *The Antique Trader* (Weekly), July 20, 1977 issue, pp. 40-44. Copy is also available in the Geography and Map Division Pamphlet File.

Kerfoot, Glenn. "Super Sleuth of the Bird's Eye Views." *The Antique Trader* (Weekly), July 29, 1981 issue, pp. 80-83. This article deals primarily with the collecting of panoramic maps by Mr. James R. Warren, Sr. Copy is also available in the Geography and Map Division Pamphlet File.

Maryland Historical Society. *A. Hoen on Stone: Lithographs of E. Weber & Co. and A. Hoen & Co. 1835-1969.* Baltimore: Maryland Historical Society, 1969. Exhibition dates: May 5-June 30, 1969.

Marzio, Peter C. "American Lithographic Technology Before the Civil War." *Prints in and of America to 1850*, edited by John D. Morse. Charlottesville, Va.: University of Virginia Press for the Henry Francis du Pont Winterthur Museum, 1970.

———. *The Democratic Art: An Exhibition on the History of Chromolithography in America 1840-1900.* Fort Worth, Tex.: Amon Carter Museum of Western Art, 1979. Exhibition dates: September 6-October 21, 1979.

Maule, Elizabeth Singer. *Bird's Eye Views of Wisconsin Communities: A Preliminary Checklist.* Madison, Wis.: State Historical Society of Wisconsin, 1977.

Peters, Harry T. *America on Stone.* Garden City, N.Y.: Doubleday, Doran & Co., 1931.

———. *California on Stone.* Garden City, N.Y.: Arno Press, 1935.

Reps, John W. *Cities of The American West: A History of Frontier Urban Planning.* Princeton, N.J.: Princeton University Press, 1979.

_____ *Cities on Stone: Nineteenth Century Lithograph Images of the Urban West.* Fort Worth, Tex.: Amon Carter Museum, 1976.

_____ *The Making of Urban America.* Princeton, N.J.: Princeton University Press, 1965.

Stout, Leon J. "Pennsylvania Towns Views, 1850-1922: A Union Catalogue." *The Western Pennsylvania Historical Magazine,* LVIII (July 1975), 409-428; (October 1975), 546-571; LIX (January 1976), 88-109.

Warren, James R., Sr. "Thaddeus Mortimer Fowler, Bird's-eye View Artist." Special Libraries Association, Geography and Map Division *Bulletin,* No. 120, June 1980, pp. 27-35.

Warren, James R., Sr., and Donald A. Wise. "Two Bird's-eye View Artists: The Bailey Brothers." Special Libraries Association, Geography and Map Division *Bulletin,* No. 124, June 1981, pp. 20-30.

Watson, Douglas S. *California in the Fifties: Fifty Views of Cities and Mining Towns in California and the West, originally drawn on stone by Kuchel & Dresel and other early San Francisco lithographers.* San Francisco, Calif.: John Howell, 1936.

Note:

The Geography and Map Division also has a complete listing of all Bailey panoramic maps which are held in the custody of the Boston Public Library. This list of electrostatic reproductions is bound in book form. It was donated to the Library of Congress by James R. Warren, Sr.

PANORAMIC MAPS
of Cities in the United States and Canada
CHECKLIST

Alabama

Entry No.	City and Date	LC Call No.	Artist	Publisher	Lithographer	Map Size (inches)
1	Anniston 1887	G3974 .A5A3 1887 .H4		Henry Wellge & Co., Milwaukee, Wisconsin	Beck & Pauli, Lith., Milwaukee, Wisconsin	18 × 24½
2	Anniston 1888	G3974 .A5A3 1888 .G6	E. S. Glover	E. S. Glover	Shober & Carqueville Litho. Co., Chicago	21 × 31
3	Anniston 1903	G3974 .A5A3 1903 .D7		C. N. Dry	Chas. Hart, Lith., New York	23½ × 34
4	Birmingham 1885	G3974 .B5A3 1885 .W4	H. Wellge	Norris, Wellge & Co., Milwaukee, Wisconsin	Beck & Pauli, Litho., Milwaukee, Wisconsin	23 × 33
5	Birmingham (Business Section) 1903	G3974 .B5A3 1903 .D7	C. N. Dry	C. N. Dry		6½ × 9½ Positive photostat
6	Gadsden 1887	G3974 .G2A3 1887 .W4	H. Welge [sic]	Henry Wellge & Co., Milwaukee, Wisconsin	Beck & Pauli Litho. Co., Milwaukee, Wisconsin	20½ × 26
7	Huntsville 1871	G3974 .H8A3 1871 .R8 Rug 202	[Albert Ruger]		Ehrgott & Krebs Lith., Cincinnati	22 × 24½
8	Montgomery 1887	G3974 .M6A3 1887 .W4	H. Wellge	Henry Wellge & Co., Milwaukee, Wisconsin	Beck & Pauli Lith. Co., Milwaukee, Wisconsin	25 × 36½
9	Selma 1887	G3974 .S4A3 1887 .W4	H. Wellge	Henry Wellge & Co., Milwaukee, Wisconsin	Beck & Pauli Lith. Co., Milwaukee, Wisconsin	21½ × 33½
10	Tuscaloosa 1887	G3974 .T8A3 1887 .W4	H. Wellge	Henry Wellge & Co., Milwaukee, Wisconsin	Beck & Pauli Lith. Co., Milwaukee, Wisconsin	20 × 25½

Arizona

Entry No.	City and Date	LC Call No.	Artist	Publisher	Lithographer	Map Size (inches)
10.1	Flagstaff 1892	Prints & Photographs Division		Jules Baumann		9 × 11½
11	Phoenix 1885	G4334 .P5A3 1885 .D9	C. J. Dyer, Phoenix	C. J. Dyer, Phoenix	W. Byrnes, Lith., San Francisco; Schmidt Label & Litho. Co., San Francisco	22 × 33
11.1	Phoenix 1885	G4334 .P5A3 1885 .D9 1977	C. J. Dyer, Phoenix; Arizona. Reproduced in 1977 by Historic Urban Plans, Ithaca, New York	C. J. Dyer, Phoenix, A. T.	W. Byrnes, Litho., S. F., Schmidt Label & Litho. Co., S. F.	12 × 18½ Facsimile

Entry No.	City and Date	LC Call No.	Artist	Publisher	Lithographer	Map Size (inches)
11.2	Prescott [1885]	G4334 .P7A3 1885 .D9 1972	C. J. Dyer	C. J. Dyer. Reproduced in 1972 by Historic Urban Plans, Ithaca, New York		17½ × 27 Facsimile

Arkansas

Entry No.	City and Date	LC Call No.	Artist	Publisher	Lithographer	Map Size (inches)
12	Hot Springs 1888	G4004 .H6A3 1888 .W4	H. Wellge	Henry Wellge & Co., Milwaukee, Wisconsin	Beck & Pauli Lith. Co., Milwaukee, Wisconsin	16½ × 26½
13	Little Rock 1871	G4004 .L7A3 1871 .R8 Rug 2	A. Ruger (Ruger Map Coll. 2)	A. Ruger		23 × 34
14	Little Rock 1887	G4004 .L7A3 1887 .H4		Henry Wellge & Co., Milwaukee, Wisconsin	Beck & Pauli Lith. Co., Milwaukee, Wisconsin	21½ × 30
15	Texarkana, Arkansas and Texas 1888	G4034 .T5A3 1888 .H4		Henry Wellge & Co., Milwaukee, Wisconsin	Beck & Pauli Co., Milwaukee, Wisconsin	16 × 26½
16	Van Buren 1888	G4004 .V3A3 1888 .W4	H. Wellge	Henry Wellge & Co., Milwaukee, Wisconsin	Beck & Pauli Lith. Co., Milwaukee, Wisconsin	17½ × 25

California

Entry No.	City and Date	LC Call No.	Artist	Publisher	Lithographer	Map Size (inches)
16.1	Anaheim [1877]	G4364 .A5A3 1877 .G5	E. S. Glover, Los Angeles, Cal.	Reproduced from original in the University of California at Berkeley Bancroft Library	A. L. Bancroft & Co., Lith., San Francisco.	8 × 10 Photograph
16.2	Azusa 1887	G4364 .A9A3 1887 .M6	E. S. Moore	Reproduced from original in University Research Library, Department of Special Collections, University of California at Los Angeles		8 × 10 Photograph
17	Bakersfield 1901	G4364 .B2A3 1901 .S7		N. J. Stone, San Francisco	Britton & Rey, San Francisco	28 × 37½
17.1	Berkeley 1891	G4364 .B5A3 1891 .M6 1977	E. S. Moore	Reproduced in 1977 by Ken Stein, Berkeley, Calif.		14 × 22 Facsimile
18	Berkeley 1909	G4364 .B5A3 1909 .G7		Charles Green, Berkeley, California		12½ × 28½
18.1	Coloma 1857	G4364 .C595A35 1857 .K7 1975	Kuchel & Dressel	Kuchel & Dressel. Reproduced in 1975 by Historic Urban Plans, Ithaca, New York		17 × 20 Facsimile

Little Rock, Arkansas, 1887. Drawn and published by
Henry Wellge & Co., Milwaukee, Wisconsin.

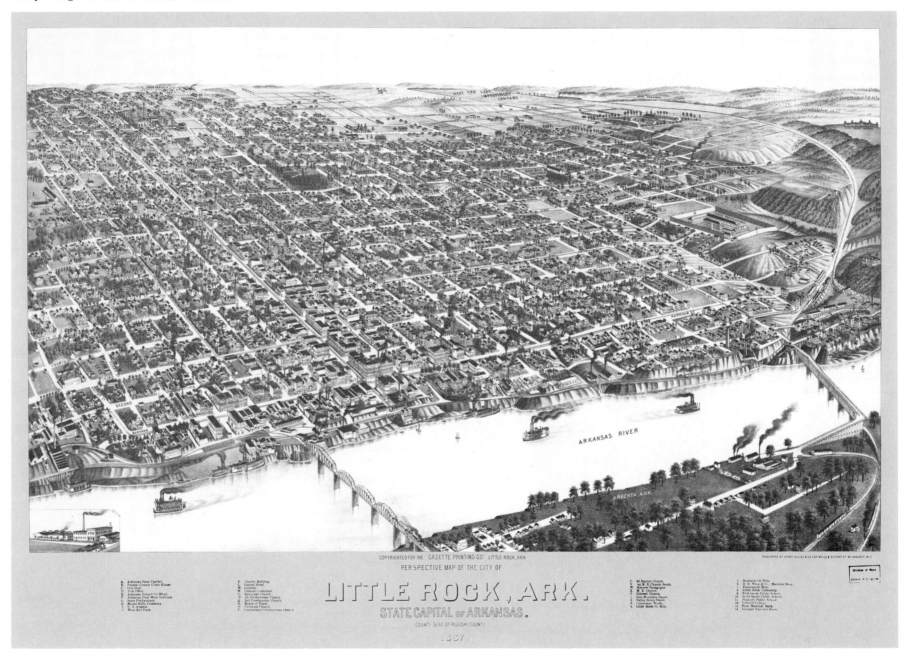

PERSPECTIVE MAP OF THE CITY OF

LITTLE ROCK, ARK.

STATE CAPITAL OF ARKANSAS.

COUNTY SEAT OF PULASKI COUNTY

1887.

Entry No.	City and Date	LC Call No.	Artist	Publisher	Lithographer	Map Size (inches)
19	Columbia 1852	G4364 .C61A35 1852 .G6 1970	E. H. Goddard	Reproduced in 1970 by Historic Urban Plans, Ithaca, New York	Pollard & Britton's Lith., S. F.	12½ × 18
19.1	Coronado Beach, San Diego Bay and City of San Diego [188-]	G4364 .C772A3 [188-] .M6	E. S. Moore	Coronado Beach Company	Crocker & Co. Lith. S. F.	18½ × 25½
20	Eureka 1902	G4364 .E9A3 1902 .N6		A. C. Noe & G. R. Georgeson	Britton & Rey, San Francisco	26½ × 38
20.1	Fresno 1901	G4364 .F8A3 1901 .K5	L. W. Klein	L. W. Klein	Britton & Rey, Photo-Lith., S. F.	26½ × 42½
21	Healdsburg and Russian River Valley 1876	G4364 .H43A3 1876 .G6	E. S. Glover	Jordan Bros.	A. L. Bancroft & Co., San Francisco	17½ × 23
22	Lakeport 1888	G4364 .L27A3 1888 .I6	Stanley Inchbold		Britton & Rey, San Francisco	18½ × 25½
22.1	Livermore & Livermore Valley 1889	G4364 .L59A3 1889 .B3	W. P. Bartlett	W. W. Elliott	Schmidt Label and Lithograph Co., S. Francisco	8 × 10 Photograph
22.2	Los Angeles 1857	G4364 .L8A35 1857 .K8 1959	Kuchel & Dressel, S. Francisco	Kuchel & Dressel. Republished by the California Historical Society, 1959	Britton & Rey	18½ × 24 Facsimile
23	Los Angeles 1857	G4364 .L8A35 1857 .K8 1969	Kuchel & Dressel, S. F.	Kuchel & Dressel. Reproduced in 1969 by Historic Urban Plans, Ithaca, New York	Britton & Rey	12 × 18 Facsimile
23.1	Los Angeles 1871	G4364 .L8A3 1871 .G6	Gores	Women's University Club of L. A.		19 × 25
24	Los Angeles 1873	G4364 .L8A35 1873 .M3 1970	A[lfred] E. Mathews	A. L. Bancroft & Co., San Francisco, Cal. Reproduced in 1970 by Historic Urban Plans, Ithaca, New York	A. L. Bancroft & Co.	13 × 20 Facsimile
25	Los Angeles 1877 (with Brooklyn Hights)	G4364 .L8A3 1877 .C6	E. S. Glover	Brooklyn Land & Building Co., Los Angeles	A. L. Bancroft & Co., San Francisco	13 × 23½
25.1	Los Angeles 1877 (with Brooklyn Hights)	G4364 .L8A3 1877 .G6 1977	E. S. Glover	Brooklyn Land and Building Co., Los Angeles, Cal. Reproduced in 1977 by Historic Urban Plans, Ithaca, New York	A. L. Bancroft & Co., Lith., S. F.	14½ × 23 Facsimile
26	Los Angeles, Santa Monica & Wilmington 1877	G4364 .L8A3 1877 .G61	E. S. Glover, Los Angeles, Cal.	E. S. Glover, Los Angeles, Cal.		21 × 33½

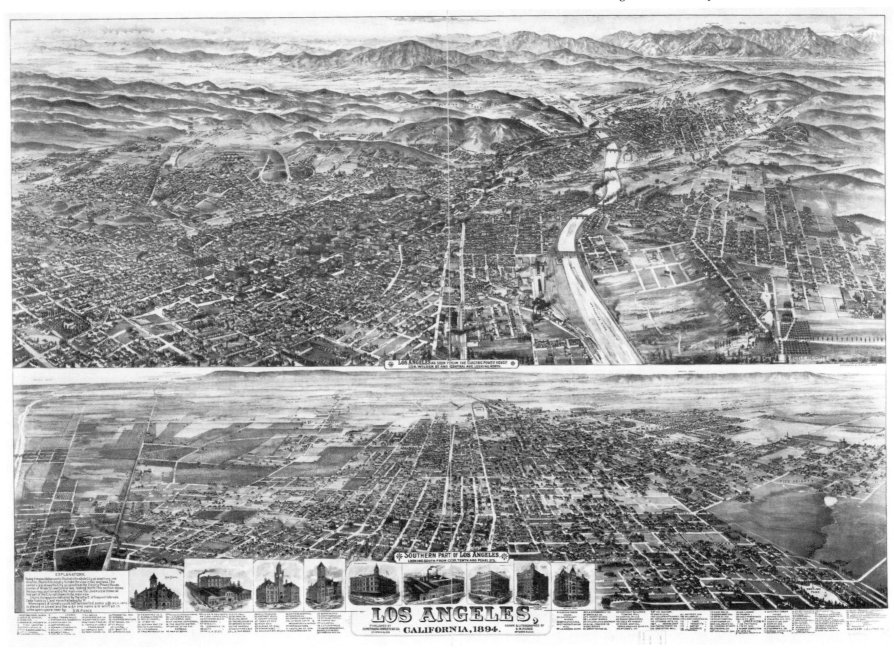

Los Angeles, California, 1894. Drawn and lithographed by B. W. Pierce. With the unofficial closing of the western frontier in 1890, Los Angeles was the fifth largest American city in the West.

Entry No.	City and Date	LC Call No.	Artist	Publisher	Lithographer	Map Size (inches)
26.1	Los Angeles [1888]	Prints & Photographs Division	S. F. Cook	A. J. Hatch & Co. San Francisco	Britton & Rey, Lith., S. F.	18 × 34
27	Los Angeles 1891	G4364 .L8A3 1891 .E6	H. B. Elliott	Southern California Land Co.	Elliott Publishing Co.	31 × 44
27.1	Los Angeles 1893	G4364 .L8A3 1893 .B4				8 × 19 Photograph
28	Los Angeles 1894	G4364 .L8A3 1894 .P5	B. W. Pierce	Semi-Tropic Homestead Co.	B. W. Pierce; L[os] A[ngeles] Lith.	31 × 44
28.1	Los Angeles 1894	G4364 .L8A3 1894 .P5 1977	B. W. Pierce	Semi-Tropic Homestead Co. Reproduced in 1977 by Historic Urban Plans, Ithaca, New York	B. W. Pierce	15 × 18 Facsimile
29	Los Angeles 1909	G4364 .L8A3 1909 .G3	Worthington Gates	Bird's Eye View Publishing Co., Los Angeles	Western Lith. Co., Los Angeles	22½ × 36
29.1	Monterey 1842	G4364 .M77A35 1842 .L3 1972	[Thomas] Larkin	[Thomas] Larkin. Reproduced in [1972?] by Historic Urban Plans, Ithaca, New York	[Francis] D'Avignon, N. Y.	13 × 21 Facsimile
29.2	Oakland [1887?]	G4364 .O2A3 1887 .O3		*Oakland Tribune*	Britton & Rey, S. F.	16½ × 23½ Negative photostat
30	Oakland 1900	G4364 .O2A3 1900 .S6	F. L.	F. & H. Soderberg	Mutual L. & Lith. Co., San Francisco	28 × 43
30.1	Pasadena 1893	G4364 .P4A3 1893 .P5 1972	B. W. Pierce, L. A., Cal.	Wood & Church. Reproduced in 1972 by Historic Urban Plans, Ithaca, New York	B. W. Pierce, L. A., Cal.	21 × 31 Facsimile
30.2	Pasadena [1903]	G4364 .P4A3 1903 .B5				17 × 28
31	Placerville 1888	G4364 .P74A3 1888 .R6 1969	R. H. & L. Roethe	*Weekly Observer.* Reproduced in 1969 by Historic Urban Plans, Ithaca, New York	W. W. Elliott, Lith., S. F.	20½ × 28 Facsimile
31.1	Sacramento 1850	Prints & Photographs Division	Geo. W. Casilear & Henry Bainbridge	Casilear & Bainbridge	[Napoleon] Sarony, New York	26 × 37
31.2	Sacramento City 1850	Prints & Photographs Division	G. V. Cooper; C. Parsons	Stringer & Townsend, New York	Wm. Endicott & Co., N. York	17 × 23½
32	Sacramento [189-?]	G4364 .S2A3 189- .E5	R. H.	W. W. Elliott; *Daily Record-Union and Weekly Union*		24 × 36

Entry No.	City and Date	LC Call No.	Artist	Publisher	Lithographer	Map Size (inches)
32.1	San Bernadino [1886]	G4364 .S3A3 1886 .E4		W. H. Syme & Co. Reproduced from original in the University of California at Berkeley Bancroft Library	W. W. Elliott	8 × 10 Photograph
32.2	San Buenaventura 1877		E. S. Glover	E. S. Glover. Reproduced from original in the University of California at Berkeley Bancroft Library	A. L. Bancroft & Co., Lith., San Francisco	8 × 10 Photograph
32.3	San Diego 1873	G4364 .S4A35 1873 .M3 1970	A. E. Mathews	A. L. Bancroft & Co., San Francisco, Cal. Reproduced in 1970 by Historic Urban Plans, Ithaca, New York	A. L. Bancroft & Co., Lith.	14 × 20 Facsimile
33	San Diego 1876	G4364 .S4A3 1876 .G6	E. S. Glover	Schneider & Kueppers, San Diego	A. L. Bancroft & Co., San Francisco	19 × 27
33.1	San Francisco [1846?]	Prints & Photographs Division	Deroy		Deroy	15½ × 20
33.2	San Francisco 1846-47	G4364 .S5A35 1847 .B6	W. F. Swasey	W. F. Swasey	Bosqui Eng. & Print. Co.	20 × 20½
34	San Francisco 1846-47	G4364 .S5A35 1847 .B6 1968	Capt. W. F. Swasey	Bosqui Eng. & Print. Co., c1884. Reproduced in 1968 by Historic Urban Plans, Ithaca, New York	Bosqui Eng. & Print. Co.	19 × 20½ Facsimile
34.1	San Francisco 1851	Prints & Photographs Division	Henry Bainbridge & Geo. W. Casilear	Geo. W. Casilear, New York City, and Atwill, San Francisco	Lith. of Sarony & Major, New York	25½ × 35½
34.2	San Francisco 1862	Prints & Photographs Division	C. B. Gifford	A. Rosenfield, S. F.	C. B. Gifford; Printed by L. Nagel, S. F.	14 × 83½
34.3	San Francisco 1864	Prints & Photographs Division	C. B. Gifford	Robinson & Snow, S. F.	C. B. Gifford; Printed by L. Nagel, S. F.	28½ × 40
35	San Francisco 1868	G4364 .S5A3 1868 .G6	George H. Goddard	Snow & May	Britton & Rey, San Francisco	27½ × 41
35.1	San Francisco 1868	G4364 .S5A3 1868 .G7 1972	W. Vallance Gray & C. B. Gifford	W. Vallance Gray & C. B. Gifford, S. F. Reproduced in [1972?] by The American West, Palo Alto, Calif.	W. Vallance Gray & C. B. Gifford	14½ × 20½ Facsimile
35.2	San Francisco 1868	G4364 .S5A3 1868 .G6 1976	George H. Goddard	Snow & Roos. Reproduced in 1976 by Historic Urban Plans, Ithaca, New York	Britton & Rey, S. F.	21 × 27 Facsimile

Entry No.	City and Date	LC Call No.	Artist	Publisher	Lithographer	Map Size (inches)
36	San Francisco 1875	G4364 .S5A3 1875 .M3	Frederick Marriott, L. R. Townsend, E. Wyneken & J. Mendenhall		Britton & Rey, San Francisco	20½ × 31
37	San Francisco & Surrounding Country 1876	G4364 .S5A3 1876 .G6	G. H. Goddard	Snow & May	Britton & Rey, San Francisco	33 × 47
37.1	San Francisco 1878	G4364 .S5A3 1878 .P3	C. R. Parsons	Currier & Ives, New York		23½ × 33
38	San Francisco 1878	G4364 .S5A3 1878 .P3 1968	C. R. Parsons	Currier & Ives, New York. Reproduced in 1968 by Historic Urban Plans, Ithaca, New York		21 × 27½ Facsimile
39	San Gabriel [1893]	G4364 .S52A3 1893 .M6		D. D. Morse		14 × 20½
39.1	San Gabriel [1893]	G4364 .S52A3 1893 .M6 1975	Morse, D. D.	Reproduced in 1975 by Historic Urban Plans, Ithaca, New York		15½ × 20 Facsimile
39.2	San Jacinto [1886]	G4364 .S55A3 1886 .M6	E. S. Moore	E. S. Moore		18 × 25½
40	San Jose 1869	G4364 .S6A3 1869 .G7	W. Vallance Gray & C. B. Gifford	Geo. H. Ware, San Jose	W. Vallance Gray & C. B. Gifford, S. F.; L. Nagel Print, S. F.	19½ × 28
41	San Jose 1875	G4364 .S6A3 1875 .G5	C. B. Gifford	W. C. Gifford, San Jose	A. L. Bancroft & Co., San Francisco	19 × 27
42	San Jose 1901	G4364 .S6A3 1901 .S7	F. L.	N. J. Stone Company, San Francisco, Cal.	Britton & Rey, S. F.	28½ × 42
42.1	San Luis Obispo 1877	G4364 .S63A3 1877 .G6 1972	E. S. Glover	E. S. Glover. Reproduced in 1972 by Historic Urban Plans, Ithaca, New York	A. L. Bancroft & Co., San Francisco	16 × 24 Facsimile
43	San Mateo 1931	G4364 .S64A3 1931 .C5		Aug. Chevalier		12½ × 24
44	San Mateo Park 1905	G4364 .S64:2S3A3 1905 .B8		Baldwin & Howell		9 × 7½
44.1	San Pedro [189-?]	G4364 .L8:2S26A3 189- .P4	B. W. Pierce, L. A. Cal.		B. W. Pierce, L. A., Cal.	16½ × 23½ Negative photostat
45	Santa Barbara 1877	G4364 .S68A3 1877 .G6	E. S. Glover	E. S. Glover	A. L. Bancroft & Co., San Francisco	20½ × 30½
45.1	Santa Barbara 1877	G4364 .S68A3 1877 .G6 1972	E. S. Glover	E. S. Glover. Reproduced in 1972 by Historic Urban Plans, Ithaca, New York	A. L. Bancroft & Co., S. F.	14 × 19½ Facsimile

Entry No.	City and Date	LC Call No.	Artist	Publisher	Lithographer	Map Size (inches)
46	Santa Barbara 1896	G4364 .S68A3 1896 .S3				5½ × 7½
47	Santa Barbara 1898	G4364 .S68A3 1898 .G5		P. E. Gifford	Los Angeles Litho. Co.	25 × 36½
48	Santa Rosa 1876	G4364 .S72A3 1876 .G6	E. S. Glover	Wm. M. Evans	A. L. Bancroft & Co., San Francisco	17½ × 25½
48.1	Santa Rosa 1885	G4364 .S72A3 1885 .E6 1972		Reproduced in 1972 by Historic Urban Plans, Ithaca, New York	Elliott & Co., Oakland, Cal.	21½ × 26 Facsimile
48.2	Shasta 1856	Prints & Photographs Division	Kuchel & Dressel, S. F.	A. Roman	Britton & Rey	12½ × 13½
49	Sonora 1852	G4364 .S795A35 1852 .G6		G. H. Goddard. Reproduced from original in New York Historical Society, New York City	Pollard & Brittons, S. F.	8 × 10 Photograph
49.1	Stockton [189-?]	G4364 .S9A35 189- .E5	C. P. Cook		W. W. Elliott, Lith., S. F.	15 × 23½ Negative photostat
50	Stockton 1895	G4364 .S9A3 1895 .D32		Dakin Publishing Co.		22 × 33
51	Stockton 1895	G4364 .S9A3 1895 .D3		Dakin Publishing Co., San Francisco		27½ × 40
52	Stockton 1895	G4364 .S9A3 1895 .M5		Dakin Publishing Co., San Francisco; John H. Mitchell		27 × 37½
53	Stockton 1895	G4364 .S9A3 1895 .D31		Dakin Publishing, San Francisco		27 × 40
53.1	Yreka & Mt. Shasta 1884	G4364 .Y7A3 1884 .W3	Fred A. Walpole	Fred A. Walpole	Beck & Pauli, Lith., Milwaukee, Wis.	43½ × 22

Colorado

Entry No.	City and Date	LC Call No.	Artist	Publisher	Lithographer	Map Size (inches)
53.2	Aspen 1893	G4314 .A72A3 1893 .K6	Augustus Koch, K. Cy., Mo.	*The Aspen Times*		21 × 27½
54	Black Hawk 1882	G4314 .B32A3 1882 .S7		J. J. Stoner, Madison, Wisconsin	Beck & Pauli, Lith., Milwaukee, Wisconsin	8 × 19
55	Buena Vista 1882	G4314 .B87A3 1882 .S7		J. J. Stoner, Madison, Wisconsin	Beck & Pauli, Lith., Milwaukee, Wisconsin	10 × 14

Colorado

Entry No.	City and Date	LC Call No.	Artist	Publisher	Lithographer	Map Size (inches)
56	Canon City 1882	G4314 .C2A3 1882 .W4	H. Wellge	J. J. Stoner, Madison, Wisconsin	Beck & Pauli, Lith., Milwaukee, Wisconsin	10 × 16½
56.1	Central City and Blackhawk 1873	G4314 .C32A3 1873 .G6 1971	E. S. Glover	Reproduced in 1971 by Historic Urban Plans, Ithaca, New York	Strobridge & Co., Lith., Cincinnati, O.	15 × 17½ Facsimile
57	Central City (imaginary place) 1887	G9930 1887 .K6		John Kohfahl, New York	Robert A. Welcke, New York	15 × 19
58	Colorado Springs, Colorado City & Manitou 1882	G4314 .C5A3 1882 .S7		J. J. Stoner, Madison, Wisconsin	Beck & Pauli, Lith., Milwaukee, Wisconsin	15 × 23
58.1	Colorado Springs, Colorado City & Manitou 1882	G4314 .C5A3 1882 .S7 1967	J. J. Stoner, Madison, Wis.	J. J. Stoner, Madison, Wisconsin. Reproduced in 1967 by Historic Urban Plans, Ithaca, New York	Beck & Pauli, Lith., Milwaukee, Wis.	16 × 23 Facsimile
58.2	Colorado Springs [1890]	G4314 .C5A3 1890 .W4		American Publishing Co., Milwaukee		18 × 42
59	Colorado Springs 1909	G4314 .C5A3 1909 .B4		Benford-Bryan Publishing Co., Denver		13 × 18½
59.1	Cripple Creek 1895	G4314 .C9A3 1895 .A4	C. H. Amerine, Cripple Creek		The Denver Lith. Co., Denver, Colo.	38 × 26½
60	Cripple Creek & Victor 1896	G4314 .C9A3 1896 .P5	Phillips & DesJardins		The Western Litho. Co., Denver	28 × 37
61	Denver 1874	G4314 .D4A3 1874 .D4 1970		Reproduced in 1970 by Historic Urban Plans, Ithaca, New York	[Strobridge & Co., Cincinnati, Ohio]	18 × 28 Facsimile
62	Denver 1874	G4314 .D4A3 1874 .S7 1971		Reproduced [in 1971] from an original lithograph in the State Historical Society of Colorado	Strobridge & Co., Cincinnati, Ohio	14½ × 23 Facsimile
63	Denver 1881	G4314 .D4A3 1881 .F6	J. H. Flett			9 × 14 Photographic copy
64	Denver 1887	G4314 .D4A3 1887 .R6		Rocky Mountain News Printing Co., Denver, Colorado	Mills Eng. Co., Denver	19 × 24
65	Denver 1889	G4314 .D4A3 1889 .W4	H. Wellge	American Publishing Co., Milwaukee, Wisconsin		27½ × 42½

Entry No.	City and Date	LC Call No.	Artist	Publisher	Lithographer	Map Size (Inches)
65.1	Denver (Harlem and Jacksons Broadway Heights Development) 1907	G4314 .D4A3 1907 .M5	A. E. Mitchell	A. F. Haraszthy & W. J. Voit, Colorado Land Headquarters, Denver, Colo.	Denver Engraving Co.	20 × 25
66	Denver 1908	G4314 .D4A3 1908 .B4		Bird's Eye View Publishing Co., Denver	The Denver Lith. Co., Denver	42½ × 62
66.1	[Fort Collins 1865?]	G4314 .F4A3 1865 .H6	[Merritt Dana Houghton]			4½ × 8 Photographic copy
67	Fort Collins 1899	G4314 .F4A3 1899 .H6	M. D. Houghton			7½ × 13 Photographic copy
67.1	Georgetown 1874	G4314 .G3A3 1874 .G6 1971	E. S. Glover	Reproduced in 1971 by Historic Urban Plans, Ithaca, New York	Strobridge & Co., Cincinnati	16 × 17½ Facsimile
68	Golden 1882	G4314 .G6A3 1882 .S7		J. J. Stoner, Madison, Wisconsin	Beck & Pauli, Lith., Milwaukee, Wisconsin	11 × 23½
69	Greeley 1882	G4314 .G8A3 1882 .S7		J. J. Stoner, Madison, Wisconsin	Beck & Pauli, Lith., Milwaukee, Wisconsin	15 × 23
70	Gunnison 1882	G4314 .G9A3 1882 .S7		J. J. Stoner, Madison, Wisconsin	Beck & Pauli, Lith., Milwaukee, Wisconsin	11 × 21
71	Leadville 1879	G4314 .L5A3 1879 .K6	Augustus Koch	Augustus Koch	Ramsey, Millett & Hudson, Kansas City, Missouri	23 × 33½
72	Leadville 1882	G4314 .L5A3 1882 .W4	H. Wellge	J. J. Stoner, Madison, Wisconsin	Beck & Pauli, Lith., Milwaukee, Wisconsin	19 × 26½
73	Maysville 1882	G4314 .M37A3 1882 .S7		J. J. Stoner, Madison, Wisconsin	Beck & Pauli, Lith., Milwaukee, Wisconsin	7 × 15
74	Pueblo 1890	G4314 .P8A3 1890 .A6		American Publishing Co., Milwaukee, Wisconsin		36 × 26
75	Salida 1882	G4314 .S3A3 1882 .S7		J. J. Stoner, Madison, Wisconsin	Beck & Pauli, Lith., Milwaukee, Wisconsin	10 × 16½
76	Trinidad 1882	G4314 .T7A3 1882 .S7		J. J. Stoner, Madison, Wisconsin	Beck & Pauli, Lith., Milwaukee, Wisconsin	13 × 17½

Leadville, Colorado, 1879. Drawn by Augustus Koch.
This 1877 view shows the amazing growth only two
years after its founding of Leadville, a typical boom to
bust mining town on the frontier.

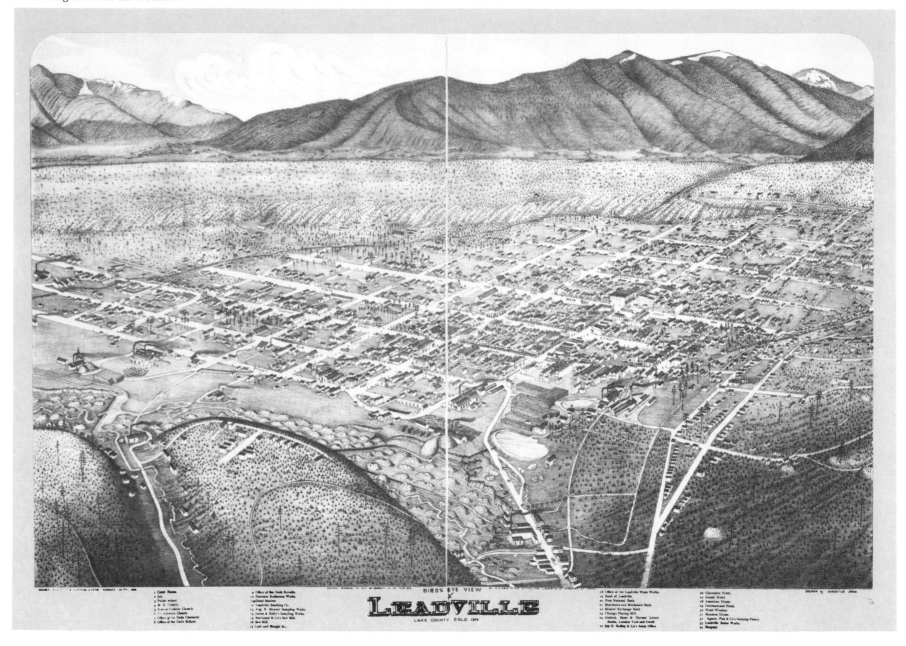

BIRDS EYE VIEW

LEADVILLE

LAKE COUNTY COLO. 1879

Connecticut

Entry No.	City and Date	LC Call No.	Artist	Publisher	Lithographer	Map Size (inches)
76.1[1]	Ansonia [187-?]	G3784 .A6A3 187- .B3	O. H. Bailey & Co.	O. H. Bailey & Co.	C. H. Vogt, J. Knauber & Co.	17½ × 23½ Negative photostat
77	Ansonia 1921	G3784 .A6A3 1921 .H8		Hughes & Bailey, Waterbury, Connecticut	[Meriden Gravure Co., Meriden, Conn.]	22½ × 32½
77.1[1]	Bethel 1879	G3784 .B5A3 1879 .B3		O. H. Bailey & Co., Boston.		17½ × 23½ Negative photostat
77.2	Birmingham 1876	G3784 .B54A3 1876 .B3	O. H. Bailey & Co., Boston	O. H. Bailey & Co., Boston	C. H. Vogt, Lith., Milwaukee	19½ × 23½
77.3	Bridgeport 1875	G3784 .B7A3 1875 .B3	O. H. Bailey & Co.	O. H. Bailey & Co.	American Oleograph Co., Milwaukee, Wisconsin	26 × 34½
77.4[1]	Bristol 1878	G3784 .B8A3 1878 .B3		O. H. Bailey & Co., Boston	Beck & Pauli, Lith.	17½ × 23½ Negative photostat
78	Bristol 1889	G3784 .B8A3 1889 .N6	Geo. E. Norris, Brockton, Mass.	Geo. E. Norris, Brockton, Mass.	The Burleigh Lith. Est., Troy, New York	19½ × 31½
79	Bristol 1907	G3784 .B8A3 1907 .H8		Hughes & Bailey, New York		31 × 35
79.1	Broad Brook [187-]	G3784 .B82A3 187- .B3		[O. H. Bailey & Co., Boston]	O. H. Bailey & Co., Lith., Boston	17½ × 23½ Negative photostat
79.2	Cheshire 1882	G3784 .C3A3 1882 .B3		O. H. Bailey & Co., Boston		19½ × 22½
79.3[1]	Chester 1881	G3784 .C39A3 1881 .B3		O. H. Bailey & Co., Boston		17½ × 23½ Negative photostat
79.4	Clinton 1881	G3784 .C4A3 1881 .B3		O. H. Bailey & Co., Boston		18½ × 24½
79.5	Danbury 1875	G3784 .D2A3 1875 .B3	O. H. Bailey	Fowler & Bailey	C. H. Vogt, Lith., Milwaukee; J. Knauber & Co.	20 × 26
79.6[1]	Danielsonville 1877	G3784 .D3A3 1877 .B3	O. H. Bailey	M. P. Dowe, Danielsonville, Conn.	Bremner & Co., Milwaukee, Wis.	17½ × 23½ Negative photostat

[1] Reproduced from the original in the Connecticut State Library, Hartford.

Entry No.	City and Date	LC Call No.	Artist	Publisher	Lithographer	Map Size (inches)
79.7	Derby 1920	G3784 .D7A3 1920 .H8 Fow 81	[T. M. Fowler] (T. M. Fowler Map Coll. 81)	Hughes & Bailey, New York		8½ × 11
80	Derby 1920	G3784 .D7A3 1920 .H8	[T. M. Fowler]	Hughes & Bailey, New York		8 × 10 Photograph
80.1[1]	East Hampton 1880	G3784 .E3A3 1880 .B3		O. H. Bailey & Co., Boston		17 × 21 Positive photostat
80.2	Essex, Centerbrook & Ivoryton 1881	G3784 .E85A3 1881 .B3	A. E. D.	O. H. Bailey & Co., Boston		20½ × 25½
80.3[1]	Hartford 1864	G3784 .H3A3 1864 .B3			John Bachmann, Lith.; F. Heppenheimer, N. Y.	17½ × 23½ Positive photostat
80.4[1]	Hartford 1877	G3784 .H3A3 1877 .B3	O. H. Bailey & Co., Boston	O. H. Bailey & Co., Boston		Negative Photostat in 2 parts, each 23½ × 17½
80.5[1]	Hartford [189-]	G3784 .H3:2B6A3 189- .B6				14 × 21 Negative photostat
80.6[1]	Hazardville 1880	G3784 .H4A3 1880 .B3		O. H. Bailey & Co., Boston		17 × 23 Negative photocopy
80.7	Higganum 1881	G3784 .H5A3 1881 .B3	A. E. D.	O. H. Bailey & Co., Boston		19½ × 21½
81	Jewett City 1889	G3784 .J4A3 1889 .B8		L. R. Burleigh, Troy, New York	The Burleigh Lith. Est., Troy, New York	16 × 26½
81.1	Madison 1881	G3784 .M13A3 1881 .B3		O. H. Bailey & Co., Boston		16 × 24
82	Manchester 1914	G3784 .M2A3 1914 .H8		Hughes & Bailey, New York	[Franklin Engraving Co., Boston, Mass.]	27 × 36½
82.1[1]	Meriden 1875	G3784 .M4A3 1875 .B3	O. H. Bailey & Co.	O. H. Bailey & Co.	C. H. Vogt, Lith.; J. Knauber & Co., Milwaukee	Negative Photostat in 2 parts, each 23 × 17
83	Meriden 1918	G3784 .M4A3 1918 .F6 Fow 65	T. M. Fowler (T. M. Fowler Map Coll. 65)	Hughes & Bailey, New York & Boston	[Meriden Gravure Co., Meriden, Conn.]	25 × 35½

[1] Reproduced from the original in the Connecticut State Library, Hartford.

Middletown, Connecticut, 1915. Drawn by T. M. Fowler.
Published by Hughes & Bailey.

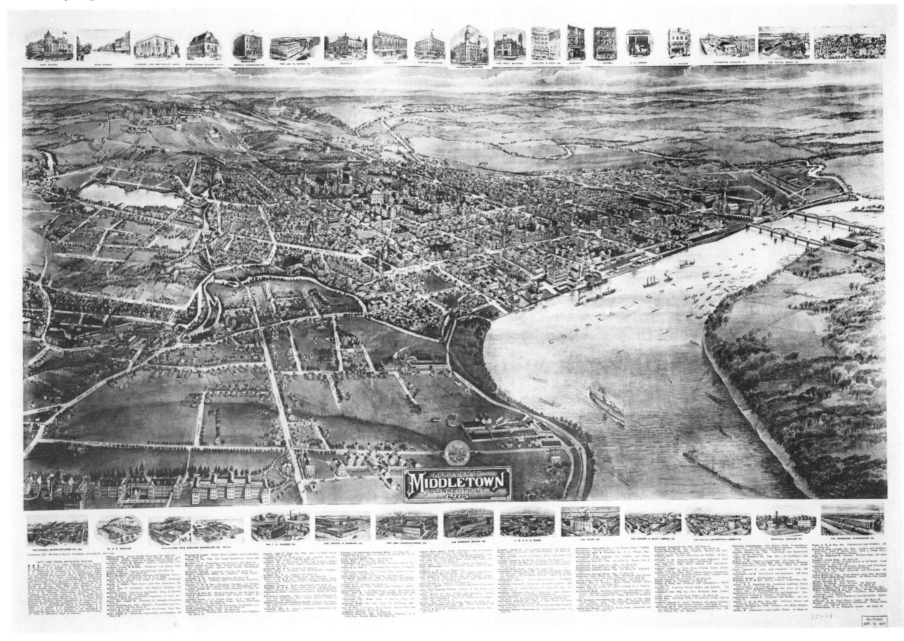

Entry No.	City and Date	LC Call No.	Artist	Publisher	Lithographer	Map Size (inches)
84	Middletown 1877	G3784 .M5A3 1877 .B3		O. H. Bailey & Co.		25 × 29
85	Middletown 1915	G3784 .M5A3 1915 .F6 Fow 80	T. M. Fowler (T. M. Fowler Map Coll. 80)	Hughes & Bailey, New York	[Meriden Gravure Co., Meriden, Conn. & National Process Co., N. Y.]	25 × 35½
85.1	Middletown 1915	G3784 .M5A3 1915 .F62	T. M. Fowler	Hughes & Bailey, New York		24½ × 35
85.2[1]	Moosup, Uniondale and Almyville 1889	G3784 .M72A3 1889 .B8	L. R. Burleigh, Troy, N. Y.	L. R. Burleigh, Troy, N. Y.	The Burleigh Lith. Est., Troy, N. Y.	13 × 21½ Negative photostat
85.3	Mystic 1879	G3784 .M92A3 1879 .B3	O. H. Bailey & J. C. Hazen, Boston	O. H. Bailey & J. C. Hazen, Boston		20 × 25½
85.4	Naugatuck 1877	G3784 .N2A3 1877 .B3	O. H. Bailey & Co., Boston	O. H. Bailey & Co., Boston	C. H. Vogt, Lith., Milwaukee	19½ × 25
86	Naugatuck 1906	G3784 .N2A3 1906 .H8		Hughes & Bailey, New York		27 × 34
86.1	New Britain 1875	G3784 .N3A3 1875 .B3	O. H. Bailey & Co.	O. H. Bailey & Co.	C. H. Vogt, Lith., Milwaukee; J. Knauber & Co.	20 × 26
86.2[1]	New Britain 1899	G3784 .N3A3 1899 .L3		Landis and Hughes, Newark, N. J.		Negative photostat in 6 parts, each 23½ × 17½
86.3[1]	New Canaan 1878	G3784 .N32A3 1878 .B3		O. H. Bailey & Co., Boston		18 × 23 Negative photostat
87	New Haven 1879	G3784 .N4A3 1879 .B3	O. H. Bailey & J. C. Hazen, Boston	O. H. Bailey & J. C. Hazen, Boston		29½ × 38
88	New London 1911	G3784 .N5A3 1911 .H8		Hughes & Bailey, New York		32 × 39½
89	New Milford 1906	G3784 .N52A3 1906 .H8		Hughes & Bailey, New York		27 × 30
90	Norwalk, South Norwalk and East Norwalk 1899	G3784 .N7A3 1899 .L3		Landis & Hughes, New York		32½ × 44½
91	Norwich 1876	G3784 .N8A3 1876 .B3	O. H. Bailey & Co.	O. H. Bailey & Co.	C. H. Vogt, Lith., Milwaukee, Wisconsin; J. Knauber & Co.	22½ × 34½

[1] Reproduced from the original in the Connecticut State Library, Hartford.

Entry No.	City and Date	LC Call No.	Artist	Publisher	Lithographer	Map Size (inches)
92	Norwich 1912	G3784 .N8A3 1912 .H8		Hughes & Bailey, New York	[Hughes & Bailey, New York]	33 × 39½
93	Plainville 1878	G3784 .P4A3 1878 .B3	O. H. Bailey & J. C. Hazen, Boston	O. H. Bailey & J. C. Hazen, Boston	C. H. Vogt	19 × 24½
94	Plainville 1907	G3784 .P4A3 1907 .B3		Hughes & Bailey, New York		19 × 29
94.1	Putnam 1877	G3784 .P9A3 1877 .B3	O. H. Bailey & Co., Boston	O. H. Bailey & Co., Boston	C. H. Vogt, Lith., Milwaukee; J. Knauber & Co.	19 × 25½
94.2	Rockville 1877	G3784 .R7A3 1877 .B3		O. H. Bailey & Co., Boston	J. Knauber & Co., Milwaukee, Wis.	21½ × 26
94.3	Seymour 1879	G3784 .S3A3 1879 .B3	O. H. Bailey & Co., Boston	O. H. Bailey & Co., Boston		19½ × 24
95	Shelton 1919	G3784 .S4A3 1919 .H8		Hughes & Bailey, Boston	[Meriden Gravure Co., Meriden, Conn.]	20 × 31
95.1[1]	South Coventry 1878	G3784 .S5A3 1878 .B3		O. H. Bailey & Co., Boston		16½ × 22½ Negative photostat
96	Southington 1914	G3784 .S6A3 1914 .H8		Hughes & Bailey	[Consolidated Engraving Co. & Federal Engraving Co., Boston, Mass.]	28 × 36
97	South Manchester 1880	G3784 .S55A3 1880 .B3 Fow 1	[T. M. Fowler] (T. M. Fowler Map Coll. 1)	O. H. Bailey & Co., Boston		18½ × 24½
97.1	Stafford Springs 1878	G3784 .S68A3 1878 .B3		O. H. Bailey & Co., Boston		20½ × 23½
97.2	Stamford 1883	G3784 .S7A3 1883 .B8	L. R. Burleigh, Troy, N.Y.		Beck & Pauli, Lith., Milwaukee, Wis.	19½ × 34
97.3[1]	Stonington 1879	G3784 .S8A3 1879 .B3		O. H. Bailey & Co., Boston		17½ × 23 Negative photostat
97.4	Thomaston 1879	G3784 .T4A3 1879 .B3		O. H. Bailey & Co., Boston		19½ × 24½
97.5[1]	Torrington 1889	G3784 .T8A3 1889 .N6	Geo. E. Norris, Brockton, Mass.	Geo. E. Norris, Brockton, Mass.	The Burleigh Lith. Est., Troy, N.Y.	Negative photostat in 2 parts, each 18½ × 16½
98	Torrington 1907	G3784 .T8A3 1907 .B3		Hughes & Bailey, New York		29 × 36

[1] Reproduced from the original in the Connecticut State Library, Hartford.

31

Entry No.	City and Date	LC Call No.	Artist	Publisher	Lithographer	Map Size (inches)
98.1[1]	Unionville 1878	G3784 .U57A3 1878 .B3		O. H. Bailey & Co., Boston	Beck & Pauli, Lith.	17½ × 22 Negative photostat
98.2[1]	Wallingford 1881	G3784 .W2A3 1881 .B3		O. H. Bailey & Co., Boston		17½ × 22½ Negative photostat
99	Wallingford 1905 (with inset of city in 1852)	G3784 .W2A3 1905 .H8		Hughes & Bailey, New York		26 × 34
100	Waterbury 1899	G3784 .W3A3 1899 .L3		Landis & Hughes, New York		36 × 44
101	Waterbury 1917	G3784 .W3A3 1917 .F6 Fow 2	T. M. Fowler (T. M. Fowler Map Coll. 2)	Hughes & Bailey, Boston	[Meriden Gravure Co., Meriden, Conn.; Tudor Press, Boston]	23 × 32
102	Watertown 1918	G3784 .W33A3 1918 .H8		Hughes & Bailey, Boston	[Meriden Gravure Co., Meriden, Conn.]	22½ × 34½
102.1[1]	Westport 1878	G3784 .W54A3 1878 .B3		O. H. Bailey & Co., Boston		18 × 21 Negative photostat
102.2[1]	Willimantic 1876	G3784 .W7A3 1876 .B3	H. H. Bailey & J. C. Hazen	H. H. Bailey & J. C. Hazen.		16 × 22 Negative photostat
102.3	Willimantic 1882	Prints & Photographs Division	Wils Porter	W. O. Laughna, Art Publishing Co., N.Y.	Charles Hart Lith., N.Y.	24½ × 32½
103	Willimantic 1909	G3784 .W7A3 1909 .B3		Hughes & Bailey, New York		29 × 33
103.1	Windsor Locks 1877	G3784 .W82A3 1877 .B3		O. H. Bailey & Co., Boston	J. Knauber & Co., Milwaukee, Wis.	18 × 26½
103.2[1]	Winsted 1877	G3784 .W83A3 1877 .B3	O. H. Bailey & Co., Boston	O. H. Bailey & Co., Boston	C. H. Vogt & Co., Lith., Milwaukee	Negative photostat in 2 parts, each 22 × 16
104	Winsted 1908	G3784 .W83A3 1908 .B3		O. H. Bailey, New York		32 × 34
104.1	Wolcottville [between 1875 and 1878]	G3784 .W865A3 1875 .B7		O. H. Bailey & Co., Boston	D. Bremner & Co., Milwaukee	19½ × 24½

[1] Reproduced from the original in the Connecticut State Library, Hartford.

Delaware

Entry No.	City and Date	LC Call No.	Artist	Publisher	Lithographer	Map Size (inches)
105	Clayton 1885	G3834 .C55A3 1885 .C5				16½ × 18 Negative photostat
106	Wilmington 1874 (with inset of the city in 1770)	G3834 .W7A3 1874 .B3	H. H. Bailey & Co.	H. H. Bailey & Co.	G. W. Lewis, Lith., Albany, New York	20 × 39

District of Columbia

Entry No.	City and Date	LC Call No.	Artist	Publisher	Lithographer	Map Size (inches)
106.1	Washington 1834	G3851 .A35 1834 .C6 1977	G. Cooke	Lewis P. Clover, N.Y. Reproduced in 1977 by Historic Urban Plans, Ithaca, New York	Commeyer & Clark, N. York	14½ × 17 Facsimile
106.2	Washington 1852	G3851 .A35 1852 .S3 1975	E. Sachse	E. Sachse & Co., Baltimore, Md. Reproduced in 1975 by Historic Urban Plans, Ithaca, New York	E. Sachse & Co.	16 × 19 Facsimile
106.3	Washington 1862	G3851 .A3 1862 .S2 1968		Reproduced in 1968 by Historic Urban Plans, Ithaca, New York	E. Sachse & Co., Lith., Baltimore, Md.	11½ × 17 Facsimile
106.4	Washington [1869]	G3851 .A3 1869 .D3 1965	Theo. R. Davis	[Harpers Weekly] Reproduced in 1965 by Historic Urban Plans, Ithaca, New York		15½ × 20½ Facsimile
106.5	Washington 1871	G3851 .A35 1871 .S3 1978		Reproduced in 1978 by Historic Urban Plans, Ithaca, New York	E. Sachse & Co., Lith., Balto.	21 × 27½ Facsimile
107	Washington 1872	G3851 .A3 1872 .M6	Geo. A. Morrison	W. H. & O. H. Morrison		14½ × 20
107.1	Washington 1880	Prints & Photographs Division	C. R. Parsons	Currier & Ives, New York		23½ × 33½
108	Washington 1882	G3851 .A3 1882 .D3 1965	Theo. R. Davis (from photographs by W. H. Jackson)	Reproduced in 1965 by Historic Urban Plans, Ithaca, New York		16 × 20 Facsimile
109	Washington 1883 (Part Showing Georgetown, Foggy Bottom and Potomac Waterfront)	G3851 .A3 1883 .S3		A. Sachse & Co., Baltimore, Maryland		41 × 33

Entry No.	City and Date	LC Call No.	Artist	Publisher	Lithographer	Map Size (inches)
110	Washington 1883-84	G3851 .A3 1884 .S3	Adolph Sachse	A. Sachse & Co., Baltimore, Maryland	A. Sachse & Co., Baltimore, Maryland	In 3 parts, 43 × 21½, 42½ × 22½, and 43 × 21½
111	Washington 1892	G3851 .A3 1892 .C8 1970		Currier & Ives, New York. Reproduced in 1970 by Historic Urban Plans, Ithaca, New York		19 × 27½ Facsimile
111.1	Washington (Brookland) [1895]	G3852 .B74A3 1895 .G4	Gedney & Roberts	Barnes & Weaver, Washington, D.C.		17½ × 22
111.2	Washington 1921	G3851 .A3 1921 .O4	William Olsen			29 × 44
111.3	Washington 1922	G3851 .A3 1922 .O4	William Olsen	Reproduced in 1922 by The Columbia Planograph Co., Washington, D.C.		29 × 44
111.4	Washington 1923	G3851 .A3 1923 .04	William Olsen			21 × 29

Florida

Entry No.	City and Date	LC Call No.	Artist	Publisher	Lithographer	Map Size (inches)
111.5	Cedar-Key 1884	G3934 .C31A3 1884 .S7		J. J. Stoner, Madison, Wis.	Beck & Pauli, Litho., Milwaukee, Wis.	11½ × 22
111.6	Cedar-Key 1884	G3934 .C31A3 1884 .S7 1976		[J. J. Stoner, Madison, Wis.]	[Beck & Pauli, Lith., Milwaukee, Wis.]	11 × 21½ Facsimile
111.7	Fernandina 1884	G3934 .F29A3 1884 .S8 1978		J. J. Stoner, Madison, Wis. Reproduced in 1978	Beck & Pauli, Litho., Milwaukee, Wis.	15 × 28 Facsimile
112	Green Cove Springs 1885	G3934 .G6A3 1885 .N6		Norris, Wellge & Co., Milwaukee, Wisconsin	Beck & Pauli, Litho., Milwaukee, Wisconsin	19½ × 27
113	Jacksonville 1876	G3934 .J2A3 1876 .K6	Augustus Koch	Alvord, Kellogg & Campbell		25 × 30½
114	Jacksonville 1893	G3934 .J2A3 1893 .K6	Augustus Koch	Augustus Koch; Hudson-Kimberly Pub. Co., Kansas City, Missouri		28½ × 39
114.1	Key West [1855]	G3934 .K6A35 1855 .C7 1974	J. C. Clapp	Reproduced in 1974 by Historic Urban Plans, Ithaca, New York	Chandlor & Co., Lith., Boston; L. Crozelier	12 × 20½ Facsimile
115	Lake City 1885	G3934 .L2A3 1885 .N6	H. Wellge	Norris, Wellge & Co., Milwaukee, Wisconsin	Beck & Pauli, Litho., Milwaukee, Wisconsin	15 × 23
116	Longwood 1885	G3934 .L84A3 1885 .M5	G. A. Miller	P. A. Demens & Co.	Forbes Co. Photo Lith.	22 × 34

Washington, D.C., 1884. Published by Adolphe Sachse & Co., Baltimore, Maryland. This portion of a three-sheet map shows the area around the Capitol three years before construction of the Library of Congress began.

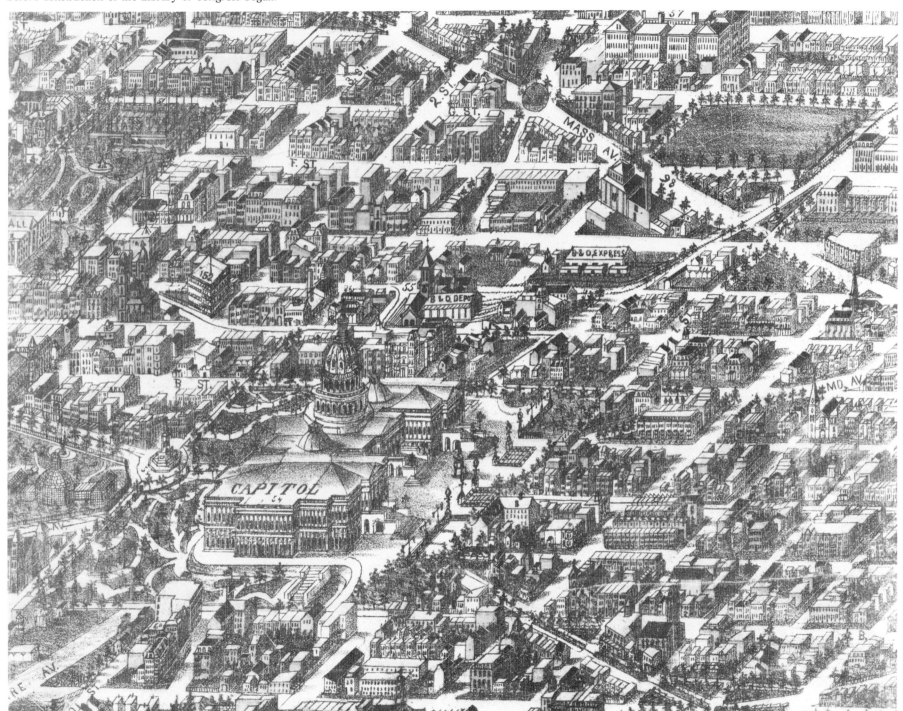

Entry No.	City and Date	LC Call No.	Artist	Publisher	Lithographer	Map Size (inches)
116.1	Palatka 1884	G3934 .P2A3 1884 .S8 1978		J. J. Stoner, Madison, Wis. Reproduced in 1978 by Forward House, Palatka, Florida	Beck & Pauli, Litho., Milwaukee, Wis.	15½ × 22½ Facsimile
117	Pensacola 1885	G3934 .P4A3 1885 .W4	H. Wellge	Norris, Wellge & Co., Milwaukee, Wisconsin	Beck & Pauli, Lith., Milwaukee, Wisconsin	21 × 26½
117.1	Pensacola 1885	G3934 .P4A3 1885 .W4 1975	H. Wellge	Norris, Wellge & Co., Milwaukee, Wis. Reproduced in 1975 by Historic Urban Plans, Ithaca, New York	Beck & Pauli, Litho., Milwaukee, Wis.	22½ × 26 Facsimile
117.2	Pensacola 1885	G3934 .P4A3 1885 .W4 1976	H. Wellge	Norris, Wellge & Co., Milwaukee, Wis. Reproduced in 1976 by the Pensacola Historical Museum, Pensacola, Florida	Beck & Pauli, Litho., Milwaukee, Wis.	17½ × 22 Facsimile
117.3	Pensacola 1896	G3934 .P4A3 1896 .K6 1976	August Koch	Thos. C. Watson & Co., Pensacola, Florida. Reproduced in 1976 by the Pensacola Historical Museum, Pensacola, Florida		16 × 23 Facsimile
118	Tallahassee 1885	G3934 .T2A3 1885 .W4	H. Wellge	Norris, Wellge & Co., Milwaukee, Wisconsin	Beck & Pauli, Litho., Milwaukee, Wisconsin	17 × 23½
118.1	Tallahassee 1885	G3934 .T2A3 1885 .W4 1971	Henry Wellge	Norris, Wellge & Co., Milwaukee, Wis. Reproduced in 1971 by Historic Urban Plans, Ithaca, New York	Beck & Pauli, Litho., Milwaukee, Wis.	16½ × 23 Facsimile
119	Tallahassee 1926	G3934 .T2A3 1926 .W9		James Wynne		19 × 15

Georgia

Entry No.	City and Date	LC Call No.	Artist	Publisher	Lithographer	Map Size (inches)
120	Albany 1885	G3924 .A3A3 1885 .N6		Norris, Wellge & Co., Milwaukee, Wisconsin	Beck & Pauli, Litho., Milwaukee, Wisconsin	14½ × 23½
121	Atlanta 1871	G3924 .A8A3 1871 .R8 Rug 3	A. Ruger, St. Louis, Mo. (Ruger Map Coll. 3)	A. Ruger, St. Louis, Mo.		20½ × 28
121.1	Atlanta 1871	G3924 .A8A3 1871 .R8 1976	A. Ruger, St. Louis, Mo.	A. Ruger, St. Louis, Mo. Reproduced in 1976 by Historic Urban Plans, Ithaca, New York		24 × 27 Facsimile

Entry No.	City and Date	LC Call No.	Artist	Publisher	Lithographer	Map Size (Inches)
122	Atlanta 1892	G3924 .A8A3 1892 .K6	Aug. Koch	H. G. Saunders & W. L. Kline	Hughes Litho. Co., Chicago	33½ × 52
123	Atlanta 1919	G3924 .A8A3 1919 .F6		Foote & Davies Co.		18 × 30
124	Columbus 1886	G3924 .C7A3 1886 .W4	H. Wellge	Henry Wellge & Co., Milwaukee, Wisconsin	Beck & Pauli Lith. Co., Milwaukee, Wisconsin	24½ × 36
124.1	Columbus 1912	G3924 .C7A3 1912 .S1		S. & O. Engraving Co., Akron, O.		5 × 9
125	Cordele 1908	G3924 .C8A3 1908 .D6 Fow 3	A. E. Downs, Boston, Mass. (T. M. Fowler Map Coll. 3)	T. M. Fowler & A. E. Downs, Morrisville, Pa.		18½ × 29
126	Fitzgerald 1908	G3924 .F5A3 1908 .F6	T. M. Fowler, Morrisville, Pa.	T. M. Fowler, Morrisville, Pa.		23 × 29
127	Macon 1887	G3924 .M3A3 1887 .W4	H. Wellge	Henry Wellge & Co., Milwaukee, Wisconsin	The Beck & Pauli Lith. Co., Milwaukee	23 × 34½
128	Macon 1912	G3924 .M3A3 1912 .B8		J. W. Burke Co.		14 × 24½
129	Ocilla 1908	G3924 .03A3 1908 .F6	T. M. Fowler, Morrisville, Pa.	T. M. Fowler, Morrisville, Pa.		19 × 23
130	Quitman 1885	G3924 .Q5A3 1885 .N6		Norris, Wellge & Co., Milwaukee, Wisconsin	Beck & Pauli, Litho., Milwaukee, Wisconsin	12 × 16½
131	Tallapoosa 1892	G3924 .T2A3 1892 .N6	Geo. E. Norris, Brockton, Mass.	Geo. E. Norris, Brockton, Mass.	The Burleigh Litho. Co., Troy, New York	25 × 31½
132	Thomasville 1885	G3924 .T5A3 1885 .W4	H. Wellge	Norris Wellge & Co., Milwaukee, Wisconsin	Beck & Pauli, Litho., Milwaukee, Wisconsin	18 × 25½
133	Thomasville 1896	G3924 .T5A3 1896 .M6	Henry Moller			5½ × 9 Photograph
133.1	Valdosta 1885	G3924 .V2A3 1885 .W4	H. Wellge	Norris, Wellge & Co., Milwaukee, Wis.	Beck & Pauli, Litho., Milwaukee, Wis.	11½ × 17½

Idaho

| 134 | Hailey & Wood River Valley 1884 | G4274 .H3A3 1884 .B7 | A. E. Browning, Salt Lake City | A. E. Browning | The Collier & Cleveland Lith. Co., Denver, Colorado | 19 × 23½ |

Illinois

Entry No.	City and Date	LC Call No.	Artist	Publisher	Lithographer	Map Size (inches)
135	Alton 1867	G4104 .A5A3 1867 .R8 Rug 4	A. Ruger (Ruger Map Coll. 4)		Chicago Lithographing Co.	20½ × 28½
136	Aurora 1867	G4104 .A9A3 1867 .R8 Rug 5	A. Ruger (Ruger Map Coll. 5)		Chicago Lithographing Co., Chicago	20½ × 28
137	Aurora 1882	G4104 .A9A3 1882 .B7	H. Brosius	J. J. Stoner, Madison, Wisconsin	Beck & Pauli, Lith., Milwaukee, Wisconsin	20½ × 32
138	Batavia 1869	G4104 .B2A3 1869 .R8 Rug 6	A. Ruger (Ruger Map Coll. 6)		Merchants' Lithographing Co., Chicago	18 × 22
139	Belleville 1867	G4104 .B3A3 1867 .R8 Rug 7	A. Ruger (Ruger Map Coll. 7)		Chicago Lithographing Co.	20 × 27½
140	Bloomington 1867	G4104 .B6A3 1867 .R8 Rug 8	A. Ruger (Ruger Map Coll. 8)		Chicago Lithographing Co.	20 × 28
140.1	Cairo [1838]	G4104 .C15A35 1838 .S7 1970	Wm. Strickland	Reproduced in 1970 by Historic Urban Plans, Ithaca, New York	A. Hoffy; P. S. Duval, Lithogr., Philadelphia	13 × 19 Facsimile
141	Cairo 1867	G4104 .C15A3 1867 .R8 Rug 9	A. Ruger (Ruger Map Coll. 9)		Chicago Lithographing Co.	20 × 28½
142	Cairo 1888	G4104 .C15A3 1888 .W4	H. Wellge	Henry Wellge & Co., Milwaukee, Wisconsin	Beck & Pauli Lith. Co., Milwaukee, Wisconsin	22 × 33½
142.1	Cairo 1888	G4104 .C15A3 1888 .W4 1970	H. Wellge	Henry Wellge & Co., Milwaukee, Wis. Reproduced in 1970 by Historic Urban Plans, Ithaca, New York	Beck & Pauli, Lith. Co., Milwaukee	19½ × 31½ Facsimile
143	Centralia 1867	G4104 .C4A3 1867 .R8 Rug 10	A. Ruger (Ruger Map Coll. 10)		Chicago Lithographing Co.	19½ × 28
144	Champaign 1869	G4104 .C5A3 1869 .R8 Rug 11	A. Ruger (Ruger Map Coll. 11)		Chicago Lithogr. Co., Chicago	20½ × 26½
145	Chenoa 1869	G4104 .C56A3 1869 .R8 Rug 12	[Albert Ruger] (Ruger Map Coll. 12)			9 × 14½
145.1	Chicago 1779-1857	G4104 .C6S1 1893 .K9 1974		Kurz & Allison, Chicago, Ill. Reproduced in 1974 by Historic Urban Plans, Ithaca, New York		21 × 23½ Facsimile
146	Chicago 1857	G4104 .C6A3 1857 .P3	Chr[istian] Inger; J. T. Palmatary	Braunhold & Sonne. Additions by Charles Sonne	Herline & Hensel, Phila.	In 2 parts, each 47 × 41

Entry No.	City and Date	LC Call No.	Artist	Publisher	Lithographer	Map Size (inches)
147	Chicago [1860]	G4104 .C6A3 1860 .C5				5 × 8
148	Chicago 1868. (Inset Chicago in 1820)	G4104 .C6A35 1868 .R8 Rug 13	A. Ruger (Ruger Map Coll. 13)		Chicago Lithographing Co., Chicago	20 × 35
149	Chicago 1871	G4104 .C6A35 1871 .D3	Theodore R. Davis	Harper's Weekly. Reproduced in 1969 by Historic Urban Plans, Ithaca, New York		14½ × 20½
149.1	Chicago [1871]	G4104 .C6A35 1871 .D3 1969	[Theodore R. Davis]	[Harper's Weekly] Reproduced in 1969 by Historic Urban Plans, Ithaca, New York		15½ × 20½ Facsimile
149.2	Chicago 1874	Prints & Photographs Division	Parsons & Atwater	Currier & Ives	Parsons & Atwater	22½ × 32½
150	Chicago 1892	G4104 .C6A3 1892 .C8		Currier & Ives		23 × 33
150.1	Chicago 1892	G4104 .C6A3 1892 .C8 1970		Currier & Ives, New York. Reproduced in 1970 by Historic Urban Plans, Ithaca, New York		20½ × 27½ Facsimile
150.2	Chicago 1892	G4104 .C6A3 1892 .C8 1972		Currier & Ives, New York. Reproduced in 1972 by Historic Urban Plans, Ithaca, New York		14½ × 18½ Facsimile
151	Chicago 1892 (Inset Chicago 1832)	G4104 .C6A3 1892 .R6		Peter Roy, Chicago		19 × 32½
152	Chicago 1893	G4104 .C6A3 1893 .T7		Reynertson & Beckerman, Chicago	Eagle Lith. Co., Chicago	32½ × 46
152.1	Chicago [1894]	G4104 .C6A3 1894 .C5		Harper's Weekly		15 × 20½
153	Chicago (Business District) 1898	G4104 .C6A3 1898 .P6		Poole Bros., Chicago		In 4 parts, each 21½ × 29
154	Chicago 1915 (Central Business District)	G4104 .C6A3 1915 .R4		Arno B. Reincke		10½ × 16 Photograph
155	Chicago (Central Business Section) 1916	G4104 .C6A3 1916 .R4		Arno B. Reincke, Chicago		20 × 30½
156	Clinton 1869	G4104 .C75A3 1869 .R8 Rug 14	A. Ruger (Ruger Map Coll. 14)		Merchant's Lithographing Co., Chicago	17 × 22½

Entry No.	City and Date	LC Call No.	Artist	Publisher	Lithographer	Map Size (inches)
157	Danville 1869	G4104 .D2A3 1869 .R8 Rug 15	A. Ruger (Ruger Map Coll. 15)		Chicago Lithogr. Co., Chicago	18½ × 26
158	Decatur 1869	G4104 .D3A3 1869 .R8 Rug 16	A. Ruger (Ruger Map Coll. 16)		Chicago Lithogr. Co.	20 × 25½
159	Elgin 1880	G4104 .E5A3 1880 .U6	A. B. Upham	A. B. Upham	Shober & Carqueville Lith. Co., Chicago	19½ × 24½
160	El Paso 1869	G4104 .E457A3 1869 .R8 Rug 17	A. Ruger (Ruger Map Coll. 17)		Chicago Lithographg Co.	14 × 21
161	Geneva 1869	G4104 .G3A3 1869 .R8 Rug 18	A. Ruger (Ruger Map Coll. 18)		Merchant's Lithographing Co., Chicago	19 × 22½
162	Highland 1894	G4104 .H48A35 1894 .H6		J. S. Hoerner, Highland, Illinois	Heinicke-Fiegel Litho. Co., St. Louis	17 × 30½
163	Homer 1869	G4104 .H68A3 1869 .R8 Rug 19	A. Ruger (Ruger Map Coll. 19)		Merchants' Lithographing Co., Chicago	9½ × 12½
164	Kankakee 1869	G4104 .K2A3 1869 .R8 Rug 20	A. Ruger (Ruger Map Coll. 20)	Ruger & Stoner, Madison, Wisconsin	Chicago Lithog. Co., Chicago	21 × 26
165	Lincoln 1869	G4104 .L6A3 1869 .R8 Rug 21	[Albert Ruger] (Ruger Map Coll. 21)	Ruger & Stoner	Merchants Lithographing Co., Chicago, Ills.	20 × 26
166	Loda 1869	G4104 .L78A3 1869 .R8 Rug 22	A Ruger (Ruger Map Coll. 22)		Chicago Lith. Co.	13 × 20
167	Manteno 1869	G4104 .M26A3 1869 .R8 Rug 23	A. Ruger (Ruger Map Coll. 23)		Merchant's Lithogr. Co., Chicago	9½ × 12½
167.1	Mattoon 1884	G4104 .M4A3 1884 .S5 Vault	J. W. Smith		Shober & Carqueville Lith. Co., Chicago	19½ × 29½
168	Moline 1869	G4104 .M6A3 1869 .R8 Rug 24	[Albert Ruger] (Ruger Map Coll. 24)	Ruger & Stoner, Madison, Wisconsin	Chicago Lithogr. Co.	17 × 22
169	Moline 1873	G4104 .M6A35 1873 .H3	A. Hageboeck, Davenport, Iowa	A. Hageboeck, Davenport, Iowa	A. Hageboeck, Davenport, Iowa	9 × 26
170	Moline 1889	G4104 .M6A3 1889 .W4	H. Wellge	American Publishing Co., Milwaukee, Wisconsin		19 × 27
171	Monmouth 1869	G4104 .M7A3 1869 .R8 Rug 25	A. Ruger (Ruger Map Coll. 25)		Merchant's Lithographing Co., Chicago	20 × 26

Entry No.	City and Date	LC Call No.	Artist	Publisher	Lithographer	Map Size (inches)
172	Mount Sterling 1869	G4104 .M88A3 1869 .R8 Rug 26	A. Ruger (Ruger Map Coll. 26)		Chicago Lithographing Co.	15½ × 22
173	Mount Vernon 1881	G4104 .M9A3 1881 .B7	H. Brosius	S. C. Polk, Mount Vernon, Illinois; J. J. Stoner, Madison, Wisconsin	Beck & Pauli, Lith., Milwaukee, Wisconsin	14 × 24½
174	Naperville 1869	G4104 .N2A3 1869 .R8 Rug 27	[Albert Ruger] (Ruger Map Coll. 27)	Ruger & Stoner, Madison, Wis.	Merchant's Lithographing Co., Chicago	18½ × 23½
175	Nauvoo [1855]	Microform Reading Room Reel Number 35575	Herrmann J. Meyer, New York	Herrmann J. Meyer, New York		6 × 7 (original photograph)
176	New Salem 1831-1837	G4104 .N35A3 1837 .B7	Arthur L. Brown	R. J. Onstott, Mason City, Ill. (1909)	J. W. Franks & Sons, Peoria, Ill.	19 × 32
176.1	Ottawa 1895	G4104 .O8A3 1895 .P3	C. J. Pauli, Milwaukee, Wis.	C. J. Pauli, Milwaukee, Wis.		9 × 13½ Photograph
177	Paxton 1869	G4104 .P25A3 1869 .R8 Rug 28	A. Ruger (Ruger Map Coll. 28)		Merchants Lithographing Co., Chicago, Ills.	15 × 20
178	Peoria 1867	G4104 .P4A3 1867 .R8 Rug 29	A. Ruger (Ruger Map Coll. 29)		Chicago Lithographing Co.	20 × 34
179	Pontiac 1869	G4104 .P8A3 1869 .R8 Rug 30	A. Ruger (Ruger Map Coll. 30)		Merchant's Lithographing Co., Chicago	17 × 22
180	Princeton 1870	G4104 .P9A3 1870 .R8 Rug 31	Ruger & Stoner, Madison, Wisconsin (Ruger Map Coll. 31)		Chicago Lithogr. Co., Chicago	20 × 26
181	Rockford 1880	G4104 .R7A3 1880 .S7		J. J. Stoner, Madison, Wisconsin	Beck & Pauli, Lith., Milwaukee, Wisconsin	18½ × 27½
182	Rockford 1891	G4104 .R7A3 1891 .P4				26 × 41
183	Rock Island 1869	G4104 .R6A3 1869 .R8 Rug 32	[Albert Ruger] (Ruger Map Coll. 32)	Ruger & Stoner, Madison, Wis.	Chicago Lithogr. Co., Chicago	20 × 26
184	Rock Island 1874	G4104 .R6A35 1874 .H3	A. Hageboeck, Davenport, Iowa	A. Hageboeck, Davenport, Iowa	A. Hageboeck, Davenport, Iowa	8 × 25
185	Rock Island 1889	G4104 .R6A3 1889 .W4	H. Wellge	American Publishing Co., Milwaukee, Wisconsin		27½ × 41

Rockford, Illinois, 1891.

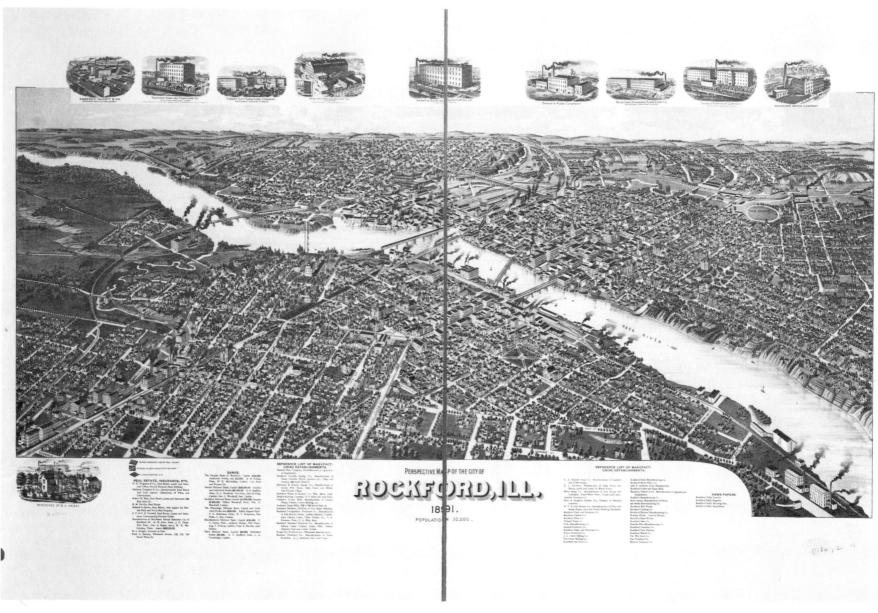

Entry No.	City and Date	LC Call No.	Artist	Publisher	Lithographer	Map Size (inches)
186	Sandwich 1869	G4104 .S25A3 1869 .R8 Rug 33	A. Ruger (Ruger Map Coll. 33)		Chicago Lith. Co., Chicago	17½ × 22
187	Shelbyville 1869	G4104 .S37A3 1869 .R8 Rug 34	A. Ruger (Ruger Map Coll. 34)		Merchant's Lithographing Co., Chicago, Ills.	20 × 26
188	Springfield 1867	G4104 .S5A3 1867 .R8 Rug 35	A. Ruger (Ruger Map Coll. 35)		Chicago Lithographing Co.	20 × 34
189	Urbana 1869	G4104 .U7A3 1869 .R8 Rug 37	[Albert Ruger] (Ruger Map Coll. 37)		Chicago Lithogr. Co., Chicago	17½ × 22
189.1	Urbana 1869	G4104 .U7A3 1869 .R8 1976	A. Ruger	Reproduced in 1976 by Historic Urban Plans, Ithaca, New York	Chicago Lithogr. Co.	17 × 19½ Facsimile
190	Young America 1869	G4104 .Y7A3 1869 .R8 Rug 38	A. Ruger (Ruger Map Coll. 38)	Ruger & Stoner, Madison, Wisconsin	Chicago Lith. Co., Chicago	14 × 20

Indiana

Entry No.	City and Date	LC Call No.	Artist	Publisher	Lithographer	Map Size (inches)
191	Attica 1869	G4094 .A6A3 1869 .R8 Rug 39	A. Ruger (Ruger Map Coll. 39)		Chicago Lithogr. Co., Chicago	15½ × 22
191.1	Cambridge City 1871	G4094 .C15A3 1871 .F6	T. M. Fowler & H. H. Bailey	T. M. Fowler & H. H. Bailey	Milwaukee Lith. & Eng. Co.; C. H. Vogt, Lith.	17½ × 21½ Positive photostat
192	Delphi 1868	G4094 .D5A3 1868 .R8 Rug 40	A. Ruger (Ruger Map Coll. 40)		Merchants Lithographing Co., Chicago	18½ × 25
193	Evansville 1888	G4094 .E9A3 1888 .W4	H. Wellge	American Publishing Co., Milwaukee, Wisconsin		27 × 40½
194	Fort Wayne 1868 (Inset Fort Wayne 1825)	G4094 .F7A3 1868 .R8 Rug 41	A. Ruger (Ruger Map Coll. 41)		Chicago Lithogr. Co.	21½ × 28
195	Fort Wayne 1907	G4094 .F7A3 1907 .G7		B. J. Griswold	W. W. Hixson, Rockford, Illinois	36 × 49
196	Kokomo 1868	G4094 .K7A3 1868 .R8 Rug 42	A. Ruger (Ruger Map Coll. 42)		Merchants Lithographing Co., Chicago	20 × 25½
197	Lafayette 1868	G4094 .L2A3 1868 .R8 Rug 43	A. Ruger (Ruger Map Coll. 43)		Chicago Lith. Co.	22 × 27½
198	Michigan City 1869	G4094 .M5A3 1869 .R8 Rug 45	A. Ruger (Ruger Map Coll. 45)		Merchant's Lithographing Co., Chicago	20 × 28

Entry No.	City and Date	LC Call No.	Artist	Publisher	Lithographer	Map Size (inches)
199	Michigan City 1869	G4094 .M5A3 1869 .R8 Rug 44	[Albert Ruger] (Ruger Map Coll. 44)		Merchants Lithographing Co., Chicago	17 × 27½
199.1	Middlebury [1874]	G1403 .E4H4 1874		In Higgins, Belden & Co. *An Illustrated Historical Atlas of Elkhart Co., Indiana* (Chicago, 1874), p. 27		12½ × 16½
199.2	Muncie 1872	G4094 .M9A3 1872 .B3	O. H. Bailey		Strobridge & Co., Lith., Cin., O.	15 × 19 Photograph
199.3	New Harmony [formerly Harmony 1825]	G4094 .N45A3 1825 .W5 1968	Stedman Whitwell	Reproduced in 1968 by Historic Urban Plans, Ithaca, New York	Ingrey & Madeley, Litho., [London]	17½ × 23½ Facsimile
200	Peru 1868	G4094 .P4A3 1868 .R8 Rug 46	[Albert Ruger] (Ruger Map Coll. 46)			20 × 25½
201	Richmond 1884	G4094 .R5A3 1884 .D6	Albert Downs	O. H. Bailey & Co., Boston	J. W. C. Gilman & Co.	28 × 39½
202	South Bend 1866	G4094 .S6A3 1866 .R8 Rug 48	A. Ruger, Battle Creek, Mich. (Ruger Map Coll. 48)	A. Ruger, Battle Creek, Mich.	Chicago Lithographing Co., Chicago	21 × 28½
203	South Bend 1874	G4094 .S6A3 1874 .R8 Rug 49	[Ruger] (Ruger Map Coll. 49)	J. J. Stoner, Madison, Wisconsin	Chas. Shober & Co., Chicago Lith. Co.	19½ × 26
204	South Bend 1890	G4094 .S6A3 1890 .P3	C. J. Pauli, Milwaukee, Wis.	C. J. Pauli, Milwaukee, Wis.		28 × 40
205	Terre Haute 1880	G4094 .T4A3 1880 .B4			Beck & Pauli, Milwaukee, Wisconsin	24 × 40

Iowa

Entry No.	City and Date	LC Call No.	Artist	Publisher	Lithographer	Map Size (inches)
205.1	Atlantic [1875. In Alfred T. Andreas' *Illustrated Historical Atlas of the State of Iowa* (Chicago, 1875), p. 14]	G1430 .A3 1875			Chas. Shober & Co., Lithographing Co., Chicago	16 × 13
206	Blairstown 1868	G4154 .B53A3 1868 .R8 Rug 50	A. Ruger (Ruger Map Coll. 50)		Merchant's Lith. Co.	10 × 12½

South Bend, Indiana, 1866. Drawn & published by
Albert Ruger.

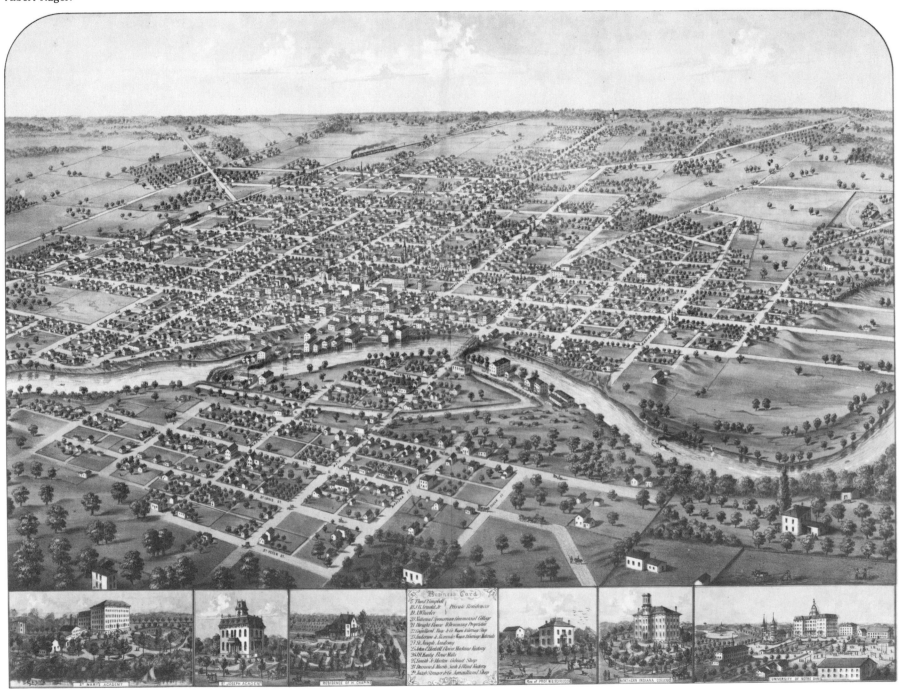

Entry No.	City and Date	LC Call No.	Artist	Publisher	Lithographer	Map Size (Inches)
207	Burlington 1889	G4154 .B9A3 1889 .W4	H. Wellge	American Publishing Co., Milwaukee, Wisconsin		22 × 32½
208	Cedar Rapids 1868	G4154 .C4A3 1868 .R8 Rug 51	A. Ruger (Ruger Map Coll. 51)		Chicago Lith. Co.	21½ × 26
208.1	Cedar Rapids 1889	G4154 .C4A3 1889 .C2 1973	C. J. Pauli & Co., Milwaukee	C. J. Pauli & Co., Milwaukee. Reproduced in 1973 by Gerald A. Noble, Hiawatha, Iowa		26½ × 33½ Positive photostat
208.2	Chariton [1875. In Alfred T. Andreas' *Illustrated Historical Atlas of the State of Iowa* (Chicago, 1875), p. 155]	G1430 .A3 1875			Chas. Shober & Co., Lithographing Co., Chicago	16 × 13
209	Council Bluffs 1868	G4154 .C8A3 1868 .R8 Rug 52	A. Ruger (Ruger Map Coll. 52)		Merchant's Lith. Co., Chicago	22 × 27½
209.1	Council Bluffs [1875. In Alfred T. Andreas' *Illustrated Historical Atlas of the State of Iowa* (Chicago, 1875), p. 8]	G1430 .A3 1875			Chas. Shober & Co., Lithographing Co., Chicago	16 × 13
209.2	Davenport [1875. In Alfred T. Andreas' *Illustrated Historical Atlas of the State of Iowa* (Chicago, 1875), opposite title page.]	G1430 .A3 1875			Chas. Shober & Co., Lithographing Co., Chicago	16 × 13
210	Davenport 1888	G4154 .D2A3 1888 .W4	H. Wellge	American Publishing Co., Milwaukee, Wisconsin		24 × 40
211	Decorah 1870	G4154 .D3A3 1870 .R8 Rug 53	[Albert Ruger] (Ruger Map Coll. 53)	Ruger & Stoner, Madison, Wisconsin	Merchant's Lith. Co., Chicago	19 × 22
212	Des Moines 1868	G4154 .D5A3 1868 .R8 Rug 54	A. Ruger (Ruger Map Coll. 54)		Merchant's Lith. Co., Chicago	22 × 28½

Entry No.	City and Date	LC Call No.	Artist	Publisher	Lithographer	Map Size (inches)
212.1	Des Moines [1875. In Alfred T. Andreas' *Illustrated Historical Atlas of the State of Iowa* (Chicago, 1875), p. 179]	G1430 .A3 1875			Chas. Shober & Co., Lithographing Co., Chicago	16 × 13
213	De Witt 1868	G4154 .D26A3 1868 .R8 Rug 55	[Albert Ruger] (Ruger Map Coll. 55)			20 × 26
214	Dubuque 1889	G4154 .D8A3 1889 .W4	H. Wellge	American Publishing Co.		27 × 40
215	Fort Madison 1889	G4154 .F8A3 1889 .W4	H. Wellge	American Publishing Co.		In 2 parts, 17½ × 18½ and 17½ × 19½
216	Guttenberg 1869	G4154 .G93A3 1869 .R8 Rug 56	[Albert Ruger] (Ruger Map Coll. 56)	Ruger & Stoner, Madison, Wisconsin	Merchants Lithographing Co., Chicago	16½ × 21½
217	Iowa City 1868	G4154 .I5A3 1868 .R8 Rug 57	A. Ruger (Ruger Map Coll. 57)		Chicago Lith. Co.	20½ × 26
218	Lyons 1868	G4154 .C6:2L9A3 1868 .R8 Rug 58	A. Ruger (Ruger Map Coll. 58)		Merchant's Lith. Co., Chicago	21½ × 28½
219	McGregor & North McGregor 1869	G4154 .M634A3 1868 .R8 Rug 59	[Albert Ruger] (Ruger Map Coll. 59)	Ruger & Stoner, Madison, Wisconsin	Chicago Lith. Co.	21 × 22
220	Marengo 1868	G4154 .M35A3 1868 .R8 Rug 60	A. Ruger (Ruger Map Coll. 60)		Merchant's Lith. Co.	22 × 26
221	Marion 1868	G4154 .M4A3 1868 .R8 Rug 61	A. Ruger (Ruger Map Coll. 61)		Merchant's Lith. Co.	20½ × 26½
222	Marshalltown 1868	G4154 .M5A3 1868 .R8 Rug 62	[Albert Ruger] (Ruger Map Coll. 62)			20 × 26
223	Montana 1868	G4154 .M745A3 1868 .R8 Rug 63	A. Ruger (Ruger Map Coll. 63)		Chicago Lith. Co.	20 × 26

Entry No.	City and Date	LC Call No.	Artist	Publisher	Lithographer	Map Size (inches)
223.1	Muscatin [1875. In Alfred T. Andreas' *Illustrated Historical Atlas of the State of Iowa* (Chicago, 1875), p. 22]	G1430 .A3 1875			Chas. Shober & Co., Lithographing Co., Chicago	16 × 13
224	Newton 1868	G4154 .N6A3 1868 .R8 Rug 64	A. Ruger (Ruger Map Coll. 64)		Merchant's Lith. Co., Chicago	21 × 26½
224.1	Red Oak [1875. In Alfred T. Andreas' *Illustrated Historical Atlas of the State of Iowa* (Chicago, 1875), p. 225]	G1430 .A3 1875			Chas. Shober & Co., Lithographing Co., Chicago	16 × 13
225	Sioux City 1888	G4154 .S6A3 1888 .W4	Henry Wellge	H. Wellge & Co.	Beck & Pauli Lith. Co., Milwaukee	25½ × 37

Kansas

Entry No.	City and Date	LC Call No.	Artist	Publisher	Lithographer	Map Size (inches)
226	Atchison 1869	G4204 .A8A3 1869 .R8 Rug 65	A. Ruger (Ruger Map Coll. 65)		Merchants Lithographing Co., Chicago	20½ × 25½
226.1	Atchison 1880	G4204 .A8A3 1880 .K6	Augustus Koch	Reproduced from original in The Kansas State Historical Society, Topeka	Ramsey, Millett & Hudson, Lith., Kansas City, Mo.	8 × 10 Photograph
226.2	Dodge City 1882	G4204 .D6A3 1882 .S8		J. J. Stoner, Madison, Wis. Reproduced from original in The Kansas State Historical Society, Topeka	Beck & Pauli, Lithographers, Milwaukee, Wis.	8 × 10 Photograph
227	Girard [1879] (Inset in map of Crawford County by W. J. Eldridge [1879])	G4203 .C9G46 1879 .E4				8 × 10 Negative photograph
228	Herington 1887	G1455 .E9 1887		In L. H. Everts & Co.'s *The Official State Atlas of Kansas...* (Philadelphia, 1887), p. 260		12 × 15

Sioux City, Iowa, 1888. Drawn and published by Henry Wellge & Co., Milwaukee, Wisconsin. When settlers first poured into the Northwest, the Missouri River was one of the important arteries of travel, and both overland and river travelers made Sioux City their supply base for the long trip ahead of them.

PERSPECTIVE MAP OF.

SIOUX CITY, IOWA.

SIOUX CITY CORN PALACE.

THE PEAVEY GRAND OPERA HOUSE. CHAMBER OF COMMERCE BUILDING.

Entry No.	City and Date	LC Call No.	Artist	Publisher	Lithographer	Map Size (inches)
245	Houlton 1894	G3734 .H67A3 1894 .N6	Geo. E. Norris, Brockton, Mass.	Geo. E. Norris, Brockton, Mass.		18½ × 27
246	Livermore Falls 1889	G3734 .L6A3 1889 .N6	Geo. E. Norris, Brockton, Mass.	Geo. E. Norris, Brockton, Mass.	Burleigh Lithographing Establishment, Troy, N.Y.	13 × 21½
246.1	Monhegan 1896	G3734 .M597A3 1896 .P6	Bert Poole			17 × 21½
246.2	Monson 1889	G3734 .M75A3 1889 .N6	Geo. E. Norris, Brockton, Mass.	Geo. E. Norris, Brockton, Mass.	Burleigh Lith. Est., Troy, N.Y.	14 × 24
246.3	New Castle & Damariscotta 1878	G3734 .N35A3 1878 .R8	A. Ruger	J. J. Stoner, Madison, Wis.		13 × 20½
246.4	North Berwick 1877	G3734 .N6A3 1877 .R8	[Albert Ruger]	Ruger & Stoner, Madison, Wis.		14 × 16
247	Peak's Island 1886	G3734 .P8:2P4A3 1886 .M6	JC	G. W. Morris, Portland, Me.	Geo. H. Walker & Co., Boston	19½ × 32
248	Pittsfield 1889	G3734 .P56A3 1889 .N6	Geo. E. Norris, Brockton, Mass.	Geo. E. Norris, Brockton, Mass.	The Burleigh Lith. Est., Troy, New York	16 × 22½
249	Portland 1876	G3734 .P8A3 1876 .W3	Jos. Warner	J. J. Stoner, Madison, Wis.	Chas. Shober & Co., Chicago Litho'g Co.	23 × 35
250	Presque Isle 1894	G3734 .P9A3 1894 .N6		Geo. E. Norris, Brockton, Mass.		16 × 23½
250.1	Richmond 1878	G3734 .R4A3 1878 .R8	A. Ruger		D. Bremner & Co., Lith., Milwaukee, Wis.	14 × 20½
251	Sanford 1889	G3734 .S35A3 1889 .N6	Geo. E. Norris, Brockton, Mass.	Geo. E. Norris, Brockton, Mass.	The Burleigh Lith. Est., Troy, New York	15 × 26

Maryland

Entry No.	City and Date	LC Call No.	Artist	Publisher	Lithographer	Map Size (inches)
252	Annapolis 1864	G3844 .A6A3 1864 .M3 1967		Chas. Magnus, New York. Reproduced in 1967 by Historic Urban Plans, Ithaca, New York		14 × 17 Facsimile
253	Baltimore 1850	G3844 .B2A35 1850 .S3 1967	E. Sachse	Casimir Bohn. Reproduced in 1967 by Historic Urban Plans, Ithaca, New York	E. Sachse & Co., Baltimore, Maryland	21 × 28 Facsimile
253.1	Baltimore 1850	G3844 .B2A35 1850 .S3 1972	E. Sachse	Casimir Bohn. Reproduced in 1972 by Historic Urban Plans, Ithaca, New York	E. Sachse & Co., Baltimore, Md.	15 × 20½ Facsimile

Entry No.	City and Date	LC Call No.	Artist	Publisher	Lithographer	Map Size (inches)
253.2	Baltimore City 1862	Prints & Photographs Division		E. Sachse & Co., Baltimore	E. Sachse & Co.	19 × 27½
254	Baltimore 1869	G3844 .B2A3 1869 .S3		E. Sachse & Co., Baltimore, Maryland	E. Sachse & Co., Baltimore, Maryland	In 4 parts: 62 × 34, 62 × 31, 62 × 32, 62 × 34
254.1	Baltimore 1880	Prints & Photographs Division	[A. Sachse]	A. Sachse & Co., Baltimore, Md.	A. Sachse & Co., Lithographers & Printers	19 × 23½
255	Baltimore 1911	G3844 .B2A3 1911 .S6	Edward W. Spofford	Norman T. A. Munder & Co., Baltimore, Maryland	Norman T. A. Munder & Co., Baltimore, Maryland	20 × 30½
256	Chestertown 1907	G3844 .C4A3 1907 .F6 Fow 79	T. M. Fowler (T. M. Fowler Map Coll. 79)	Fowler & Kelley, Morrisville, Pennsylvania		21 × 25½
257	Cumberland 1906	G3844 .C9A3 1906 .F6	Thaddeus M. Fowler, Morrisville, Pa.	Fowler & Kelly, Morrisville, Pa.		15 × 20
258	Elkton 1907	G3844 .E6A3 1907 .F6 Fow 59	[T. M. Fowler] (T. M. Fowler Map Coll. 59)	Fowler & Kelly, Morrisville, Pennsylvania		18 × 22
258.1	Ellicotts Mills 1854	Prints & Photographs Division		John Schofield, Ellicotts Mills	E. Sachse & Co., Baltimore	21½ × 29
259	Frostburg 1905	G3844 .F8A3 1905 .F6 Fow 4	T. M. Fowler, Morrisville, Pa. (T. M. Fowler Map Coll. 4)	T. M. Fowler, Morrisville, Pa.		20½ × 25
260	Havre de Grace 1907	G3844 .H4A3 1907 .F6	T. M. Fowler, Morrisville, Pa.	Fowler & Kelly, Morrisville, Pa.		20½ × 23
261	Mountain Lake Park 1906	G3844 .M87A3 1906 .F6		Fowler & Kelly, Morrisville, Pennsylvania		22½ × 29½
262	Oakland 1906	G3844 .O3A3 1906 .F6	Fowler & Kelly, Morrisville, Pa.	Fowler & Kelly, Morrisville, Pa.		16 × 20½
263	Rising Sun 1907	G3844 .R4A3 1907 .F6	T. M. Fowler, Morrisville, Pa.	Fowler & Kelly, Morrisville, Pa.		17½ × 20½
263.1	St. Mary's City 1634	G3844 .S27A3 1634 .C3	[Cary Carson]	St. Mary's City Commission		9 × 12

Baltimore, Maryland, 1869. Published by E. Sachse &
Co., Baltimore, Maryland. This portion of the twelve-
sheet map shows the inner harbor and the original
Washington Monument.

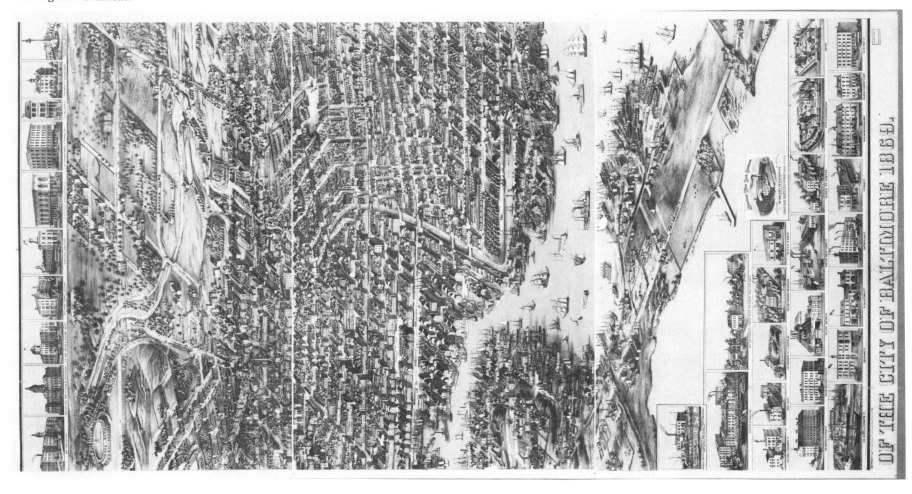

Entry No.	City and Date	LC Call No.	Artist	Publisher	Lithographer	Map Size (inches)
263.2	St. Mary's City 1690's	G3844 .S27A3 1690 .C3	[Cary Carson]	[St. Mary's City Commission]		9 × 12

Massachusetts

Entry No.	City and Date	LC Call No.	Artist	Publisher	Lithographer	Map Size (inches)
263.3[2]	Amesbury & Salisbury Mills 1880	G3764 .A4A3 1880 .B5		E. H. Bigelow, Framingham, Mass.	Beck & Pauli, Milwaukee, Wis.	8 × 10 Photograph
264	Amesbury 1890	G3764 .A4A3 1890 .N6	Geo. E. Norris, Brockton, Mass.	Geo. E. Norris, Brockton, Mass.	The Burleigh Lith. Est., Troy, New York	20 × 33½
265	Amesbury 1914	G3764 .A4A3 1914 .H8 Fow 62	(T. M. Fowler Map Coll. 62)	Hughes & Bailey, New York	[Meriden Gravure Co., Meriden, Conn.]	21 × 29½
266	Amherst 1886	G3764 .A5A3 1886 .B8		L. R. Burleigh, Troy, New York	The Burleigh Lith. Est., Troy, New York	18 × 30
267	Ashburnham 1886	G3764 .A72A3 1886 .B8	L. R. Burleigh, Troy, New York	L. R. Burleigh, Troy, New York		13 × 20½
268	Ashland 1878	G3764 .A78A3 1878 .B3	O. H. Bailey & J. C. Hazen, Boston	O. H. Bailey & J. C. Hazen, Boston		20 × 24½
269	Athol 1887	G3764 .A8A3 1887 .B8	L. R. Burleigh, Troy, New York	L. R. Burleigh, Troy, New York	L. R. Burleigh, Troy, New York	17½ × 24½
270	Ayer 1886	G3764 .A99A3 1886 .B8		L. R. Burleigh, Troy, New York		13 × 23½
271	Baldwinville 1886	G3764 .B18A3 1886 .B8		L. R. Burleigh, Troy, New York	Beck & Pauli, Lith., Milwaukee, Wisconsin	13 × 24½
271.1	Barnstable 1884	G3764 .B2A3 1884 .P6 1975	A. F. Poole	A. F. Poole, Brockton, Mass. Reprinted and copyrighted in 1975 by Great Marshes Press, Barnstable, Massachusetts 02630	Geo. H. Walker & Co. Lith., Boston	13½ × 32½ Facsimile
271.2	Barre [189-?]	G3764 .B23A3 189-? .S6		W. R. Spooner, Publ.		10½ × 24½
271.3	Barre 1891	G3764 .B23A3 1891 .02		O. H. Bailey & Co., Boston	O. H. Bailey & Co., Boston	22 × 26
271.4	Beverly 1886	G3764 .B5A3 1886 .G7		W. A. Greenough & Co., Boston		19½ × 25
272	Beverly Farms 1886	G3764 .B52A3 1886 .W3		O. W. Walker, Boston		16½ × 30½

[2]Map may not be reproduced without written permission from the Merrimac Valley Textile Museum, North Andover, Massachusetts 01845

Entry No.	City and Date	LC Call No.	Artist	Publisher	Lithographer	Map Size (inches)
272.1	Boston [1768]	G3764 .B6A35 1768 .P6 1970	Thomas Pownal	Reproduced in 1970 by Historic Urban Plans, Ithaca, New York	P. C. Canot	15½ × 20½ Facsimile
272.2	Boston [1774]	G3764 .B6A35 1774 .R4 1973	[Paul Revere]	Reproduced in 1973 by Historic Urban Plans, Ithaca, New York		15½ × 20½ Facsimile
272.3	Boston 1850	G3764 .B6A35 1850 .B3 1973	J. Bachmann	John Bachmann, New York. Reproduced in 1973 by Historic Urban Plans, Ithaca, New York	Sarony & Major, New York	22 × 28½ Facsimile
273	Boston 1870	G3764 .B6A3 1870 .F8	F. Fuchs	John Weik, Philadelphia	New England Lith. Co., Boston	28½ × 36½
274	Boston [187-?]	G3764 .B6A3 187- .S8	T. Sulman			13 × 19½
275	Boston 1873	G3764 .B6A3 1873 .P3	Parsons & Atwater	Currier & Ives, New York		22½ × 33
275.1	Boston 1873	G3764 .B6A3 1873 .P3 1975	Parsons & Atwater	Currier & Ives, New York. Reproduced in 1975 by Historic Urban Plans, Ithaca, New York		16 × 19 Facsimile
275.2	Boston 1873	G3764 .B6A3 1873 .P3 1976	Parsons & Atwater	Currier & Ives, New York. Reproduced in 1976 by Historic Urban Plans, Ithaca, New York		21 × 27½ Facsimile
276	Boston 1877	G3764 .B6A3 1877 .B3	J. Bachmann	L. Prang & Co.	J. Bachmann	20 × 25
276.1	Boston 1877	G3764 .B6A3 1877 .B3 1975	J. Bachmann	L. Prang & Co. Reproduced in 1975 by Historic Urban Plans, Ithaca, New York	J. Bachmann	16 × 19 Facsimile
276.2	Boston 1877	G3764 .B6A3 1877 .B3 1976	J. Bachmann	L. Prang & Co. Reproduced in 1976 by Historic Urban Plans, Ithaca, New York	J. Bachmann	22 × 27½ Facsimile
277	Boston 1879	G3764 .B6A3 1879 .B3		O. H. Bailey & J. C. Hazen, Boston	Armstrong & Co., Riverside Press, Cambridge	29 × 44
278	Boston 1880	G3764 .B6A3 1880 .R6	H. H. Rowley & Co., Hartford, Conn.	H. H. Rowley & Co., Hartford, Conn.	Beck & Pauli, Milwaukee, Wisconsin	33½ × 54½
278.1	Boston 1880	G3764 .B6A3 1880 .R6 1970	H. H. Rowley & Co., Hartford, Conn.	H. H. Rowley & Co., Hartford, Conn. Reproduced in 1970 by Historic Urban Plans, Ithaca, New York	Beck & Pauli, Milwaukee, Wis.	32 × 54 In 3 parts, each 32 × 17 Facsimile
279	Boston 1899	G3764 .B6A3 1899 .D6	E. A. Downs, Boston [A. E. Downs]	E. A. Downs, Boston [A. E. Downs]	Geo. H. Walker & Co., Boston	25 × 38

Boston, Massachusetts, 1899. Drawn by A. E. Downs.

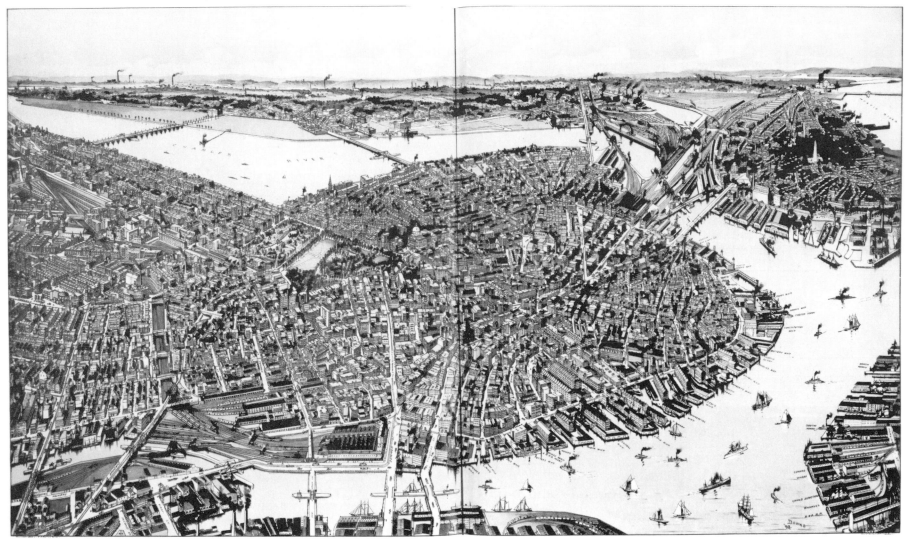

Entry No.	City and Date	LC Call No.	Artist	Publisher	Lithographer	Map Size (inches)
279.1	Boston 1902	G3764 .B6A35 1902 .W3		Geo. H. Walker & Co., Boston		18 × 24½
280	Boston 1905	G3764 .B6A3 1905 .P6	Bert Poole	F. D. Nichols Co., Boston	A. W. Elson & Co., Boston	22 × 30
280.1	Boston 1905	G3764 .B6A3 1905 .W3			Geo. H. Walker & Co., Boston	20 × 28
281	Boston Highlands 1888	G3764 .B6A3 1888 .F3	Favour	O. H. Bailey & Co.		31 × 41
282	Brockton 1882	G3764 .B8A3 1882 .P6	A. F. Poole	J. J. Stoner, Madison, Wisconsin	Beck & Pauli, Lith., Milwaukee, Wisconsin	26 × 39
283	Canton 1918	G3764 .C3A3 1918 .H8		Hughes & Bailey, Boston	[Meriden Gravure Co., Meriden, Conn.]	26 × 36
283.1	Chicopee 1878	G3764 .C5A3 1878 .B7		Galt & Hoy, New York	D. Bremner & Co., Lith., Milwaukee, Wis.	20 × 26
283.2[2]	Clinton 1876	G3764 .C6A3 1876 .B4	O. H. Bailey & Co.	O. H. Bailey & Co.	J. Knauber & Co.; C. H. Vogt	8 × 10 Photograph
284	Dalton 1884	G3764 .D15A3 1884 .B8	L. R. Burleigh, Troy, N.Y.	L. R. Burleigh, Troy, N.Y.	Beck & Pauli, Litho., Milwaukee, Wis.	15 × 30
285	East Boston 1879	G3764 .B6:3E2A3 1879 .B3	O. H. Bailey & Co., Boston	O. H. Bailey & Co., Boston		21 × 24
286	East Douglas 1886	G3764 .E17A3 1886 .B8	L. R. Burleigh, Troy, New York		C. H. Vogt, Lith., The Burleigh Lith. Est., Troy, New York	15 × 24
287	East Pepperell 1886	G3764 .E22A3 1886 .B8	L. R. Burleigh, Troy, New York		C. H. Vogt, Lith.	15 × 21
288	East Walpole 1898	G3764 .E26A3 1898 .P6	The Bert Poole Co., Boston	The Bert Poole Co., Boston		15 × 22½
289	Edgartown [1886]	G3764 .E35A3 1886 .W3			Geo. H. Walker & Co., Boston	13 × 19
289.1	Edgartown [1886]	G3764 .E35A3 1886 .W3 1976		Reproduced in 1976 by Historic Urban Plans, Ithaca, New York	Geo. H. Walker & Co., Boston	14½ × 21 Facsimile
290	Fall River 1877	G3764 .F3A3 1877 .B3	O. H. Bailey & J. C. Hazen, Boston	O. H. Bailey & J. C. Hazen, Boston	C. H. Vogt, Lith., Milwaukee; J. Knauber & Co.	27 × 42
291	Fitchburg 1882	G3764 .F5A3 1882 .B8	L. R. Burleigh, Troy, New York	L. R. Burleigh, Troy, New York	C. H. Vogt, Lith., Cleveland, Ohio	22 × 31½

[2]Map may not be reproduced without written permission from the Merrimac Valley Textile Museum, North Andover, Massachusetts 01845

Entry No.	City and Date	LC Call No.	Artist	Publisher	Lithographer	Map Size (inches)
292	Fitchburg 1915	G3764 .F5A3 1915 .H8 Fow 66	T. M. Fowler (T. M. Fowler Map Coll. 66)	Hughes & Bailey, New York	[Meriden Gravure Co., Meriden, Conn.]	24 × 35
292.1	Foxborough 1879	G3764 .F65A3 1879 .B3	O. H. Bailey & J. C. Hazen, Boston	O. H. Bailey & J. C. Hazen, Boston		20 × 25½
293	Graniteville 1886	G3764 .G63A3 1886 .F3	[C.] Fausel	L. R. Burleigh, Troy, New York	The Burleigh Lith. Est., Troy, New York	15 × 22
294	Great Barrington 1884	G3764 .G66A3 1884 .B8	L. R. Burleigh, Troy, New York	L. R. Burleigh, Troy, New York	Beck & Pauli, Lith., Milwaukee, Wisconsin	17½ × 30
294.1	Greenfield 1877	G3764 .G7A3 1887 .B3	O. H. Bailey & Co., Boston	O. H. Bailey & Co., Boston		20 × 24½
295	Groton 1886	G3764 .G85A3 1886 .B8		L. R. Burleigh, Troy, New York	The Burleigh Lith. Est., Troy, New York	16 × 24
296	Haverhill 1893	G3764 .H5A3 1893 .B3		O. H. Bailey & Co., Boston	O. H. Bailey & Co., Boston	25 × 36
297	Haverhill 1914	G3764 .H5A3 1914 .F6	Fowler & Downs	Hughes & Bailey	[Franklin Engraving Co. & Federal Engraving Co., Boston, Mass.]	28 × 31
298	Haydenville 1886	G3764 .H53A3 1886 .B8		L. R. Burleigh	Northern Lith. Co., Troy, New York	13 × 20½
298.1	Highlandville 1887	G3764 .N33A3 1887 .B3		O. H. Bailey & Co., Boston	O. H. Bailey & Co., Boston	21 × 25
299	Hingham and South Hingham 1885	G3764 .H62A3 1885 .P6	A. F. Poole and C. E. Jörgensen	A. F. Poole, Brockton, Mass.	Geo. H. Walker & Co., Boston	24½ × 33
300	Hinsdale 1887	G3764 .H63A3 1887 .B8	L. R. Burleigh, Troy, New York	L. R. Burleigh, Troy, New York	C. H. Vogt, Cleveland; Burleigh Lith. Est., Troy, New York	14 × 22
301	Holyoke and South Hadley Falls 1881	G3764 .H7A3 1881 .P6	A. F. Poole	J. J. Stoner, Madison, Wisconsin	Beck & Pauli, Lith., Milwaukee, Wisconsin	27 × 38
302	Hopedale 1899	G3764 .H72A3 1899 .P6	The Bert Poole Co., Boston	The Bert Poole Co., Boston		16 × 22½
303	Housatonic 1890	G3764 .H76A3 1890 .B8	L. R. Burleigh, Troy, New York	L. R. Burleigh, Troy, New York		17 × 23
304	Huntington 1886	G3764 .H86A3 1886 .B8	L. R. Burleigh, Troy, New York		The Burleigh Lith. Est., Troy, New York	13 × 21

Entry No.	City and Date	LC Call No.	Artist	Publisher	Lithographer	Map Size (inches)
304.1[2]	Lawrence 1876	G3764 .L31A3 1876 .L3	H. H. Bailey & J. C. Hazen	H. H. Bailey & J. C. Hazen	J. Knauber & Co.; C. H. Vogt	8 × 10 Photograph
304.2	Lawrence 1876	G3764 .L31A3 1876 .B3 1976	H. H. Bailey & J. C. Hazen	H. H. Bailey & J. C. Hazen. Reproduced in 1976 by Historic Urban Plans, Ithaca, New York	J. Knauber & Co.; C. H. Vogt	22 × 27½ Facsimile
305	Leominster 1886	G3764 .L5A3 1886 .B8	L. R. Burleigh, Troy, New York	L. R. Burleigh, Troy, New York	Burleigh Lith. Est., Troy, New York	16½ × 29½
305.1[2]	Lowell 1876	G3764 .L7A3 1876 .B3	H. H. Bailey & J. C. Hazen	H. H. Bailey & J. C. Hazen	J. Knauber & Co.; C. H. Vogt	8 × 10 Photograph
305.2	Lowell 1876	G3764 .L7A3 1876 .B3 1976	H. H. Bailey & J. C. Hazen	H. H. Bailey & J. C. Hazen. Reproduced in 1976 by Historic Urban Plans, Ithaca, New York	J. Knauber & Co.; C. H. Vogt	22½ × 28 Facsimile
306	Lynn 1820	G3764 .L9:2M3A35 1820 .06	Wm. T. Oliver (Drawn in 1874)	Wm. T. Oliver		6 × 16
307	Lynn 1881	G3764 .L9A3 1881 .S6		C. A. Shaw & H. J. Hutchinson	Armstrong & Co., Lith., Boston	27 × 39
307.1	Manchaug 1891	G3764 .M22A3 1891 .B3		O. H. Bailey & Co., Boston	O. H. Bailey & Co., Boston	11 × 14 Photograph
308	Marblehead Shore 1886			O. W. Walker, Boston		17½ × 30½
309	Maynard 1879	G3764 .M47A3 1879 .B3	O. H. Bailey & J. C. Hazen, Boston	O. H. Bailey & J. C. Hazen, Boston		22 × 26
310	Merrimac 1889	G3764 .M64A3 1889 .N6	Geo. E. Norris, Brockton, Mass.	Geo. E. Norris, Brockton, Mass.		16 × 27
310.1	Monson 1879	G3764 .M86A3 1879 .B3		O. H. Bailey & Co., Boston		19 × 25½
311	Nantasket Beach 1879	G3764 .H84:2N3A3 1879 .M3	R. P. Mallory	George H. Walker & Co.		17 × 25½
311.1	Nantasket Beach [1879]	G3764 .H84:2N3A3 1879 .M31	R. P. Mallory		Geo. H. Walker & Co.	16½ × 25
311.2	Nantasket Beach [1879]	G3764 .H84:2N3A3 1879 .M32	R. P. Mallory		Geo. H. Walker & Co.	16½ × 25

[2]Map may not be reproduced without written permission from the Merrimac Valley Textile Museum, North Andover, Massachusetts 01845

Entry No.	City and Date	LC Call No.	Artist	Publisher	Lithographer	Map Size (inches)
312	Nantucket 1881 (Inset of Siasconset)	G3764 .N18A3 1881 .S7		J. J. Stoner, Madison, Wis.	Beck & Pauli, Lith., Milwaukee, Wis.	20 × 28½
312.1	Nantucket 1881	G3764 .N18A3 1881 .S7 1976		J. J. Stoner, Madison, Wis. Reproduced in 1976 by Historic Urban Plans, Ithaca, New York	Beck & Pauli, Lith., Milwaukee, Wis.	21 × 29 Facsimile
312.2	Newton (comprising wards 1 and 7) 1878	G3764 .N5A3 1878 .B3		O. H. Bailey & Co., Boston		20 × 25½
312.3	Newton (comprising wards 1 and 7) 1897	G3764 .N5A3 1897.B3		O. H. Bailey & Co., Boston	O. H. Bailey & Co., Boston	16½ × 25
312.4	Newton Centre 1897	G3764 .N52A3 1897 .B3		O. H. Bailey & Co., Boston	O. H. Bailey & Co., Boston	20 × 27½
313	North Attleborough 1878	G3764 .N7A3 1878 .B3	O. H. Bailey & J. C. Hazen, Boston	O. H. Bailey & J. C. Hazen, Boston	C. H. Vogt, Lith.	22 × 27
314	North Billerica 1887	G3764 .N72A3 1887 .B8	L. R. Burleigh, Troy, New York	L. R. Burleigh, Troy, New York	The Burleigh Lith. Est., Troy, New York	15 × 24
314.1[2]	Northboro 1887	G3764 .N82A3 1887 .N6	Geo. E. Norris, Brockton, Mass.	Geo. E. Norris, Brockton, Mass.	Burleigh Litho. Establishment, Troy, N.Y.	8 × 10 Photograph
314.2	Northborough 1887	G3764 .N82A3 1887 .V5				18½ × 26½
315	North Bridgewater 1844	G3764 .B8A35 1844 .P6	A. F. Poole (Drawn in 1882)	J. J. Stoner, Madison, Wisconsin	Beck & Pauli, Lith., Milwaukee, Wisconsin	12 × 17
316	North Leominster 1887	G3764 .N774A3 1887 .B8	L. R. Burleigh	L. R. Burleigh	Burleigh Lith. Est., Troy, New York	17 × 27
316.1	Norton 1891	G3764 .N86A3 1891 .B3		O. H. Bailey & Co., Boston	O. H. Bailey & Co., Boston	18½ × 25½
317	Oak Bluffs 1890 [Formerly Cottage City]	G3764 .O2A3 1890 .W4			Robert A. Welcke, Lith., New York	20 × 25
318	Peabody 1877	G3764 .P3A3 1877 .B3	O. H. Bailey & J. C. Hazen, Boston	O. H. Bailey & J. C. Hazen, Boston	J. Knauber & Co., Milwaukee, Wisconsin	20½ × 26

[2]Map may not be reproduced without written permission from the Merrimac Valley Textile Museum, North Andover, Massachusetts 01845

Massachusetts

Entry No.	City and Date	LC Call No.	Artist	Publisher	Lithographer	Map Size (Inches)
318.1[2]	Plymouth 1882	G3764 .P7A3 1882 .B3		O. H. Bailey & Co., Boston		8 × 10 Photograph
319	Provincetown 1877	G3764 .P78A35 1877 .R6		F. K. Rogers, Boston		17 × 26
320	Provincetown 1910	G3764 .P78A3 1910 .W31		Walker Lith. & Pub. Co., Boston	Walker Lith. & Pub. Co., Boston	11 × 17½ Postitive photostat
321	Quincy 1877	G3764 .Q6A3 1877 .W5	E. Whitefield	E. Whitefield		20 × 33
321.1	Salem 1883	G3764 .S2A3 1883 .B8 1976	L. R. Burleigh	D. Mason & Co., Syracuse, N.Y. Reproduced in 1976 by Historic Urban Plans, Ithaca, New York	J. Lyth	20 × 34½ Facsimile
322	South Acton 1886	G3764 .S415A3 1886 .B8		L. R. Burleigh	The Burleigh Lith. Est., Troy, New York	11 × 22
323	South Weymouth 1885	G3764 .S52A3 1885 .J6	C. E. Jörgensen	A. F. Poole & Co., Brockton, Mass.	Geo. H. Walker & Co., Boston	20 × 25½
324	Spencer 1877	G3764 .S67A3 1877 .B3	O. H. Bailey & J. C. Hazen, Boston	O. H. Bailey & J. C. Hazen, Boston		20 × 24½
325	Springfield 1875	G3764 .S7A3 1875 .B3		O. H. Bailey & Co.		27½ × 35
325.1	Taunton 1875	G3764 .T2A3 1875 .B3	O. H. Bailey & Co.	O. H. Bailey & Co.	American Oleograph Co., Lith., Milwaukee, Wis.	22½ × 31
325.2	Turners Falls 1877	G3764 .T8A3 1877 .B3	O. H. Bailey & Co., Boston	O. H. Bailey & Co., Boston	C. H. Vogt & Co., Milwaukee	20 × 28
326	Uxbridge 1880	G3764 .U9A3 1880 .B5		E. H. Bigelow, Framingham, Massachusetts	Beck & Pauli, Milwaukee, Wisconsin	23½ × 24½
326.1[2]	Ware 1878	G3764 .W26A3 1878 .G3		J. L. Galt & Co.	Beck & Pauli, Milwaukee, Wis.	8 × 10 Photograph
327	Wareham and Onset Bay Grove 1885	G3764 .W272A3 1885 .W3		O. W. Walker	Geo. H. Walker & Co., Boston	18 × 24
327.1	Webster 1892	G3764 .W36A3 1892 .B3		O. H. Bailey & Co., Boston	O. H. Bailey & Co., Boston	22 × 27½
327.2	Westfield 1875	G3764 .W6A3 1875 .B3	O. H. Bailey & Co.	O. H. Bailey & Co.	J. Knauber & Co., Printers; C. H. Vogt, Lith., Milwaukee	21 × 28

[2]Map may not be reproduced without written permission from the Merrimac Valley Textile Museum, North Andover, Massachusetts 01845

Entry No.	City and Date	LC Call No.	Artist	Publisher	Lithographer	Map Size (inches)
328	Westford 1886	G3764 .W62A3 1886 .B8		L. R. Burleigh	The Burleigh Lith. Est., Troy, New York	12 × 20
328.1	West Medway 1887	G3764 .W48A3 1887 .02	[T. M. Fowler]	O. H. Bailey & Co.	O. H. Bailey & Co.	19½ × 25½
329	Williamstown 1889	G3764 .W77A3 1889 .B8	L. R. Burleigh	L. R. Burleigh	The Burleigh Lith. Est., Troy, New York	19 × 29
330	Winchester 1898	G3764 .W8A3 1898 .R6	Robbins	Robbins & Enrich	Heliotype Co., Boston	18 × 26
331	Winthrop 1894	G3764 .W84A3 1894 .P6		Bert [A. F.] Poole		15 × 24½
331.1	Woburn 1883	G3764 .W86A3 1883 .M3	L. R. Burleigh	D. Mason & Co., Syracuse, N.Y.		20½ × 32
331.2	Wollaston 1890	G3764 .Q6:2W6A3 1890 .Q2		O. H. Bailey & Co. Lith. & Pub., Boston, Mass.	O. H. Bailey & Co. Lith. & Pub., Boston, Mass.	16½ × 22½ Facsimile

Michigan

Entry No.	City and Date	LC Call No.	Artist	Publisher	Lithographer	Map Size (inches)
332	Adrian 1866	G4114 .A2A3 1866 .R8 Rug 75	A. Ruger, Battle Creek, Mich. (Ruger Map Coll. 75)	A. Ruger, Battle Creek, Mich.	Chicago Lith. Co., Chicago	22 × 34
333	Albion [1868]	G4114 .A3A3 1868 .R8 Rug 76	A. Ruger, Battle Creek, Mich. (Ruger Map Coll. 76)	A. Ruger, Battle Creek, Mich.	Chicago Lith. Co.	19½ × 28
334	Ann Arbor 1880	G4114 .A8A3 1880 .R8 Rug 77	[Albert Ruger] (Ruger Map Coll. 77)	J. J. Stoner, Madison, Wisconsin	Beck & Pauli, Lith., Milwaukee, Wisconsin	15 × 27
334.1	Ann Arbor 1880	G4114 .A8A3 1880 .R8 1970		J. J. Stoner, Madison, Wis. Reproduced in 1970 by Historic Urban Plans, Ithaca, New York	Beck & Pauli, Lith., Milwaukee, Wis.	19 × 27 Facsimile
335	Battle Creek [1869]	G4114 .B2A35 1869 .R8 Rug 78	A. Ruger, Battle Creek, Mich. (Ruger Map Coll. 78)	A. Ruger, Battle Creek, Mich.		13 × 20½
336	Battle Creek [1870?]	G4114 .B2A3 1870 .R8 Rug 79	A. Ruger, Battle Creek, Mich. (Ruger Map Coll. 79)	A. Ruger, Battle Creek, Mich.		21½ × 28

Entry No.	City and Date	LC Call No.	Artist	Publisher	Lithographer	Map Size (inches)
337	Battle Creek [188-?]	G4114 .B2A3 188- .B4				26 × 41½
338	Bay City, Portsmouth, Wenona & Salzburg 1867	G4114 .B3A3 1867 .R8 Rug 80	A. Ruger (Ruger Map Coll. 80)		Chicago Lith. Co.	20 × 28½
339	Benton Harbor 1889	G4114 .B4A3 1889 .P3	C. J. Pauli & Co., Milwaukee, Wis.	C. J. Pauli & Co., Milwaukee, Wis.		23 × 29
340	Bessemer 1886	G4114 .B56A3 1886 .N6		Norris, Wellge & Co., Milwaukee, Wisconsin	Beck & Pauli, Lith., Milwaukee, Wisconsin	10 × 17
340.1	Calumet, Hecla & Red Jacket 1881	G4114 .C22 1881 .W4	H. Wellge		J. J. Stoner, Madison, Wis.	15 × 25
341	Coldwater [1868?]	G4114 .C7A3 1868 .R8 Rug 81	A. Ruger, Battle Creek, Mich. (Ruger Map Coll. 81)	A. Ruger, Battle Creek, Mich.	Chicago Litho. Co.	19 × 28½
341.1	Coldwater ca. 1868	G4114 .C7A3 1868 .R8 1976	A. Ruger, Battle Creek	A. Ruger, Battle Creek. Reproduced in 1976 by the Branch County Historical Society, 1976	Chicago Lithographing Co.	13 × 19 Reprint of original with modifications
341.2	Coldwater 1883	G4114 .C7A3 1883 .S7 1976		J. J. Stoner, Madison, Wis. Reproduced in 1976 by the Branch County Historical Society	Beck & Pauli, Lith., Milwaukee, Wis.	12½ × 19 Facsimile
342	Detroit 1889	G4114 .D4A3 1889 .B4			The Calvert Lith. Co., Detroit	11½ × 19½
342.1	Detroit 1906	G4114 .D4A3 1906 .H81		Hurd-Wheeler Co., Detroit		5 × 9½ Photograph
343	Detroit 1818 & 1906	G4114 .D4A3 1818 .H8		Hurd Wheeler Co., Detroit		5½ × 9½ Photograph
343.1	Detroit 1906	G4114 .D4A3 1906 .H8		Hurd Wheeler Co., Detroit		5 × 10 Photograph
343.2	Escanaba 1881	G4114 .E8A3 1881 .S7		J. J. Stoner, Madison, Wis.	Beck & Pauli, Lith., Milwaukee, Wis.	6½ × 10½ Photograph
344	Fenton 1880	G4114 .F3A3 1880 .W3	Jos. Warner	J. J. Stoner, Madison, Wisconsin		8 × 10 Photograph
345	Flint 1867	G4114 .F6A3 1867 .R8	A. Ruger, Battle Creek, Mich.	A. Ruger, Battle Creek, Mich.		16 × 20 Photograph

Entry No.	City and Date	LC Call No.	Artist	Publisher	Lithographer	Map Size (inches)
346	Flint 1880	G4114 .F6A3 1880 .P3				15 × 20 Photograph
347	Flint 1890	G4114 .F6A3 1890 .P3	C. J. Pauli, Milwaukee	C. J. Pauli, Milwaukee		14 × 20 Photograph
348	Grand Haven 1868	G4114 .G4A3 1868 .R8 Rug 82	A. Ruger (Ruger Map Coll. 82)	E. S. Glover	Merchant's Lith. Co., Chicago	17 × 24
349	Grand Haven 1874	G4114 .G4A3˙ 1874 .R8 Rug 83	[Albert Ruger] (Ruger Map Coll. 83)	J. J. Stoner, Madison, Wisconsin	Chas. Shober & Co., Props., Chicago Lith. Co.	18 × 24
349.1	Grand Ledge 1881	G4114 .G45A3 1881 .S7 1976		J. J. Stoner, Madison, Wis. Reproduced in 1976 by the Grand Ledge Area Historical Society	Beck & Pauli, Lith., Milwaukee, Wis.	11 × 16½ Facsimile
349.2	Grand Ledge 1881	G4114 .G45A3 1881 .S71 1976		J. J. Stoner, Madison, Wis.	Beck & Pauli, Lith., Milwaukee, Wis.	14½ × 20 Facsimile
349.3	Grand Ledge 1881	G4114 .G45A3 1881 .S73 1977		J. J. Stoner, Madison, Wis. Reproduced in 1977 "From the collection of Lyle V. Huhn."	Beck & Pauli, Lith., Milwaukee, Wis.	13½ × 20 Positive photostat
350	Grand Rapids 1868	G4114 .G5A3 1868 .R8 Rug 84	A. Ruger (Ruger Map Coll. 84)		Chicago Litho. Co.	22½ × 34½
351	Hillsdale 1866	G4114 .H65A3 1866 .R8 Rug 85	A. Ruger, Battle Creek, Mich. (Ruger Map Coll. 85)	A. Ruger, Battle Creek, Mich.	Chicago Litho. Co.	19½ × 28
352	Hudson 1868	G4114 .H86A3 1868 .R8 Rug 86	A. Ruger (Ruger Map Coll. 86)	E. S. Glover	Chicago Litho. Co.	17½ × 23½
353	Ionia 1868	G4114 .I4A3 1868 .R8 Rug 87	A. Ruger (Ruger Map Coll. 87)		Chicago Litho. Co.	22½ × 28
354	Ironwood 1886	G4114 .I7A3 1886 .W4	H. Wellge	Norris, Wellge & Co., Milwaukee, Wisconsin	Beck & Pauli, Litho., Milwaukee, Wisconsin	9½ × 18
354.1	Ishpeming 1871	G4114 .I8A3 1871 .B3	H. H. Bailey		C. H. Vogt, Lith; Milwaukee Lith. & Engr. Co.	15½ × 18 Positive and negative photostats

Entry No.	City and Date	LC Call No.	Artist	Publisher	Lithographer	Map Size (inches)
355	Jackson [1868]	G4114 .J2A3 1868 .R8 Rug 88	A. Ruger, Battle Creek, Mich. (Ruger Map Coll. 88)	A. Ruger, Battle Creek, Mich.	Chicago Litho. Co.	20½ × 34
356	Jackson 1881	G4114 .J2A3 1881 .R8 Rug 89	A. Ruger (Ruger Map Coll. 89)	J. J. Stoner, Madison, Wisconsin	Beck & Pauli, Milwaukee, Wisconsin	15½ × 30½
357	Kalamazoo 1874	G4114 .K2A3 1874 .R8 Rug 90	[Albert Ruger] (Ruger Map Coll. 90)	J. J. Stoner, Madison, Wisconsin	Chas. Shober & Co., Chicago Lith. Co.	20½ × 28½
358	Kalamazoo 1883	G4114 .K2A3 1883 .W4	H. Wellge & A. F. Poole	J. J. Stoner, Madison, Wisconsin	Beck & Pauli, Milwaukee, Wisconsin	17 × 28½
358.1	Kalamazoo 1883	G4114 .K2A3 1883 .W4 1976	H. Wellge & A. F. Poole	J. J. Stoner, Madison, Wis. Reproduced in 1976 by the Kalamazoo Historical Commission	Beck & Pauli, Lithographers, Milwaukee, Wis.	22½ × 27 Facsimile
359	Lansing 1866	G4114 .L3A3 1866 .R8 Rug 91	A. Ruger, Battle Creek, Mich. (Ruger Map Coll. 91)	A. Ruger, Battle Creek, Mich.	Chicago Litho. Co.	22 × 28½
359.1	Ludington 1880	G4114 .L9A3 1880 .S7		J. J. Stoner, Madison, Wis.	Beck & Pauli, Lith., Milwaukee, Wis.	13 × 18 Positive photostat
359.2	Ludington 1892	G4114 .L9A3 1892 .P3	C. J. Pauli, Milwaukee, Wis.	C. J. Pauli, Milwaukee, Wis.		25 × 35½ Positive photostat
359.3	Manistee 1830	G4114 .M2A3 1830 .S7		J. J. Stoner, Madison, Wis.		8 × 10 Photograph
359.4	Manistee 1891	G4114 .M2A3 1891 .P3	C. J. Pauli, Milwaukee, Wis.	C. J. Pauli, Milwaukee, Wis.		8 × 10 Photograph
360	Marquette 1897 (Inset Marquette 1849)	G4114 .M3A3 1897 .L3				23 × 41½
361	Marshall [1868?]	G4114 .M32A3 1868 .R8 Rug 92	A. Ruger, Battle Creek, Mich. (Ruger Map Coll. 92)	A. Ruger, Battle Creek, Mich.	Chicago Lith. Co.	19 × 28

Entry No.	City and Date	LC Call No.	Artist	Publisher	Lithographer	Map Size (inches)
361.1	Midland City 1884	G4114 .M5A3 1884 .O2		O. H. Bailey & Co. Pub., Boston		8½ × 11 Positive Photostat
362	Monroe 1866	G4114 .M6A3 1866 .R8 Rug 93	A. Ruger, Battle Creek, Mich. (Ruger Map Coll. 93)	A. Ruger, Battle Creek, Mich.	Chicago Lith. Co.	19 × 27½
363	Mt. Clemens 1881	G4114 .M7A3 1881 .S7		J. J. Stoner, Madison, Wisconsin	Beck & Pauli, Lith., Milwaukee, Wisconsin	12½ × 22
364	Muskegon 1868	G4114 .M9A3 1868 .R8 Rug 94	A. Ruger (Ruger Map Coll. 94)		Chicago Lith. Co.	19½ × 28
365	Muskegon 1874	G4114 .M9A3 1874 .R8 Rug 95	[Albert Ruger] (Ruger Map Coll. 95)		Chas. Shober & Co., Chicago Lith. Co.	18 × 26
366	Muskegon 1889	G4114 .M9A3 1889 .G6	E. S. Glover	A. J. Little	Shober-Carqueville Lith. Co., Chicago	21 × 37½
367	Negaunee 1871	G4114 .N3A3 1871 .B3	H. H. Bailey		C. H. Vogt, Lith.; Milwaukee Lith. & Engr. Co.	16½ × 24
368	Niles [1868?]	G4114 .N6A3 1868 .R8 Rug 96	A. Ruger, Battle Creek, Mich. (Ruger Map Coll. 96)	A. Ruger, Battle Creek, Mich.	Chicago Lith. Co.	21 × 28
369	Pontiac 1867	G4114 .P6A3 1867 .R8 Rug 97	A. Ruger, Battle Creek, Mich. (Ruger Map Coll. 97)	A. Ruger, Battle Creek, Mich.	Chicago Lith. Co.	18½ × 28½
370	Port Huron & Gratiot, Michigan 1867 (with Sarnia & Port Edwards, Ontario)	G4114 .P7A3 1867 .R8 Rug 98	A. Ruger, Battle Creek, Mich. (Ruger Map Coll. 98)	A. Ruger, Battle Creek, Mich.	Chicago Lith. Co.	19½ × 28½
371	Port Huron 1894	G4114 .P7A3 1894 .P3	C. J. Pauli, Milwaukee, Wis.	C. J. Pauli, Milwaukee, Wis.		20½ × 39
371.1	Portland 1881	G4114 .P83A3 1881 .S7 1976		J. J. Stoner, Madison, Wis.	Beck & Pauli, Lith., Milwaukee, Wis.	13 × 20 Facsimile
371.2	Quincy 1883	G4114 .Q5A3 1883 .P2 1976		Reproduced in 1976 by the Branch County Historical Society		12 × 18½ Facsimile

Entry No.	City and Date	LC Call No.	Artist	Publisher	Lithographer	Map Size (inches)
372	Romeo 1868	G4114 .R62A3 1868 .R8 Rug 99	A. Ruger (Ruger Map Coll. 99)	E. S. Glover	Chicago Lith. Co.	17 × 24½
373	Saginaw 1867	G4114 .S2A3 1867 .R8 Rug 100	A. Ruger (Ruger Map Coll. 100)		Chicago Lith. Co.	20½ × 28½
374	East Saginaw and Saginaw 1887	G4114 .E43A3 1887 .B3		O. H. Bailey & Co., Boston	O. H. Bailey & Co., Boston	5½ × 8½ Photograph
375	Saint Clair 1868	G4114 .S28A3 1868 .R8 Rug 101	A. Ruger (Ruger Map Coll. 101)	E. S. Glover	Chicago Lith. Co.	17 × 23½
376	Saint Johns 1868	G4114 .S37A3 1868 .R8 Rug 102	A. Ruger (Ruger Map Coll. 102)		Chicago Lith. Co.	16 × 24
377	Saranac 1910	G4114 .S48A3 1910 .P4		H. Peake		10 × 16 Photograph
378	Tecumseh 1868	G4114 .T3A3 1868 .R8 Rug 103	A. Ruger (Ruger Map Coll. 103)	E. S. Glover	Chicago Lith. Co.	17½ × 23½
378.1	Union City 1880	G4114 .U5A3 1880 .S7 1976		J. J. Stoner, Madison, Wis. Reproduced in 1976 by the Branch County Historical Society	Beck & Pauli, Lith., Milwaukee, Wis.	13 × 18 Facsimile
379	Wyandotte 1896	G4114 .W8A3 1896 .F6 Fow 69	T. M. Fowler, Morrisville, Pa. (T. M. Fowler Map Coll. 69)	T. M. Fowler & James B. Moyer		23 × 32½
380	Ypsilanti [1868?]	G4114 .Y6A3 1868 .R8 Rug 104	A. Ruger, Battle Creek, Mich. (Ruger Map Coll. 104)	A. Ruger, Battle Creek, Mich.	Chicago Lith. Co.	20½ × 28

Minnesota

Entry No.	City and Date	LC Call No.	Artist	Publisher	Lithographer	Map Size (inches)
380.1	Albert Lea 1879	G4144 .A4A3 1879 .S7 1977		J. J. Stoner, Madison, Wis.	Beck & Pauli, Lith., Milwaukee, Wis.	10½ × 16 Facsimile
381	Anoka 1869	G4144 .A6A3 1869 .R8 Rug 105	A. Ruger (Ruger Map Coll. 105)		Merchant's Lith. Co., Chicago	17½ × 20

Entry No.	City and Date	LC Call No.	Artist	Publisher	Lithographer	Map Size (inches)
382	Appleton 1874 [In Alfred T. Andreas' *An Illustrated Historical Atlas of the State of Minnesota (Chicago, 1874),* p. 83]	G1425 .A3 1874				5×6
383	Austin 1870	G4144 .A9A3 1870 .R8 Rug 106	[Albert Ruger] (Ruger Map Coll. 106)	Ruger & Stoner, Madison, Wisconsin	Chicago Lith. Co., Chicago	17×20
384	Brainerd 1914	G4144 .B7A3 1914 .M3		Brainerd Townsite Co., Duluth	McCoy Duluth Photo-Engraving Co., Duluth, Minnesota	20×26½
385	Duluth 1883	G4144 .D9A3 1883 .W4	H. Wellge	J. J. Stoner, Madison, Wisconsin	Beck & Pauli Lith. Co., Milwaukee, Wisconsin	16×40
386	Duluth 1887	G4144 .D9A3 1887 .W4	H. Wellge, Milwaukee, Wis.	The Duluth News Co.	Beck & Pauli Lith. Co., Milwaukee, Wisconsin	22×41
387	Faribault 1869	G4144 .F4A3 1869 .R8 Rug 107	Prof. A. Ruger (Ruger Map Coll. 107)		Merchant's Lith. Co., Chicago	21×22½
388	Granite Falls 1874 [In Alfred T. Andreas' *An Illustrated Historical Atlas of the State of Minnesota (Chicago, 1874),* p. 86]	G1425 .A3 1874				7×12
389	Hastings 1867	G4144 .H4A3 1867 .R8 Rug 108	A. Ruger (Ruger Map Coll. 108)		Chicago Lith. Co., Chicago	20×24
390	Lake City 1867	G4144 .L2A3 1867 .R8 Rug 109	A. Ruger (Ruger Map Coll. 109)		Chicago Lith. Co., Chicago	19×24
391	Luverne 1883	G4144 .L9A3 1883 .B7	H. Brosius	J. J. Stoner, Madison, Wisconsin; *Rock Co. Herald*	Beck & Pauli, Milwaukee, Wisconsin	14×21½
392	Mankato 1870	G4144 .M3A3 1870 .R8	[Albert Ruger]	Ruger & Stoner, Madison, Wis.	Merchants Lithographing Co., Chicago	21×26

Entry No.	City and Date	LC Call No.	Artist	Publisher	Lithographer	Map Size (inches)
393	Minneapolis & Saint Anthony 1867	G4144 .M5A3 1867 .R8 Rug 110	A. Ruger (Ruger Map Coll. 110)		Chicago Lith. Co., Chicago	22½ × 28
393.1	Minneapolis and Saint Anthony 1867	G4144 .M5A3 1867 .R8 1972	A. Ruger	Reproduced in 1972 by Historic Urban Plans, Ithaca, New York	Chicago Lithographing Co.	22 × 26½ Facsimile
394	Minneapolis 1873	G4144 .M5A35 1873 .H3	A. Hageboeck, Davenport, Iowa	A. Hageboeck, Davenport, Iowa	A. Hageboeck, Davenport, Iowa	7½ × 24½
394.1	Minneapolis 1874	Prints & Photographs Division	Hoffman	Geo. H. Ellsbury & V. Green	Chas. Shober & Co. Props. Chicago Litho. Co.	17½ × 29½
395	Minneapolis 1879	G4144 .M5A3 1879 .R8	A. Ruger	J. J. Stoner, Madison, Wisconsin	Beck & Pauli, Lith., Milwaukee, Wisconsin	20½ × 32½
396	Minneapolis 1885	G4144 .M5A3 1885 .H4	W. V. Herancourt	J. Monasch, Minneapolis		27½ × 40½
396.1	Minneapolis 1886	G4144 .M5A35 1886 .H3 1967	A. Hageboeck	A. Hageboeck, Minneapolis, Minn. Reproduced in 1967 by Historic Urban Plans, Ithaca, New York	A. Hageboeck, Minneapolis, Minn.	13 × 17 Facsimile
397	Minneapolis 1891	G4144 .M5A3 1891 .P4	Frank Pezolt	A. M. Smith	E. G. Christoph Lith. Co., Chicago	29 × 41
398	Minneapolis 1891	G4144 .M5A3 1891 .P41	Frank Pezolt	A. M. Smith		15½ × 21½
399	Montevideo 1874 [In Alfred T. Andreas' *An Illustrated Historical Atlas of the State of Minnesota* (Chicago, 1874), p. 86]	G1425 .A3 1874				7½ × 12
400	New Ulm 1870	G4144 .N4A3 1870 .R8 Rug 112	A. Ruger (Ruger Map Coll. 112)	A. Ruger & Stoner, Madison, Wisconsin	Chicago Lith. Co., Chicago	15½ × 20½
401	Northfield 1869	G4144 .N8A3 1869 .R8 Rug 113	[Albert Ruger] (Ruger Map Coll. 113)	Ruger & Stoner, Madison, Wisconsin	Chicago Lith. Co., Chicago	17 × 20
402	Owatonna 1870	G4144 .O9A3 1870 .R8 Rug 114	[Albert Ruger] (Ruger Map Coll. 114)	Ruger & Stoner, Madison, Wisconsin	Merchant's Lith. Co., Chicago	18 × 20½

Minneapolis, Minnesota, 1891. Drawn by Frank Pezolt.

Entry No.	City and Date	LC Call No.	Artist	Publisher	Lithographer	Map Size (inches)
403	Preston 1874 [In Alfred T. Andreas' *An Illustrated Historical Atlas of the State of Minnesota* (Chicago, 1874), p. 188]	G1425 .A3 1874	E. S. Moore			7½ × 12
404	Redwing 1868	G4144 .R4A3 1868 .R8 Rug 115	A. Ruger (Ruger Map Coll. 115)		Robert Teufel, Chicago	18½ × 24½
405	Rochester 1869	G4144 .R7A3 1869 .R8 Rug 116	[Albert Ruger] (Ruger Map Coll. 116)	Ruger & Stoner, Madison, Wisconsin	Merchant's Lith. Co., Chicago	20½ × 22
406	Saint Cloud 1869	G4144 .S2A3 1869 .R8 Rug 117	A. Ruger (Ruger Map Coll. 117)		Merchant's Lith Co., Chicago	21 × 24
406.1	St. Paul 1853	G4144 .S4A35 1853 .R5	Strobel	Thompson Ritchie	J. Queen; P. S. Duval & Co., steam lith. press, Philada.	15 × 20
407	St. Paul 1867	G4144 .S4A3 1867 .R8 Rug 118	A. Ruger (Ruger Map Coll. 118)		Chicago Lith. Co., Chicago	22½ × 28
407.1	St. Paul 1867	G4144 .S4A3 1867 .R8 1975		Reproduced in 1975 by Historic Urban Plans, Ithaca, New York	Chicago Lith. Co., Chicago	23½ × 28 Facsimile
408	St. Paul 1873	G4144 .S4A35 1873 .H3	A. Hageboeck, Davenport, Iowa	A. Hageboeck, Davenport, Iowa	A. Hageboeck, Davenport, Iowa	7½ × 24½
409	St. Paul [1874]	G4144 .S4A35 1874 .E5	Hoffman	George Ellsbury & Vernon Green		16½ × 29½
409.1	St. Paul 1883	G4144 .S4A3 1883 .W4	H. Wellge	J. J. Stoner, Madison, Wis.	Beck & Pauli, Lithographers, Milwaukee, Wis.	26½ × 40
409.2	St. Paul 1888	G4144 .S4A3 1888 .M3	Marr-Richards Engravers, Milwaukee, Wis.	Baker, Collins & Co., St. Paul, Minn.	Marr-Richards Engravers, Milwaukee, Wis.	17 × 28
410	St. Paul 1893	G4144 .S4A3 1893 .B7		Brown, Tracy & Co.		8 × 10½
411	St. Paul 1906	G4144 .S4A3 1906 .S3		Robert M. Saint, St. Paul		16½ × 30½
412	Saint Peter 1870	G4144 .S44A3 1870 .R8 Rug 119	[Albert Ruger] (Ruger Map Coll. 119)	Ruger & Stoner, Madison, Wisconsin	Merchant's Lith. Co., Chicago	17½ × 20½

Entry No.	City and Date	LC Call No.	Artist	Publisher	Lithographer	Map Size (inches)
413	Shakopee 1869	G4144 .S56A3 1869 .R8 Rug 120	A. Ruger & Stoner, Madison, Wis. (Ruger Map Coll. 120)		Chicago Lith. Co., Chicago	16 × 20½
414	Stillwater 1870	G4144 .S9A3 1870 .R8 Rug 121	A. Ruger (Ruger Map Coll. 121)		Merchant's Lith. Co., Chicago	20½ × 22½
414.1	Winona 1866 [In L. G. Bennett and A. C. Smith's *Map of Winona County, Minnesota 1867.* Frontispiece]	G1428 .W8B4 1867	Geo. H. Ellsburg		Chas. Shober & Co., Lith., Chicago	11½ × 21
415	Winona 1867	G4144 .W8A3 1867 .R8 Rug 122	A. Ruger (Ruger Map Coll. 122)		Chicago Lith. Co., Chicago	22½ × 28½
416	Winona 1874	G4144 .W8A3 1874 .E6		George H. Ellsbury & Vernon Green	Chas. Shober & Co., Chicago Lith. Co.	18 × 28½
417	Winona 1889	G4144 .W8A3 1889 .P3	C. J. Pauli	C. J. Pauli & Co., Milwaukee, Wisconsin		18 × 40

Missouri

Entry No.	City and Date	LC Call No.	Artist	Publisher	Lithographer	Map Size (inches)
417.1	Aurora 1891	G4164 .A8A3 1891 .F6	T. M. Fowler, Morrisville, Pa; A. E. D.	T. M. Fowler & James B. Moyer		17 × 26
418	Brookfield 1869	G4164 .B8A3 1869 .R8 Rug 123	A. Ruger (Ruger Map Coll. 123)			17 × 20½
419	California 1869	G4164 .C14A3 1869 .R8 Rug 124	A. Ruger (Ruger Map Coll. 124)			17 × 18
420	Carthage 1891	G4164 .C3A3 1891 .F6 Fow 5	T. M. Fowler, Morrisville, Pa. (T. M. Fowler Map Coll. 5)	T. M. Fowler & James B. Moyer		16½ × 32
421	Chillicothe 1869	G4164 .C5A3 1869 .R8 Rug 125	A. Ruger (Ruger Map Coll. 125)			21 × 26
422	Columbia 1869	G4164 .C8A3 1869 .R8 Rug 126	A. Ruger (Ruger Map Coll. 126)			17½ × 22

Entry No.	City and Date	LC Call No.	Artist	Publisher	Lithographer	Map Size (inches)
423	Hannibal 1869	G4164 .H2A3 1869 .R8 Rug 127	A. Ruger (Ruger Map Coll. 127)			22½ × 26
423.1	Hannibal 1869	G4164 .H2A3 1869 .R8 1970	A. Ruger	Reproduced in 1970 by Historic Urban Plans, Ithaca, New York		21½ × 23 Facsimile
424	Hermann 1869	G4164 .H4A3 1869 .R8 Rug 128	A. Ruger (Ruger Map Coll. 128)			14 × 16½
425	Holden 1869	G4164 .H7A3 1869 .R8 Rug 129	A. Ruger (Ruger Map Coll. 129)			11 × 12
426	Independence 1868	G4164 .I3A3 1868 .R8 Rug 130	A. Ruger (Ruger Map Coll. 130)			21½ × 26½
427	Jefferson City 1869	G4164 .J4A3 1869 .R8 Rug 131	A. Ruger (Ruger Map Coll. 131)			20 × 26
428	Kansas City 1869 (Inset Kansas City 1855)	G4164 .K2A3 1869 .R8 Rug 132	A. Ruger (Ruger Map Coll. 132)	Ruger & Stoner, Madison, Wisconsin	Merchant's Lith. Co., Chicago	22 × 28
429	Kansas City (West Bottoms) 1895	G4164 .K2A3 1895 .K6		Augustus Koch		32½ × 49½
430	Lexington 1869	G4164 .L6A3 1869 .R8 Rug 133	A. Ruger (Ruger Map Coll. 133)			20½ × 26
431	Macon City 1869	G4164 .M13A3 1869 .R8 Rug 134	A. Ruger (Ruger Map Coll. 134)			20½ × 26
432	Mexico 1869	G4164 .M5A3 1869 .R8 Rug 135	A. Ruger (Ruger Map Coll. 135)			20 × 26
433	Pacific 1869 (Formerly Franklin)	G4164 .P15A3 1869 .R8 Rug 136	A. Ruger (Ruger Map Coll. 136)			10 × 12
434	Palmyra 1869	G4164 .P3A3 1869 .R8 Rug 137	A. Ruger (Ruger Map Coll. 137)			20 × 26
435	Pleasant Hill 1869	G4164 .P7A3 1869 .R8 Rug 138	A. Ruger (Ruger Map Coll. 138)			14 × 18
436	Saint Charles 1869	G4164 .S2A3 1869 .R8 Rug 139	A. Ruger (Ruger Map Coll. 139)			20½ × 26
437	Saint Joseph 1868	G4164 .S3A3 1868 .R8 Rug 140	A. Ruger (Ruger Map Coll. 140)		Merchant's Lith. Co., Chicago	22½ × 28

Hannibal, Missouri, 1869. Drawn by Albert Ruger. This famous town on the Mississippi River is the hometown of Mark Twain.

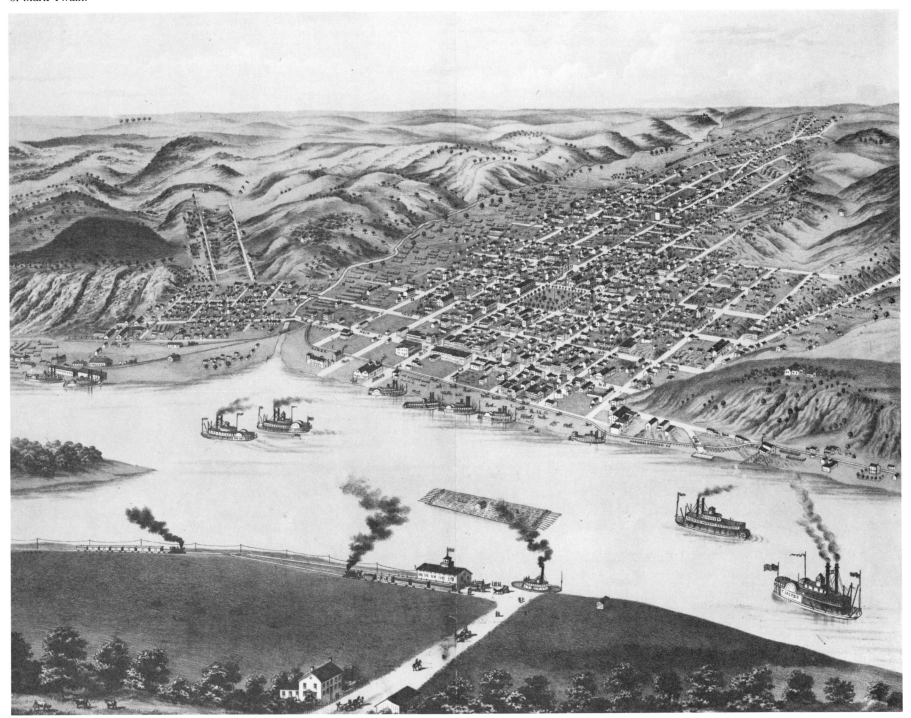

Entry No.	City and Date	LC Call No.	Artist	Publisher	Lithographer	Map Size (inches)
438	St. Louis [1848]	G4164 .S4A35 1848 .K4	J. M. Kershaw, St. Louis	J. M. Kershaw, St. Louis	J. M. Kershaw, St. Louis	8½ × 10½
438.1	St. Louis 1859	Prints & Photographs Division		Hagen & Pfau	A. Janicke & Co., St. Louis	17½ × 22
438.2	St. Louis 1873	Prints & Photographs Division		Geo. Degen, New York		15½ × 23
438.3	St. Louis 1874	Prints & Photographs Division	Parsons & Atwater	Currier & Ives, New York	Parsons & Atwater	22½ × 32½
439	St. Louis 1875	G1439 .S4C6 1876	Camille N. Dry	Compton & Co. (1876)	St. Louis Globe-Democrat Job Printing Co.	Atlas in 110 plates, each plate 13 × 18½
439.1	St. Louis 1876	G4164 .S4A35 1876 .L6	Lord, C. K.		[Woodward, Tiernan, and Hale]	12 × 24
440	St. Louis 1784 & 1884	G4164 .S4A35 1884 .V6			J. E. Lawton Printing Co.	18½ × 26
441	St. Louis 1893	G4164 .S4A3 1893 .G7	Fred Graf	Fred Graf, St. Louis	Fred Graf, St. Louis	25½ × 39½
442	St. Louis 1894	G4164 .S4A3 1894 .J9	Chas. Juehne	Chas. Juehne		18 × 24
443	St. Louis 1895	G4164 .S4A3 1895 .J9		Chas. Juehne	Chas. Juehne	23 × 40
444	St. Louis 1896	G4164 .S4A3 1896 .G7	Fred Graf, St. Louis	Graf Eng. Co., St. Louis		26 × 40½
445	St. Louis 1896	G4164 .S4A3 1896 .J9	Chas. Juehne	Chas. Juehne	Chas. Juehne	23½ × 40
446	St. Louis 1897	G4164 .S4A3 1897 .S3				8½ × 9½
447	St. Louis 1904 (Wholesale & Office District)	G4164 .S4A3 1904 .J9	Charles Juehne	Charles Juehne		5 × 10½
448	St. Louis 1907	G4164 .S4A3 1907 .G7	Fred Graf	Fred Graf Engraving Co., St. Louis		19½ × 24½
449	Sedalia 1869	G4164 .S5A3 1869 .R8 Rug 141	A. Ruger (Ruger Map Coll. 141)			21 × 26½
450	Warrensburg 1869	G4164 .W2A3 1869 .R8 Rug 142	A. Ruger (Ruger Map Coll. 142)			16 × 20
451	Washington 1869	G4164 .W3A3 1869 .R8 Rug 143	A. Ruger (Ruger Map Coll. 143)			21 × 26

Entry No.	City and Date	LC Call No.	Artist	Publisher	Lithographer	Map Size (inches)
452	Billings 1904	G4254 .B4A3 1904 .W4	H. Wellge	H. Wellge, Milwaukee, Wisconsin		18 × 28½
453	Butte-City 1884	G4254 .B9A3 1884 .W4	H. Wellge	J. J. Stoner, Madison, Wisconsin	Beck & Pauli, Lith., Milwaukee, Wisconsin	20 × 29 Positive photostat
453.1	Butte-City 1884	G4254 .B9A3 1884 .W4 1974	H. Wellge	J. J. Stoner, Madison, Wis. Reproduced in 1974 by Historic Urban Plans, Ithaca, New York	Beck & Pauli, Litho., Milwaukee, Wis.	21 × 27 Facsimile
454	Great Falls 1891	G4254 .G7A3 1891 .A6		American Publishing Co., Milwaukee, Wisconsin		24 × 33
455	Helena 1875	G4254 .H5A3 1875 .G6	E. S. Glover	C. K. Wells, Helena, Montana Territory	A. L. Bancroft & Co., San Francisco, California	20½ × 27
456	Helena 1883	G4254 .H5A3 1883 .S7		J. J. Stoner, Milwaukee, Wisconsin	Beck & Pauli, Lith., Milwaukee, Wisconsin	17 × 26
457	Helena 1890	G4254 .H5A3 1890 .A4		American Publishing Co., Milwaukee, Wisconsin		27 × 40
457.1	Helena 1890	G4254 .H5A3 1890 .A5 1970		American Publishing Co., Milwaukee, Wis. Reproduced in 1970 by Historic Urban Plans, Ithaca, New York		22 × 28½ Facsimile
458	Livingston 1883	G4254 .L6A3 1883 .S7		J. J. Stoner, Madison, Wisconsin	Beck & Pauli, Lith., Milwaukee, Wisconsin	16 × 22½
459	Miles City 1883	G4254 .M5A3 1883 .S7		J. J. Stoner, Madison, Wisconsin	Beck & Pauli, Lith., Milwaukee, Wisconsin	14 × 22
460	Missoula 1884	G4254 .M6A3 1884 .W4	H. Wellge	J. J. Stoner, Madison, Wisconsin	Beck & Pauli, Lith., Milwaukee, Wisconsin	16 × 24
461	Missoula 1891	G4254 .M6A3 1891 .A6		American Publishing Co., Milwaukee, Wisconsin		22 × 33½
461.1	Virginia City 1868	G4254 .V55A3 1868 .M3 1974	A. E. Mathews, N.Y.	Reproduced in 1974 by Historic Urban Plans, Ithaca, New York	A. E. Mathews, Lith., N.Y.	14 × 21 Facsimile
461.2	Virginia City 1875	G4254 .V55A35 1875 .G5	E. S. Glover, Salt Lake City, Utah	Reproduced from original in The Montana Historical Society, Helena	Chas. Shober & Co. Prop's Chicago Lith. Co.	8 × 10 Photograph

Nebraska

Entry No.	City and Date	LC Call No.	Artist	Publisher	Lithographer	Map Size (inches)
462	Kearney 1889	G4194 .K4A3 1889 .W4	H. Wellge	American Publishing Co., Milwaukee, Wisconsin		24 × 36½
463	Lincoln 1880	G4194 .L6A3 1880 .K6 1970	Augustus Koch	Reproduced in 1970 by Historic Urban Plans, Ithaca, New York	Ramsey, Millett & Hudson, Kansas City, Mo.	20½ × 25½ Facsimile
464	Lincoln 1889	G4194 .L6A3 1889 .W4	H. Wellge	American Publishing Co., Milwaukee, Wisconsin		22½ × 32
465	Nebraska City 1868	G4194 .N3A3 1868 .R8 Rug 144	A. Ruger (Ruger Map Coll. 144)		Merchant's Lith. Co., Chicago	21 × 26
466	Norfolk 1889 (Inset Norfolk 1884)	G4194 .N7A3 1889 .W4	H. Wellge	American Publishing Co., Milwaukee, Wisconsin		18 × 24½
467	Omaha 1868	G4194 .O4A3 1868 .R8 Rug 145	A. Ruger (Ruger Map Coll. 145)		Chicago Lith. Co.	22½ × 28
467.1	Omaha 1868	G4194 .O4A3 1868 .R8 1977	A. Ruger	Reproduced in 1977 by Historic Urban Plans, Ithaca, New York	Chicago Lithographing Co., Chicago	16½ × 19 Facsimile
467.2	Omaha 1876	G4194 .O4A3 1876 .K6	Augustus Koch		[Charles Sho]ber & Co., Prop's	8 × 10 Photograph
468	Omaha 1906	G4194 .O4A3 1905 .A8	Edw. J. Austen	Bee Publishing Co.		17 × 32

Nevada

Entry No.	City and Date	LC Call No.	Artist	Publisher	Lithographer	Map Size (inches)
468.1	Carson City 1875	G4354 .C4A3 1875 .K6	Augustus Koch	Reproduced from original in the University of California at Berkeley Bancroft Library	Britton, Rey & Co. Lith., S. F.	8 × 10 Photograph
468.2	Reno [1890]	G4354 .R4A3 1890 .C7 1972		C. C. Powning; Reproduced in 1972 from an original lithograph in the Nevada Historical Society, Reno, by Historic Urban Plans, Ithaca, New York	H. S. Crocker & Co., Lith.	17½ × 23½ Facsimile
468.3	Virginia City 1861	Prints & Photographs Division	Grafton T. Brown	Grafton T. Brown	C. C. Kuchel, Lith., S. Francisco, Cal.	21 × 27
469	Virginia City 1875	G4354 .V4A3 1875 .K6	Augustus Koch		Britton, Rey & Co., San Francisco	24 × 28½

Entry No.	City and Date	LC Call No.	Artist	Publisher	Lithographer	Map Size (Inches)
469.1	Virginia City 1875	G4354 .V4A3 1875 .K6 1970	Augustus Koch	Reproduced in 1970 by Historic Urban Plans, Ithaca, New York	Britton, Rey & Co., Lith.	22 × 23½ Facsimile

New Hampshire

Entry No.	City and Date	LC Call No.	Artist	Publisher	Lithographer	Map Size (Inches)
469.2	Alton and Alton Bay 1888	G3744 .A45A3 1888 .N6	Geo. E. Norris, Brockton, Mass.	Geo. E. Norris, Brockton, Mass.	Burleigh Lith. Est., Troy, N.Y.	14½ × 23
469.3	Antrim and Clinton Village 1887	G3744 .A57A3 1887 .N6	Geo. E. Norris, Brockton, Mass.	Geo. E. Norris, Brockton, Mass.	The Burleigh Litho. Establishment, Troy, N.Y.	17 × 26½
470	Ashland 1883	G3744 .A8A3 1883 .P6		Poole & Norris, Brockton, Massachusetts	Beck & Pauli, Milwaukee, Wisconsin	15½ × 14½
471	Bethlehem 1883	G3744 .B43A3 1883 .P6	A. F. Poole	Poole & Norris, Brockton, Massachusetts	Beck & Pauli, Milwaukee, Wisconsin	16 × 20
471.1	Bristol 1884	G3744 .B74A3 1884 .N6		Geo. E. Norris, Brockton, Mass.	Beck & Pauli, Litho., Milwaukee, Wis.	19 × 23
472	Claremont 1877	G3744 .C5A3 1877 .R8 Rug 146	A. Ruger (Ruger Map Coll. 146)		Shober & Carqueville Litho. Co., Chicago	20 × 24½
473	Concord 1899	G3744 .C7A3 1899 .P6		Bert Poole		22½ × 28
474	Concord 1899	G3744 .C7A3 1899 .P61		G. M. Clough, Boston		22½ × 28
475	Dover 1877	G3744 .D6A3 1877 .R8 Rug 147	A. Ruger (Ruger Map Coll. 147)		D. Bremner & Co., Milwaukee, Wisconsin	23½ × 25
475.1	Dover 1888	G3744 .D6A3 1888 .P6	[Al]bert Poole	Interstate Art Publishing Co., Boston	Interstate Art Publishing Co., Boston	24½ × 30
476	Exeter 1884	G3744 .E9A3 1884 .W4	H. Wellge	Norris & Wellge, Brockton, Massachusetts		17½ × 21½
477	Exeter 1896	G3744 .E89A3 1896 .M6		A. W. Moore Co., Boston	A. W. Moore Co., Boston	27½ × 32
477.1	Farmington 1877	G3744 .F3A3 1877 .B5				17 × 18
478	Franklin and Franklin Falls 1884 (Inset Franklin Falls 1856)	G3744 .F7A3 1884 .W4	H. Wellge	Norris & Wellge, Brockton, Massachusetts		17 × 20
478.1	Goffstown 1887	G3744 .G6A3 1887 .N6	Geo. E. Norris, Brockton, Mass.	Geo. E. Norris, Brockton, Mass.	Burleigh Litho. Establishment, Troy, N.Y.	16 × 20

Entry No.	City and Date	LC Call No.	Artist	Publisher	Lithographer	Map Size (inches)
478.2	Gorham 1888	G3744 .G63A3 1888 .N6	Geo. E. Norris, Brockton, Mass.	Geo. E. Norris, Brockton, Mass.	Burleigh Lith. Est., Troy, N.Y.	21 × 25½
479	Great Falls, New Hampshire and Berwick, Maine 1877	G3744 .G7A3 1877 .R8 Rug 148	A. Ruger (Ruger Map Coll. 148)	J. J. Stoner, Madison, Wisconsin	C. H. Vogt & Co., Milwaukee	23 × 24
480	Greenville 1886 (View of Mason Village 1847)	G3744 .G77A3 1886 .B8		L. R. Burleigh, Troy, N.Y.	The Burleigh Lith. Establishment, Troy, N.Y.	13½ × 20
480.1	Henniker 1889	G3744 .H4A3 1889 .N6	Geo. E. Norris, Brockton, Mass.	Geo. E. Norris, Brockton, Mass.	Burleigh Lith. Est., Troy, N.Y.	14½ × 21
481	Hillsborough-Bridge 1884	G3744 .H5A3 1884 .W4	H. W. [H. Wellge]	Norris & Wellge, Brockton, Massachusetts		15 × 18
482	Hinsdale [1886]	G3744 .H53A3 1886 .B8	L. R. Burleigh, Troy, New York	L. R. Burleigh, Troy, New York	C. H. Vogt & Son, Cleveland, Ohio	14 × 24½
483	Laconia 1883	G3744 .L2A3 1883 .P6		Poole & Norris, Brockton, Massachusetts	Beck & Pauli, Milwaukee, Wisconsin	17 × 21
484	Lake Village 1883	G3744 .L23A3 1883 .P6		Poole & Norris, Brockton, Massachusetts	Beck & Pauli, Milwaukee, Wisconsin	13 × 19
485	Lancaster 1883	G3744 .L3A3 1883 .P6	A. F. Poole	Poole & Norris, Brockton, Massachusetts	Beck & Pauli, Milwaukee, Wisconsin	16 × 19½
486	Littleton 1883	G3744 .L7A3 1883 .P6	A. Poole	Poole & Norris, Brockton, Massachusetts	Beck & Pauli, Milwaukee, Wisconsin	19 × 21½
487	Meredith Village 1889	G3744 .M4A3 1889 .N6	George E. Norris, Brockton, Mass.	George E. Norris, Brockton, Mass.	The Burleigh Lith. Est., Troy, New York	16 × 25
488	Milford 1886	G3744 .M5A3 1886 .B8	C. H. Vogt; L. R. Burleigh, Troy, New York	L. R. Burleigh, Troy, New York		16 × 24½
488.1	Milton 1888	G3744 .M53A3 1888 .N6	Geo. E. Norris, Brockton, Mass.	Geo. E. Norris, Brockton, Mass.	The Burleigh Lith. Est., Troy, N.Y.	14 × 24
488.2	Nashua 1883	G3744 .N2A3 1883 .N2				25 × 33½
489	Penacook [1887]	G3744 .P45A3 1887 .B8	L. R. Burleigh, Troy, New York	L. R. Burleigh, Troy, New York		16 × 24½

Entry No.	City and Date	LC Call No.	Artist	Publisher	Lithographer	Map Size (inches)
490	Peterborough 1886 (with South Peterboro & West Peterboro)	G3744 .P46A3 1886 .B8	L. R. Burleigh, Troy, New York	L. R. Burleigh, Troy, New York	Burleigh Lith. Est.	16½ × 25
491	Pittsfield 1884	G3744 .P5A3 1884 .N6		Geo. E. Norris, Brockton, Massachusetts	Beck & Pauli, Milwaukee, Wisconsin	18 × 24
492	Portsmouth 1877	G3744 .P8A3 1877 .R82	A. Ruger	[J. J. Stoner, Madison, Wisconsin]	D. Bremner & Co., Milwaukee, Wisconsin	22 × 26½
492.1	Portsmouth 1877	G3744 .P8A3 1877 .R8 Rug 149	A. Ruger (Ruger Map Coll. 149)	J. J. Stoner, Madison, Wis.	D. Bremner & Co. Lith., Milwaukee, Wis.	22 × 27
492.2	Rochester 1877	G3744 .R6A3 1877 .S7		J. J. Stoner, Madison, Wis.	C. H. Vogt & Co., Milwaukee	19 × 22½
493	Rochester 1884 (with Gonic & East Rochester)	G3744 .R6A3 1884 .W4	H. Wellge	Norris & Wellge, Brockton, Massachusetts		17 × 20
494	Salmon Falls 1877	G3744 .R65A3 1877 .R8 Rug 201	[Albert Ruger] (Ruger Map Coll. 201)		Jos. B. Richards & Co., Boston	10½ × 12½
495	South New Market 1884	G3744 .N44A3 1884 .N6		Norris & Wellge, Brockton, Massachusetts		15 × 18
496	Tilton 1884	G3744 .T5A3 1884 .W4	H. Wellge	Norris & Wellge, Brockton, Massachusetts		16 × 20
497	West Lebanon, New Hampshire & White River Junction, Vermont 1889	G3744 .W42A3 1889 .N6	Geo. E. Norris, Brockton, Mass.	Geo. E. Norris, Brockton, Mass.	The Burleigh Lith. Est., Troy, New York	17½ × 25½
498	Whitefield 1883	G3744 .W5A3 1883 .P6	A. F. Poole	Poole & Norris, Brockton, Massachusetts	Beck & Pauli, Milwaukee, Wisconsin	16 × 19
498.1	Winchester 1887	G3744 .W55A3 1887 .N6	Geo. E. Norris, Brockton, Mass.	Geo. E. Norris, Brockton, Mass.	The Burleigh Litho. Establishment, Troy, N.Y.	15½ × 22½
499	Wolfeborough, Lake Winnipesaukee 1889 (with South Wolfboro)	G3744 .W6A3 1889 .N6	Geo. E. Norris, Brockton, Mass.	Geo. E. Norris, Brockton, Mass.	The Burleigh Lith. Est., Troy, New York	17 × 25½

Entry No.	City and Date	LC Call No.	Artist	Publisher	Lithographer	Map Size (inches)
524.2	Easton, Pa. & Phillipsburg, N.J. 1900	G3824 .E3A3 1900 .L31		Landis & Alsop, Newark, New Jersey		37 × 55
525	Plainfield and North Plainfield 1899	G3814 .P6A3 1899 .L3		Landis & Hughes, New York		31 × 47½
526	Rutherford 1904	G3814 .R9A3 1904 .H8		T. J. Hughes, New York		22 × 27
527	Somers-Point 1925	G3814 .S485A3 1925 .C5	R. Cinquin	Hughes & Cinquin, Brooklyn, New York	[Meriden Gravure Co., Meriden, Conn.]	25 × 34
527.1	Somerville 1882	G3814 .S5A3 1882 .F6 Vault	T. M. Fowler	Fowler & Evans, Ashbury Park, N.J.	Beck & Pauli, Lithographers, Milwaukee, Wis.	15 × 25
527.2	South Orange 1877	G3814 .S7A3 1877 .F6 1976	T. M. Fowler	T. M. Fowler. Reproduced in 1976	D. Bremner & Co., Lith., Milwaukee, Wis.	18½ × 23½ Facsimile
527.3	Trenton 1874	G3814 .T7A3 1874 .F6		Fowler and Bailey. Reproduced from the original in the Trenton Public Library	H. J. Toudy & Co., Phila.	27 × 32½ Positive photostat
528	Vineland 1885	G3814 .V7A3 1885 .B3		O. H. Bailey & Co., Boston	O. H. Bailey & Co., Boston	23½ × 32½
529	Westfield 1929	G3814 .W5A3 1929 .C5	Rene Cinquin	Hughes & Cinquin, New York	[Meriden Gravure Co., Meriden, Conn.]	27 × 31
530	Westwood 1924	G3814 .W54A3 1924 .C5	Rene Cinquin	Hughes & Cinquin, Brooklyn, New York	[Meriden Gravure Co., Meriden, Conn.]	22½ × 34
531	Woodbury 1886	G3814 .W8A3 1886 .B3		O. H. Bailey & Co., Boston	O. H. Bailey & Co., Boston	25 × 32½

New Mexico

Entry No.	City and Date	LC Call No.	Artist	Publisher	Lithographer	Map Size (inches)
531.1	Albuquerque 1886	G4324 .A4A3 1886 .K6	Augustus Koch	Reproduced from original in the University of California at Berkeley Bancroft Library		8 × 10 Photograph
532	Las Vegas 1882	G4324 .L4A3 1882 .S7		J. J. Stoner, Madison, Wisconsin	Beck & Pauli, Milwaukee, Wisconsin	17 × 21½
533	Santa Fe 1882	G4324 .S3A3 1882 .W4	H. Wellge	J. J. Stoner, Madison, Wisconsin	Beck & Pauli, Milwaukee, Wisconsin	13 × 19
533.1	Santa Fe 1882	G4324 .S3A3 1882 .W4 1971	[Henry Wellge]	J. J. Stoner, Madison, Wis. Reproduced in 1971 by Historic Urban Plans, Ithaca, New York	Beck & Pauli, Lithographers, Milwaukee, Wis.	14½ × 19½ Facsimile

New York

Entry No.	City and Date	LC Call No.	Artist	Publisher	Lithographer	Map Size (inches)
533.2	Albany 1853	G3804 .A3A35 1853 .H5 1978	J. W. Hill	Smith Bros. & Co., N. Y. Reproduced in 1978 by Historic Urban Plans	Hatch & Severy, N.Y.	21 × 27½ Facsimile
534	Albany 1879	G3804 .A3A3 1879 .R6	H. H. Rowley & Co., Hartford, Conn.	H. H. Rowley & Co., Hartford Connecticut	Beck & Pauli, Milwaukee, Wisconsin	30 × 44½
535	Amityville 1925	G3804 .A5A3 1925 .C5	Rene Cinquin, New York	Metropolitan Aero-View Co., New York		25 × 38
536	Antwerp 1888	G3804 .A64A3 1888 .F3	C. F. [Fausel]		The Burleigh Lith. Est., Troy, New York	17 × 24
537	Bainbridge 1889	G3804 .B17A3 1889 .B8	L. R. Burleigh, Troy, New York	L. R. Burleigh, Troy, New York	The Burleigh Lith. Est., Troy, New York	14½ × 23½
537.1	Ballston Spa [189-?]	G3804 .B24A3 189- .F3	C. Fausel, Troy, N.Y.	A. M. Vandecarr, South Schodack, N.Y.		18½ × 28½
537.2	Bay Side Park [Queens 1915]	G3804 .N4:3Q4A3 1915 .N6		North Shore Realty Co., New York		22½ × 25
538	Binghamton 1901	G3804 .B6A3 1901 .L3		Landis & Alsop, Newark, New Jersey		In 2 parts, each 40 × 28½
539	Brewster 1887	G3804 .B71A3 1887 .B8		The Burleigh Litho. Est., Troy, New York		13 × 21
540	Bronx 1897 (Vicinity of Grand Concourse)	G3804 .N4:3B7A3 1897 .K6	Wm. W. Klein	Department of Street Improvements, 23rd & 24th Wards	Robert A. Welcke Photo Lith., New York	In 2 parts, each 17 × 35½
541	Brooklyn 1879	G3804 .N4:3B8A3 1879 .P3	C. R. Parsons	Currier & Ives, New York		23 × 33½
541.1	Brooklyn [1897]	G3804 .N4:3B8A3 1897 .W4	Geo. Welch			20 × 35
541.2	Brooklyn 1908	G3804 .N4:3B8A3 1908 .A9	August R. Ohman & Co.	August R. Ohman & Co., N.Y.	August R. Ohman & Co., N.Y.	23 × 19
542	Buffalo 1880	G3804 .B9A3 1880 .H8		E. H. Hutchinson, Buffalo, N.Y.	Maerz Lithographing Co., Buffalo, N.Y.	25 × 37½
543	Buffalo 1902	G3804 .B9A3 1902 .L3		Landis & Alsop, Newark, N.J.		41 × 58½

Entry No.	City and Date	LC Call No.	Artist	Publisher	Lithographer	Map Size (inches)
544	Caledonia 1892	G3804 .C14A3 1892 .B8		Burleigh Litho. Co., Troy, New York		17 × 25
545	Cambridge 1886	G3804 .C15A3 1886 .B8		L. R. Burleigh, Troy, New York	Burleigh Lith. Est., Troy, New York	17 × 27½
545.1	Camden 1885	G3804 .C162A3 1885 .B8	L. R. Burleigh, Troy, N.Y.	L. R. Burleigh, Troy, N.Y.	Beck & Pauli, Litho., Milwaukee, Wis.	14½ × 25
546	Canastota 1885	G3804 .C22A3 1885 .B8 Fow 9	L. R. Burleigh, Troy, N.Y. (T. M. Fowler Map Coll. 9)	L. R. Burleigh, Troy, N.Y.	C. H. Vogt & Son, Lith., Cleveland, O.	14½ × 24
547	Canton 1885	G3804 .C24A3 1885 .B8	L. R. Burleigh, Troy, New York	L. R. Burleigh, Troy, New York	C. H. Vogt & Son, Cleveland, Ohio	15 × 24½
548	Carthage 1888	G3804 .C27A3 1888 .B8	L. R. Burleigh, Troy, New York	L. R. Burleigh, Troy, New York	Burleigh Lith. Est., Troy, New York	18 × 28
549	Catskill 1889	G3804 .C3A3 1889 .B8	L. R. Burleigh, Troy, New York	L. R. Burleigh, Troy, New York	The Burleigh Lith. Est., Troy, New York	19 × 29½
550	Cazenovia 1890	G3804 .C36A3 1890 .B8		L. R. Burleigh, Troy, New York	Burleigh Lith. Est., Troy, New York	18 × 31
551	Chatham 1886	G3804 .C49A3 1886 .B8		L. R. Burleigh, Troy, New York	The Burleigh Lith. Est., Troy, New York	14 × 29½
551.1	Clifton Springs 1892	G3804 .C56A3 1892 .B8			Burleigh Litho. Co., Troy, N.Y.	17½ × 28
552	Clinton 1885	G3804 .C57A3 1885 .B8	L. R. Burleigh, Troy, New York	L. R. Burleigh, Troy, New York	Beck & Pauli, Litho., Milwaukee, Wisconsin	15 × 26
553	Cooperstown 1890	G3804 .C67A3 1890 .B8		L. R. Burleigh, Troy, New York	Burleigh Lith. Est., Troy, New York	17 × 28½
553.1	Cooperstown 1890	G3804 .C67A3 1890 .B8 1975		L. R. Burleigh, Troy, N.Y. Reproduced in 1975 by Historic Urban Plans, Ithaca, New York	Burleigh Lithographing Establishment, Troy, N.Y.	19½ × 28 Facsimile
554	Corinth and Palmer Falls 1888	G3804 .C69A3 1888 .B8	L. R. Burleigh, Troy, New York	L. R. Burleigh, Troy, New York	The Burleigh Lith. Est., Troy, New York	17 × 27
554.1	Cuba 1882	G3804 .C95A3 1882 .B7 1974	H. Brosius	J. J. Stoner, Madison, Wis.	Beck & Pauli, Lithographers, Milwaukee, Wis.	15 × 24½ Facsimile
555	Delhi 1887	G3804 .D42A3 1887 .B8	L. R. Burleigh, Troy, New York	L. R. Burleigh, Troy, New York	Burleigh Lith. Est., Troy, New York	15½ × 20½
555.1	Depew 1898	G3804 .D5A3 1898 .M3		Matthews-Northrup Co., Buffalo, N.Y.		29½ × 42½

Entry No.	City and Date	LC Call No.	Artist	Publisher	Lithographer	Map Size (inches)
556	Deposit 1887	G3804 .D53A3 1887 .B8	L. R. Burleigh, Troy, New York	L. R. Burleigh, Troy, New York	The Burleigh Lith. Est., Troy, New York	15 × 24½
556.1	Dolgeville 1890	G3804 .D7A3 1890 .D6		Alfred Dolge, Dolgeville, N.Y.	Burleigh Litho. Establishment, Troy, N.Y.	15½ × 25½
557	East Syracuse 1885	G3804 .E47A3 1885 .B8	L. R. Burleigh, Troy, New York	L. R. Burleigh, Troy, New York	C. H. Vogt & Son, Cleveland, Ohio	12½ × 25
558	Ellenville 1887	G3804 .E66A3 1887 .B8	L. R. Burleigh, Troy, New York	L. R. Burleigh, Troy, New York	The Burleigh Lith. Est., Troy, New York	17 × 27
559	Elmira & Elmira Heights 1901	G3804 .E7A3 1901 .L3		Landis & Alsop, Newark, New Jersey		In 4 parts, each 18 × 26
560	Fairport 1884	G3804 .F2A3 1884 .B8	L. R. Burleigh, Troy, New York	L. R. Burleigh, Troy, New York	Beck & Pauli, Litho., Milwaukee, Wisconsin	15 × 24
560.1	Fairport 1885	G3804 .F2A3 1885 .B8	L. R. Burleigh, Troy, N.Y.	L. R. Burleigh, Troy, N.Y.	Beck & Pauli, Litho., Milwaukee, Wis.	15½ × 24
561	Farmingdale 1925	G3804 .F3A3 1925 .C5	Rene Cinquin	Metropolitan Aero-View Co., New York		22 × 34
562	Fishkill-on-the-Hudson 1886	G3804 .F48A3 1886 .B8	L. R. Burleigh, Troy, New York	L. R. Burleigh, Troy, New York	Burleigh Lith. Est., Troy, New York	17 × 26
563	Fort Plain & Nelliston 1891	G3804 .F64A3 1891 .B8		L. R. Burleigh, Troy, New York	Burleigh Lith. Est., Troy, New York	20 × 27
564	Frankfort 1887	G3804 .F66A3 1887 .B8	L. R. Burleigh, Troy, New York	L. R. Burleigh, Troy, New York	Burleigh Lith. Est., Troy, New York	17 × 24
565	Freeport 1909	G3804 .F8A3 1909 .H8		Hughes & Bailey, New York		21 × 34½
566	Freeport 1925	G3804 .F8A3 1925 .C5	R. Cinquin	Metropolitan Aero-View Co., New York		23½ × 34
567	Glens Falls 1884	G3804 .G5A3 1884 .B8	L. R. Burleigh, Troy, New York	L. R. Burleigh, Troy, New York	Beck & Pauli, Litho., Milwaukee, Wisconsin	18½ × 30
568	Gloversville 1875	G3804 .G6A3 1875 .B3	H. H. Bailey & Co.	H. H. Bailey & Co.	G. W. Lewis, Albany, New York	18½ × 24
568.1	Goshen c1922	G3804 .G63A3 1922 .H8		Hughes & Fowler, Brooklyn, N.Y.		22 × 32
569	Gouverneur 1885	G3804 .G64A3 1885 .B8	L. R. Burleigh, Troy, New York	L. R. Burleigh, Troy, New York	Beck & Pauli, Litho., Milwaukee, Wisconsin	15 × 30
570	Granville 1886	G3804 .G67A3 1886 .B8		L. R. Burleigh, Troy, New York	Beck & Pauli, Litho., Milwaukee, Wisconsin	14 × 24

Entry No.	City and Date	LC Call No.	Artist	Publisher	Lithographer	Map Size (inches)
570.1	Greene 1890	G3804 .G82A3 1890 .B8		L. R. Burleigh, Troy, N.Y.	Burleigh Lithographing Establishment, Troy, N.Y.	18 × 25½
570.2	Hempstead, Long Island 1876	G3804 .H4A3 1876 .F6	Fowler & Bulger	Fowler & Bulger	C. H. Vogt Lith., Milwaukee; Printed by J. Knauber & Co.	10 × 13½ Positive photostat
571	Hicksville 1925	G3804 .H5A3 1925 .C5	Rene Cinquin	Metropolitan Aero-View Co., New York		26 × 36
572	Hoosick Falls 1889	G3804 .H66A3 1889 .B8	L. R. Burleigh, Troy, New York	L. R. Burleigh, Troy, New York	The Burleigh Lith. Est., Troy, New York	19 × 31½
573	Hunter 1890	G3804 .H88A3 1890 .B8		L. R. Burleigh, Troy, New York	Burleigh Lith. Est., Troy, New York	17½ × 26½
574	Ithaca 1836	G3804 .I8A35 1836 .W3 1968	H[enry] Walton	Reproduced in 1968 by Historic Urban Plans, Ithaca, New York	Bufford's Lithography, N.Y.	16½ × 27 Facsimile
574.1	Ithaca 1836	G3804 .I8A35 1836 .W3 1977	H. Walton	Reproduced in 1977 by Historic Urban Plans, Ithaca, New York	Bufford's Lithography, N.Y.	14½ × 19½ Facsimile
574.2	Ithaca 1873	G3804 .I8A3 1873 .B5 1972		Reproduced in 1972 by Historic Urban Plans, Ithaca, New York		21½ × 25 Facsimile
574.3	Ithaca 1882	G3804 .I8A3 1882 .B8 1970	L. R. Burleigh	Reproduced in 1970 by Historic Urban Plans, Ithaca, N.Y.		21 × 29 Facsimile
575	Jamestown 1882	G3804 .J3A3 1882 .B7	H. Brosius & A. F. Poole	J. J. Stoner, Madison, Wisconsin	Beck & Pauli, Litho., Milwaukee, Wisconsin	27½ × 42
576	Johnsonville 1887	G3804 .J62A3 1887 .B8	L. R. Burleigh, Troy, New York	L. R. Burleigh, Troy, New York	Burleigh Lith. Est., Troy, New York	12½ × 22
577	Johnstown 1888	G3804 .J65A3 1888 .B8	L. R. Burleigh, Troy, New York	L. R. Burleigh, Troy, New York	Burleigh Lith., Troy, New York	17½ × 29½
578	Keeseville 1887	G3804 .K3A3 1887 .B8	L. R. Burleigh, Troy, New York	L. R. Burleigh, Troy, New York	Burleigh, Lith. Est., Troy, New York	15 × 24
578.1	Lancaster 1892	G3804 .L312A3 1892 .B8			Burleigh Litho. Co., Troy, N.Y.	19½ × 29
579	Larchmont 1904	G3804 .L32A3 1904 .H8		Hughes & Bailey, New York		21 × 25
580	Le Roy 1892	G3804 .L38A3 1892 .B8		Burleigh Litho. Co., Troy, New York		19½ × 30½
580.1	Lima [1895?]	G3804 .L46A3 1895 .B8 1976		Reprinted in [1976?]	Burleigh Lith. Co., Troy, N.Y.	8 × 16 Photostatic reprint

Entry No.	City and Date	LC Call No.	Artist	Publisher	Lithographer	Map Size (inches)
581	Lindenhurst 1926	G3804 .L48A3 1926 .C5	R. Cinquin, New York	Metropolitan Aero-View Co., New York		27 × 32
582	Lowville 1885	G3804 .L76A3 1885 .B8	L. R. Burleigh, Troy, New York	L. R. Burleigh, Troy, New York	Beck & Pauli, Litho., Milwaukee, Wisconsin	17 × 24
583	Luzerne & Hadley 1888	G3804 .L78A3 1888 .B8	L. R. Burleigh, Troy, New York	L. R. Burleigh, Troy, New York		18 × 24½
584	Malone 1886	G3804 .M2A3 1886 .B8	L. R. Burleigh, Troy, New York	L. R. Burleigh, Troy, New York	C. H. Vogt & Son, Cleveland, Ohio	16 × 30½
584.1	Manhattan [1899-1900?]	G3804 .N4:2M3A3 190- .B5				87 × 42
584.2	New York 1905 (Borough of Manhattan)	Prints & Photographs Division		Joseph Koehler, N.Y.	Charles Hart, N.Y.	26 × 37½
585	Matteawan 1886	G3804 .B4A3 1886 .B81	L. R. Burleigh, Troy, New York	L. R. Burleigh, Troy, New York	Burleigh Lith. Est., Troy, New York	17 × 23
586	Mechanicville [188-?]	G3804 .M47A3 188- .B8	L. R. Burleigh, Troy, New York	L. R. Burleigh, Troy, New York	Beck & Pauli, Litho., Milwaukee, Wisconsin	15 × 25½
587	Middletown 1887	G3804 .M6A3 1887 .B8	L. R. Burleigh, Troy, New York	L. R. Burleigh, Troy, New York		18 × 30½
588	Middletown 1921	G3804 .M6A3 1921 .H8 Fow 10	[T. M. Fowler] (T. M. Fowler Map Coll. 10)	Hughes & Fowler		23 × 35
589	Middletown 1922	G3804 .M6A3 1922 .H8	[T. M. Fowler]	Hughes & Fowler, Brooklyn, New York		26½ × 36½
590	Middleville 1890	G3804 .M62A3 1890 .B8		L. R. Burleigh, Troy, New York	Burleigh Lith. Est., Troy, New York	17 × 23
591	Millerton 1887 (with Irondale)	G3804 .M66A3 1887 .B8	L. R. Burleigh, Troy, New York	L. R. Burleigh, Troy, New York	The Burleigh Lith. Est., Troy, New York	15 × 18½
592	Monroe 1923	G3804 .M74A3 1923 .H8		Hughes & Bailey	[Meriden Gravure Co., Meriden, Conn.]	18 × 32
593	Newburgh 1900	G3804 .N6A3 1900 .H8	Thos. J. Hughes			16½ × 32½

Entry No.	City and Date	LC Call No.	Artist	Publisher	Lithographer	Map Size (inches)
594	Newport 1890	G3804 .N66A3 1890 .B8		L. R. Burleigh, Troy, New York	Burleigh Lith. Est., Troy, New York	16 × 25
594.1	New-York et Brooklyn [1850]	G3804 .N4A35 1850 .S5 1975	Simpson	Reproduced in 1975 by Historic Urban Plans, Ithaca, New York	Th. Muller	16 × 19½ Facsimile
594.2	New York [1851]	Prints & Photographs Division	Heine, J. Kummer & Döpler	W. Schaus	Himely; Printed by Goupil & Co., Paris	25 × 37½
594.3	New-York & Brooklyn 1851	Prints & Photographs Division	J. Bachmann	A. Guerber & Co. N. York	J. Bachman	25 × 32½
594.4	New York 1856	G3804 .N4A35 1856 .P3 1975	C. Parsons	N. Currier, New York. Reproduced in 1975 by Historic Urban Plans, Ithaca, New York	C. Parsons; N. Currier, New York	16 × 19½ Facsimile
594.5	New York 1858	Prints & Photographs Division	C. Parsons	Currier & Ives, New York	Currier & Ives, N.Y.	22½ × 33½
594.6	New York 1865	G3804 .N4A3 1865 .B3	J. Bachmann	Kimmel & Forster, N.Y.		13 × 18
594.7	New York [1867]	G3804 .N4A3 1867 .L4	R. Lerow		H. Peters, N.Y.; R. Kupfer, N.Y.	21½ × 27½
594.8	New York 1867	G3804 .N4A3 1867 .L4 1967	R. Lerow	Reproduced in 1967 by Historic Urban Plans, Ithaca, New York	H. Peters, N.Y.; R. Kupfer, N.Y.	19½ × 23½ Facsimile
595	New York 1870	G3804 .N4A3 1870 .C8		Currier & Ives, New York		22 × 33
595.1	New York 1873	Prints & Photographs Division		Geo. Degen, New York	Ferd. Mayers & Sons, Liths., N.Y.	15½ × 23½
595.2	New York 1873	Prints & Photographs Division		Geo. Degen, N.Y.	G. Schlegel, N.Y.	17 × 24
595.3	New York 1874	Prints & Photographs Division	J. Bachman	John Bachman	G. Schlegel, N.Y.	22½ × 32
595.4	New York 1874	Prints & Photographs Division	[John Bachman]	Tamsen & Dethlefs, N.Y.	G. Schlegel, N.Y.	22½ × 32
596	New York and Brooklyn 1875	G3804 .N4A3 1875 .P3	Parsons & Atwater	Currier & Ives		24 × 33½
597	New York 1876	G3804 .N4A3 1876 .P3	Parsons & Atwater	Currier & Ives, New York		23½ × 34
597.1	New York 1876	G3804 .N4A3 1876 .P3 1976	Parsons & Atwater	Currier & Ives, New York. Reproduced in 1976 by Historic Urban Plans, Ithaca, New York		21½ × 27½ Facsimile
597.2	New York 1876	Prints & Photographs Division	T. Sulman	*Illustrated London News*	R. Loudans	21½ × 45½

New York City, New York, 1879. Drawn by Will L.
Taylor. This portion of Manhattan around Central Park
shows the dense urban settlement about to engulf it.
This is one of the most detailed panoramic maps of a
major metropolitan area.

Entry No.	City and Date	LC Call No.	Artist	Publisher	Lithographer	Map Size (inches)
598	New York and Brooklyn 1877	G3804 .N4A3 1877 .P3	Parsons & Atwater	Currier & Ives, New York		24 × 33
599	New York 1879	G3804 .N4A3 1879 .T3	Will L. Taylor	Galt & Hoy, New York	Galt & Hoy, New York	In 4 parts, each 37 × 21
600	New York 1879	G3804 .N4A3 1879 .W5	J. W. Williams	Root & Tinker, New York		25½ × 18
601	New York 1879	G3804 .N4A3 1879 .W51	J. W. Williams	Root & Tinker		11½ × 8
602	New York 1884	G3804 .N4A3 1884 .C8		Currier & Ives, New York		25 × 35
603	New York 1886	G3804 .N4A3 1886 .P3	Parsons & Atwater	Currier & Ives, New York		25 × 34
604	New York 1889	G3804 .N4A3 1889 .P3	Parsons & Atwater	Currier & Ives, New York		25 × 34
605	New York 1891	G3804 .N4A3 1891 .T3	Howard P. Taylor		The Courier Lith. Co., Buffalo, New York	40 × 28½
606	New York 1892	G3804 .N4A3 1892 .C8		Currier & Ives, New York		26 × 36
607	New York & Brooklyn 1892	G3804 .N4A3 1892 .P3	Parsons & Atwater	Currier & Ives, New York		24½ × 33½
607.1	New York 1907	G3804 .N4A3 1907 .O4	August R. Ohman, New York	August R. Ohman, New York	August R. Ohman, New York	26½ × 39
608	Niagara Falls 1882	G3804 .N7A3 1882 .W4 Rug 150	H. Wellge (Ruger Map Coll. 150)	J. J. Stoner, Madison, Wisconsin	Beck & Pauli, Lith., Milwaukee, Wisconsin	21 × 29
609	Olean 1882 (Inset of Boardmanville)	G3804 .O4A3 1882 .B7	H. Brosius	J. J. Stoner, Madison, Wisconsin	Beck & Pauli, Lith., Milwaukee, Wisconsin	26 × 40
609.1	Oswego [1855]	Prints & Photographs Division	Lewis Bradley	Smith Brothers & Co., N.Y.	D. W. Moody	24 × 35½
610	Oxford 1888	G3804 .O89A3 1888 .B8	L. R. Burleigh, Troy, New York	L. R. Burleigh, Troy, New York	The Burleigh Lith. Est., Troy, New York	16½ × 25
611	Patchogue 1906	G3804 .P2A3 1906 .H8		Hughes & Bailey, New York		28 × 33
612	Patchogue 1911			Great South Bay Development Co.	Moessner-Blanchard Art Service, N.Y.	14½ × 30
613	Pawling 1909	G3804 .P23A3 1909 .S6	P. H. Smith	W. G. Tice	Knickerbocker Litho. Co., New York	19 × 25
614	Pearl River 1924	G3804 .P26A3 1924 .C5	Rene Cinquin	Hughes & Bailey, Brooklyn, New York	[Stankovits & Co., New York, New York]	19 × 32

Niagara Falls, New York, 1882. Drawn by H. Wellge.

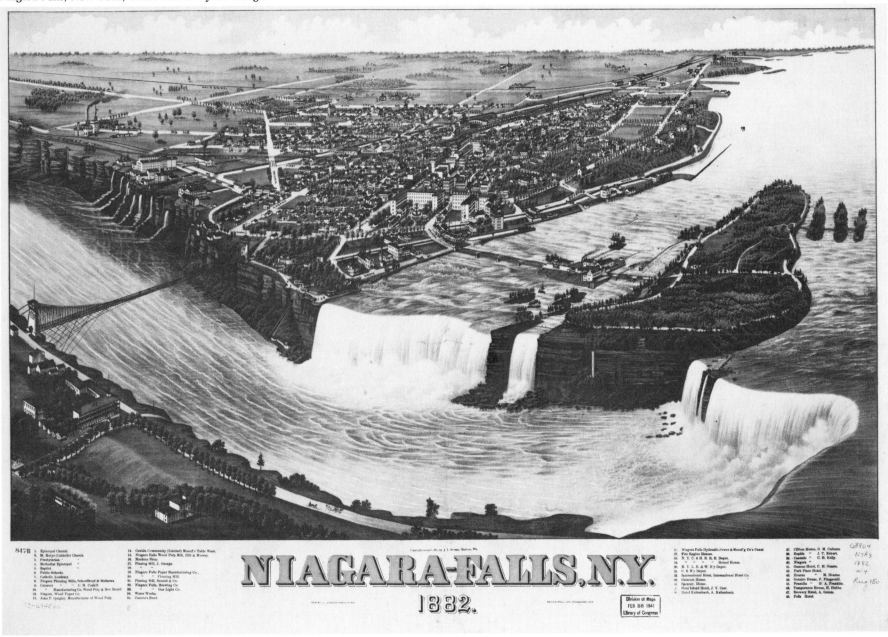

NIAGARA-FALLS, N.Y.
1882.

93

Entry No.	City and Date	LC Call No.	Artist	Publisher	Lithographer	Map Size (inches)
615	Peekskill 1911	G3804 .P3A3 1911 .H8	Fowler & Hughes	Hughes & Bailey, New York	[Consolidated Engraving Co., New York, New York]	25 × 33 Photo-engraved
615.1	Perry 1892	G3804 .P4A3 1892 .N6		Geo. E. Norris, Brockton, Mass.	Burleigh Litho. Co., Troy, N.Y.	11 × 14 Photograph
616	Plattsburgh 1877	G3804 .P5A3 1877 .R8 Rug 151	A. Ruger (Ruger Map Coll. 151)	J. J. Stoner, Madison, Wisconsin	C. H. Vogt & Co., Milwaukee	23 × 24½
617	Plattsburgh 1899	G3804 .P5A3 1899 .F3	C. Fausel		L. R. Burleigh, Lith., Troy, New York	21½ × 32½
618	Poland 1890	G3804 .P55A3 1890 .B8		L. R. Burleigh, Troy, New York	Burleigh Lith. Est., Troy, New York	16 × 23
619	Port Henry 1889	G3804 .P65A3 1889 .B8	L. R. Burleigh, Troy, New York	L. R. Burleigh, Troy, New York		19 × 29
620	Port Jervis 1920	G3804 .P67A3 1920 .H8 Fow 11	[T. M. Fowler] (T. M. Fowler Map Coll. 11)	Hughes & Fowler, Brooklyn, N.Y.		24 × 32
621	Potsdam 1885	G3804 .P76A3 1885 .B8	L. R. Burleigh, Troy, New York	L. R. Burleigh, Troy, New York	Beck & Pauli, Litho., Milwaukee, Wisconsin	16 × 26½
622	Pulaski 1885	G3804 .P82A3 1885 .B8	L. R. Burleigh, Troy, New York	L. R. Burleigh, Troy, New York	C. H. Vogt & Son, Cleveland	17 × 24½
623	Rhinebeck 1890	G3804 .R43A3 1890 .B8	L. R. Burleigh, Troy, New York	L. R. Burleigh, Troy, New York		16 × 25
624	Richfield Springs 1885	G3804 .R46A3 1885 .B8	L. R. Burleigh, Troy, New York	L. R. Burleigh, Troy, New York	C. H. Vogt & Son, Cleveland	16 × 26½
624.1	Rochester 1853	G3804 .R6A35 1853 .H5 1973	J. W. Hill	Smith Bros. & Co., N.Y. Reproduced in 1973 by Historic Urban Plans, Ithaca, New York		18½ × 27 Facsimile
625	Rochester 1880	G3804 .R6A3 1880 .R6	H. H. Rowley & Co., Hartford, Conn.	H. H. Rowley & Co., Hartford, Conn.	Beck & Pauli, Milwaukee, Wisconsin	36 × 44½
626	Rome 1886	G3804 .R7A3 1886 .B8	L. R. Burleigh, Troy, New York	L. R. Burleigh, Troy, New York	Beck & Pauli, Litho., Milwaukee, Wisconsin	19 × 34
626.1	Rome [1886]	G3804 .R7A3 1886 .B8 1972	L. R. Burleigh, Troy, N.Y.	L. R. Burleigh, Troy, N.Y. Reproduced in 1972 by Rome Historical Society, New York	Beck & Pauli, Litho., Milwaukee, Wis.	10½ × 21½ Facsimile
627	St. Johnsville 1890	G3804 .S18A3 1890 .B8		L. R. Burleigh, Troy, New York	Burleigh Lith. Est., Troy, New York	17 × 23

Entry No.	City and Date	LC Call No.	Artist	Publisher	Lithographer	Map Size (inches)
628	Salem 1889 (Inset of Salem 1789)	G3804 .S22A3 1889 .B8	L. R. Burleigh, Troy, New York	L. R. Burleigh, Troy, New York	The Burleigh Lith. Est., Troy, New York	19 × 29½
629	Sandy Hill 1884 (Now called Hudson Falls)	G3804 .S26A3 1884 .B8	L. R. Burleigh, Troy, New York	L. R. Burleigh, Troy, New York	Beck & Pauli, Litho., Milwaukee, Wisconsin	17½ × 30½
630	Saratoga Springs 1888	G3804 .S3A3 1888 .B8	L. R. Burleigh, Troy, New York	L. R. Burleigh, Troy, New York	The Burleigh Lith. Est., Troy, New York	22 × 34
631	Schaghticoke 1889	G3804 .S384A3 1889 .S3				16½ × 22
632	Schuylerville 1889	G3804 .S43A3 1889 .B8	L. R. Burleigh, Troy, New York	L. R. Burleigh, Troy, New York	The Burleigh Lith. Est., Troy, New York	17 × 25½
633	Sherburne 1887	G3804 .S54A3 1887 .B8	L. R. Burleigh, Troy, New York	L. R. Burleigh, Troy, New York	The Burleigh Lith. Est., Troy, New York	15 × 24½
633.1	Shushan 1890	G3804 .S595A3 1890 .B8 1972		L. R. Burleigh, Troy, N.Y.	Burleigh Lithographing Establishment, Troy, N.Y.	10½ × 16½ Facsimile
634	Sidney 1887	G3804 .S6A3 1887 .B8	L. R. Burleigh, Troy, New York	L. R. Burleigh, Troy, New York	The Burleigh Lith. Est., Troy, New York	15 × 23½
635	Skaneateles 1884	G3804 .S63A3 1884 .B8	L. R. Burleigh, Troy, New York	L. R. Burleigh, Troy, New York	Beck & Pauli, Litho., Milwaukee, Wisconsin	16 × 29½
636	Stamford 1890	G3804 .S83A3 1890 .B8		L. R. Burleigh, Troy, New York	Burleigh Lith. Est., Troy, New York	17 × 26
637	Stillwater 1889	G3804 .S85A3 1889 .B8	L. R. Burleigh, Troy, New York	L. R. Burleigh, Troy, New York	The Burleigh Lith. Est., Troy, New York	17 × 26½
638	Syracuse 1868	G3804 .S9A3 1868 .L2	J. C. Laass & L. Laass	E. Sachse & Co., Baltimore, Maryland	E. Sachse & Co., Baltimore, Maryland	In 2 parts, each 28½ × 78
639	Ticonderoga 1884	G3804 .T5A3 1884 .B8	L. R. Burleigh, Troy, New York	L. R. Burleigh, Troy, New York	Beck & Pauli, Litho., Milwaukee, Wisconsin	18 × 24½
640	Ticonderoga 1891	G3804 .T5A3 1891 .A3		R. M. Adkins, Ticonderoga, New York	Burleigh Lith. Est., Troy, New York	18½ × 25
641	Troy 1881	G3804 .T7A3 1881 .B4			Beck & Pauli, Milwaukee, Wisconsin	29 × 36½
642	Unadilla 1887	G3804 .U5A3 1887 .B8	L. R. Burleigh, Troy, New York	L. R. Burleigh, Troy, New York	The Burleigh Lith. Est., Troy, New York	14 × 25
643	Utica 1873	G3804 .U8A3 1873 .B7	H. Brosius			25 × 33

Entry No.	City and Date	LC Call No.	Artist	Publisher	Lithographer	Map Size (inches)
644	Valley Falls 1887	G3804 .V38A3 1887 .B8	L. R. Burleigh, Troy, New York	L. R. Burleigh, Troy, New York	Burleigh Lith. Est., Troy, New York	12 × 20
645	Valley Stream 1924	G3804 .V39A3 1924 .C5	Rene Cinquin	Hughes & Cinquin, Brooklyn, New York	[Meriden Gravure Co., Meriden, Conn.]	22 × 34½
646	Walden 1887	G3804 .W14A3 1887 .B8	L. R. Burleigh, Troy, New York	L. R. Burleigh, Troy, New York	The Burleigh Lith. Est., Troy, New York	15 × 24½
647	Walton 1887	G3804 .W16A3 1887 .B8	L. R. Burleigh, Troy, New York	L. R. Burleigh, Troy, New York	Burleigh Lith. Est., Troy, New York	15 × 24
648	Wappingers Falls 1889	G3804 .W22A3 1889 .B8	L. R. Burleigh, Troy, New York	L. R. Burleigh, Troy, New York	The Burleigh Lith. Est., Troy, New York	18 × 28
649	Warrensburgh 1891	G3804 .W24A3 1891 .B8		L. R. Burleigh, Troy, New York	Burleigh Lith. Est., Troy, New York	18 × 31
650	Warsaw 1885	G3804 .W25A3 1885 .B8	L. R. Burleigh, Troy, New York	L. R. Burleigh, Troy, New York	Beck & Pauli, Litho., Milwaukee, Wisconsin	15 × 28
651	Warwick 1887	G3804 .W26A3 1887 .B8	L. R. Burleigh, Troy, New York	L. R. Burleigh, Troy, New York	The Burleigh Lith. Est., Troy, New York	14 × 20½
652	Watertown 1891	G3804 .W3A3 1891 .K5		J. C. Kimball, Watertown, New York	Burleigh Litho. Co., Troy, New York	20 × 35½
652.1	Waterville 1885	G3804 .W35A3 1885 .B8	L. R. Burleigh, Troy, N.Y.	L. R. Burleigh, Troy, N.Y.	C. H. Vogt, Lith., Cleveland, O.	15 × 24½
653	Waverly 1881	G3804 .W42A35 1881 .M6	John Moray	John Moray	Thomas Hunter, Lith., Philadelphia, Pennsylvania	19 × 23
654	Weedsport 1885	G3804 .W45A3 1885 .B8	L. R. Burleigh, Troy, New York	L. R. Burleigh, Troy, New York	C. H. Vogt & Son, Cleveland	13 × 26½
654.1	West Chazy 1899	G3804 .W474A3 1899 .F3	C. Fausel, Troy, N.Y.	C. Fausel, Troy, N.Y.	L. R. Burleigh Lith., Troy, N.Y.	15½ × 24½
655	White Plains 1887	G3804 .W7A3 1887 .B8	L. R. Burleigh, Troy, New York	L. R. Burleigh, Troy, New York	The Burleigh Lith. Est., Troy, New York	16 × 28½
656	Windsor 1887	G3804 .W83A3 1887 .B8	L. R. Burleigh, Troy, New York	L. R. Burleigh, Troy, New York	The Burleigh Lith. Est., Troy, New York	16 × 21
657	Yonkers 1899	G3804 .Y5A3 1899 .L3		Landis & Hughes, New York		In 2 parts, each 43½ × 30

North Carolina

Entry No.	City and Date	LC Call No.	Artist	Publisher	Lithographer	Map Size (inches)
658	Asheville 1891	G3904 .A8A3 1891 .R8		Ruger & Stoner, Madison, Wisconsin	Burleigh Lith. Est., Troy, New York	26 × 31
659	Asheville 1912	G3904 .A8 A3 1912 .F6	T. M. Fowler, Passaic, N.J.	T. M. Fowler, Passaic, N.J.	Charles Hart, Photo., New York	24 × 34
660	Black Mountain 1912	G3904 .B66A3 1912 .F6	[T. M. Fowler]	Fowler & Browning, Asheville, North Carolina	[Manhattan Photo Engraving Co., New York, New York]	24 × 32
661	Durham 1891 (with inset of East Durham)	G3904 .D9A3 1891 .R8		Ruger & Stoner, Madison, Wisconsin	Burleigh Lith. Est., Troy, New York	18 × 29½
662	Greensboro 1891	G3904 .G7A3 1891 .R8		Ruger & Stoner, Madison, Wisconsin	Burleigh Lith. Est., Troy, New York	17½ × 29
663	Hendersonville 1913	G3904 .H5A3 1913 .F6	[T. M. Fowler]	Fowler & Browning, Asheville, North Carolina	[Manhattan Photo Engraving Co., New York, New York]	21½ × 31½
664	[Hickory 1907-08]	G3904 .H6A3 1907 .D6 Fow 12	[A. E. Downs] (T. M. Fowler Map Coll. 12)			18 × 28½ Manuscript
665	High Point 1913	G3904 .H7A3 1913 .F3 Fow 13	T. M. Fowler (T. M. Fowler Map Coll. 13)	J. J. Farris, High Point, N.C.	Charles Hart Litho., N.Y.	19 × 28
665.1	New Berne 1864	G3904 .N4A35 1864 .C6 1974	V. Combe	Reproduced in 1974 by Historic Urban Plans, Ithaca, New York	Major & Knapp, New York	20½ × 27½ Facsimile
666	Raleigh 1872	G3904 .R2A3 1872 .D7	C. N. Drie, Raleigh, N.C.	C. N. Drie, Raleigh, N.C.		24 × 29
666.1	Raleigh 1872	G3904 .R2A3 1872 .D7 1975	C. Drie	C. Drie. Reproduced in 1975 by Historic Urban Plans, Ithaca, New York		23½ × 27½ Facsimile
667	Rocky Mount 1907	G3904 .R7A3 1907 .F6 Fow 14	T. M. Fowler, Morrisville, Pa. (T. M. Fowler Map Coll. 14)	T. M. Fowler, Morrisville, Pa.	Chas. Hart Photo-Lith., New York	22 × 28
668	South Rocky Mount [1907]	G3904 .R7:2S6 19-- .F6 Fow 15	T. M. Fowler, Morrisville, Pa. (T. M. Fowler Map Coll. 15)			13½ × 18

Entry No.	City and Date	LC Call No.	Artist	Publisher	Lithographer	Map Size (inches)
678	Ashtabula Harbor 1896	G4084 .A8A3 1896 .F6	T. M. Fowler, Morrisville, Pa.	T. M. Fowler & James B. Moyer		20 × 26½
679	Barnesville 1899	G4084 .B22A3 1899 .F6	T. M. Fowler, Morrisville, Pa.	T. M. Fowler & James B. Moyer		16 × 25½
680	Bellaire 1882 (Inset Benwood, West Virginia)	G4084 .B3A3 1882 .W4	H. Wellge	J. J. Stoner, Madison, Wisconsin	Beck & Pauli, Milwaukee, Wisconsin	15 × 25
680.1	Belle Centre [1875. In D. J. Stewart's *Combination Atlas Map of Logan County, Ohio*, p. 15]	G1398 .L6S8 1875				13½ × 15
681	Bellevue 1888	G4084 .B34A3 1888 .B8		Burleigh & Norris, Troy, New York	The Burleigh Lith. Est., Troy, New York	18 × 28½
682	Bowling Green 1888	G4084 .B6A3 1888 .B8		Burleigh & Norris, Troy, New York	Burleigh Lith. Est., Troy, New York	19 × 27
683	Cambridge 1899	G4084 .C2A3 1899 .F6 Fow 17	T. M. Fowler, Morrisville, Pa. (T. M. Fowler Map Coll. 17)	T. M. Fowler & James B. Moyer		19 × 32
683.1	Camp Chase [186-?]	G4084 .C372A3 186- .R8 Rug 155	A. Ruger (Ruger Map Coll. 155)		Ehrgott, [For]briger & Co., Lith. Cin.	18½ × 24½
684	Canal Dover 1899	G4084 .D7A3 1899 .D6 Fow 18	A. E. Downs, Boston, Mass. (T. M. Fowler Map Coll. 18)	T. M. Fowler & A. E. Downs		21 × 28½
684.1	Cincinnati [1856]	G4084 .C4A35 .1856 .M5 1979		Middleton, Wallace & Co., Cin. Reproduced in 1979 by Historic Urban Plans, Ithaca, New York	Middleton, Wallace & Co., Cin.	15 × 19 Facsimile
685	Cincinnati 1900	G4084 .C4A3 1900 .T7	J. L. Trout, Cincinnati, Ohio	J. L. Trout, Cincinnati, Ohio	The Henderson Lith. Co., Cincinnati, Ohio	31 × 46
686	Circleville 1876	G4084 .C42A3 1876 .R8 Rug 156	[Albert Ruger] (Ruger Map Coll. 156)	J. J. Stoner, Madison, Wisconsin	Krebs Lithographing Co., Cincinnati	21 × 25
687	Cleveland 1877	G4084 .C5A3 1877 .R8	A. Ruger	J. J. Stoner, Madison, Wisconsin	Shober & Carqueville, Chicago	20½ × 34

Entry No.	City and Date	LC Call No.	Artist	Publisher	Lithographer	Map Size (inches)
687.1	Cleveland 1877	G4084 .C5A3 1877 .R8 1975	A. Ruger	J. J. Stoner, Madison, Wis. Reproduced in 1975 by Historic Urban Plans, Ithaca, New York	Shober & Carqueville, Chicago	18½ × 27½ Facsimile
687.2	Cleveland 1877	G4084 .C5A3 1877 .R8	A. Ruger (Ruger Map Coll. 157)	J. J. Stoner, Madison, Wis.	Shober & Carqueville, Chicago	20½ × 34
688	Cleveland 1883	G4084 .C5A3 1883 .C5				10½ × 15 Photographic print
689	Cleveland 1887	G4084 .C5A3 1887 .V6	C. H. Vogt & Son, Cleveland	C. H. Vogt & Son, Cleveland		15 × 21
690	Conneaut 1896	G4084 .C7A3 1896 .F6 Fow 19	T. M. Fowler, Morrisville, Pa. (T. M. Fowler Map Coll. 19)	T. M. Fowler & James B. Moyer		20 × 29
691	Dayton 1870	G4084 .D2A3 1870 .R8 Rug 158	[Albert Ruger] (Ruger Map Coll. 158)		Merchant's Lith. Co., Chicago	22½ × 31½
691.1	DeGraff [1875. In D. J. Stewart's *Combination Atlas Map of Logan County, Ohio*, p. 25]	G1398 .L6S8 1875				13½ × 15
691.2	Edgerton 1881	G4084 .E63A3 1881 .S7		J. J. Stoner, Madison, Wis. Reprint of original map in the Edgerton Historical Society, Edgerton, Ohio	Beck & Pauli, Lith., Milwaukee, Wis.	9 × 14½ Positive photostat
692	Elyria 1868	G4084 .E8A3 1868 .R8 Rug 159	A. Ruger (Ruger Map Coll. 159)		Chicago Lith. Co., Chicago	21 × 24½
693	Findlay 1889	G4084 .F5A3 1889 .B8		Burleigh & Norris, Troy, New York	The Burleigh Lith. Est., Troy, New York	22 × 34½
693.1	Guysville 1875 [In D. J. Lake's *Atlas of Athens Co., Ohio*, pp. 62-63]	G1398 .A8L3 1875	TMF			9 × 25½
694	Jefferson 1901	G4084 .J4A3 1901 .F6 Vault	T. M. Fowler, Morrisville, Pa.	T. M. Fowler & James B. Moyer		14 × 22 Pencilled Manuscript

Entry No.	City and Date	LC Call No.	Artist	Publisher	Lithographer	Map Size (Inches)
695	Kent 1882	G4084 .K3A3 1882 .R8 Rug 160	[Albert Ruger] (Ruger Map Coll. 160)	Ruger & Stoner, Madison, Wis.	Beck & Pauli, Lith., Milwaukee, Wisconsin	18 × 26
696	Lakeside 1884	G4084 .L17A3 1884 .H3		A. J. Hare, Sandusky, Ohio	Sinz & Fausel Lith., Cleveland, Ohio	20½ × 25
697	Lima 1892	G4084 .L5A3 1892 .S6		Smith & Buckingham	Geo. S. Harris & Sons, Philadelphia	30 × 39½
698	Martin's Ferry 1899	G4084 .M34A3 1899 .F6 Fow 20	T. M. Fowler, Morrisville, Pa. (T. M. Fowler Map Coll. 20)	T. M. Fowler & James B. Moyer		19 × 24
699	Massillon 1870	G4084 .M4A3 1870 .R8 Rug 161	[Albert Ruger] (Ruger Map Coll. 161)	Ruger & Stoner, Madison, Wisconsin	Merchant's Lith. Co., Chicago, Illinois	21 × 24½
700	Mingo Junction 1899	G4084 .M7A3 1899 .F6	T. M. Fowler, Morrisville, Pa	T. M. Fowler & James B. Moyer		15 × 23½
701	Mount Vernon 1870	G4084 .M9A3 1870 .R8 Rug 162	[Albert Ruger] (Ruger Map Coll. 162)	Ruger & Stoner, Madison, Wisconsin	Merchant's Lith. Co., Chicago, Illinois	22½ × 24½
702	Niles 1882	G4084 .N6A3 1882 .R8 Rug 163	[Albert Ruger] (Ruger Map Coll. 163)	Ruger & Stoner, Madison, Wisconsin	Beck & Pauli, Lith., Milwaukee, Wisconsin	16½ × 22½
703	Norwalk 1870	G4084 .N8A3 1870 .R8 Rug 164	[Albert Ruger] (Ruger Map Coll. 164)	Ruger & Stoner, Madison, Wisconsin	Merchant's Lith. Co., Chicago	20 × 24½
704	Ravenna 1882	G4084 .R2A3 1882 .R8 Rug 165	[Albert Ruger] (Ruger Map Coll. 165)			18½ × 21
705	Sandusky 1870	G4084 .S3A3 1870 .R8 Rug 166	A. Ruger (Ruger Map Coll. 166)	Ruger & Stoner, Madison, Wisconsin	Chicago Lith. Co.	21 × 25½
706	Sandusky 1883	G4084 .S3A3 1883 .H3		A. J. Hare, Sandusky, Ohio	W. J. Morgan & Co., Cleveland, Ohio	26½ × 39½
706.1	Sandusky 1883	G4084 .S3A3 1883 .H3 1975		A. J. Hare, Sandusky, O. Reproduced in 1975 by Historic Urban Plans, Ithaca, New York		21 × 27½ Facsimile
707	Sandusky 1898	G4084 .S3A3 1898 .A6		The Alvord-Peters Co., Sandusky, Ohio	The Gugler Litho. Co., Milwaukee, Wisconsin	17 × 36½

Entry No.	City and Date	LC Call No.	Artist	Publisher	Lithographer	Map Size (inches)
708	Scio 1899	G4084 .S32A3 1899 .F6	T. M. Fowler, Morrisville, Pa.	T. M. Fowler, Morrisville, Pa.	Wheeling News Publishing Co.	17 × 24½
709	Scio 1899 [2nd edition, April 1899]	G4084 .S32A3 1899 .F61	T. M. Fowler, Morrisville, Pa.	T. M. Fowler & James B. Moyer		16 × 24½
709.1	Stewart 1875 [In D. J. Lake's *Atlas of Athens Co., Ohio*, p. 75]	G1398 .A8L3 1875	TMF			8 × 13
710	Toledo 1876	G4084 .T6A35 1876 .R3 Rug 167	A. Ruger (Ruger Map Coll. 167)	J. J. Stoner, Madison, Wisconsin	Chas. Shober & Co., Chicago Lith. Co.	12 × 26
711	Toronto 1899	G4084 .T64A3 1899 .D6 Fow 21	A. E. Downs, Boston, Mass. (T. M. Fowler Map Coll. 21)	A. E. Downs & James B. Moyer		22 × 33½
712	Warren 1870	G4084 .W2A3 1870 .R8 Rug 168	[Albert Ruger] (Ruger Map Coll. 168)	Ruger & Stoner, Madison, Wisconsin	Merchant's Lith. Co., Chicago, Illinois	21 × 26½
712.1	Youngstown 1882	G4084 .Y8A3 1882 .R8	A. Ruger	J. J. Stoner, Madison, Wis.; Ruger & Stoner, Madison, Wis.	Beck & Pauli, Lithographers, Milwaukee, Wis.	20½ × 28
713	Youngstown 1882	G4084 .Y8A3 1882 .R8 Rug 169	A. Ruger (Ruger Map Coll. 169)	Ruger & Stoner, Madison, Wisconsin	Beck & Pauli, Lith., Milwaukee, Wisconsin	20½ × 28½
713.1	Zanesville 1885	G4084 .Z3A3 1885 .R8 1975		Ruger & Stoner, Madison, Wis. Reproduced in 1975 by National Roads, Zane Grey Museum, Norwich, Ohio	Beck & Pauli, Litho., Milwaukee, Wis.	22 × 28½ Facsimile

Oklahoma

Entry No.	City and Date	LC Call No.	Artist	Publisher	Lithographer	Map Size (inches)
713.2	Ardmore 1891 [Indian Territory]	G4024 .A8A3 1891 .F6 Vault	T. M. Fowler, Morrisville, Pa.	T. M. Fowler & James B. Moyer		14 × 23½
714	Bartlesville 1917	G4024 .B3A3 1917 .F6 Fow 22	T. M. Fowler (T. M. Fowler Map Coll. 22)	Fowler & Kelley, Passaic, N.J.		14 × 29
714.1	Edmond 1891 [Oklahoma Territory]	G4024 .E3A3 1891 .F6	T. M. Fowler, Morrisville, Pa.	T. M. Fowler & James B. Moyer		11½ × 19½

Youngstown, Ohio, 1882. Drawn by Albert Ruger.

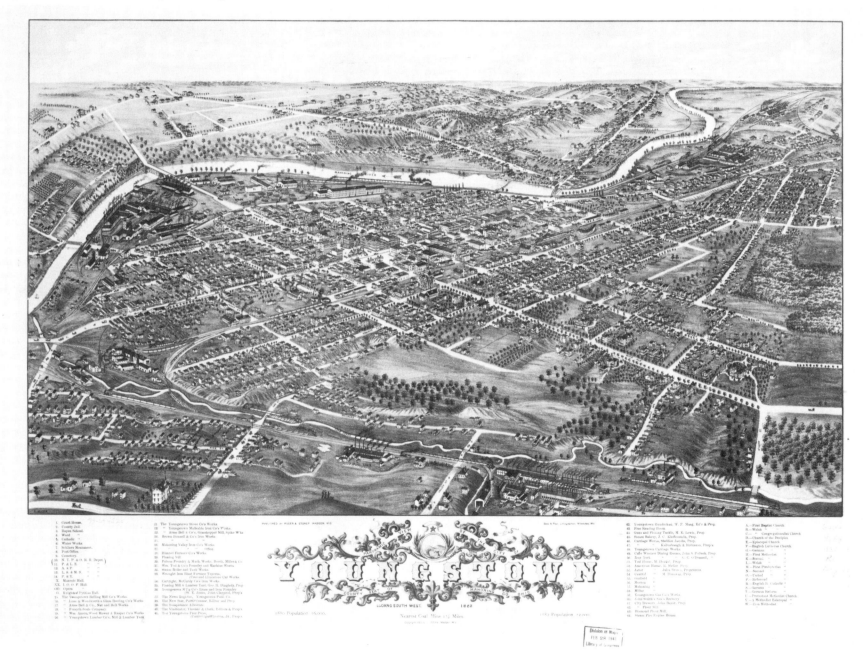

Entry No.	City and Date	LC Call No.	Artist	Publisher	Lithographer	Map Size (inches)
714.2	Fort Reno 1891 [Oklahoma Territory]	G4024 .E5:2F6A3 1891 .F6 Vault	T. M. Fowler, Morrisville, Pa.	T. M. Fowler & James B. Moyer	A. E. Downs, Lith., Boston	11½ × 23½
715	Lawton 1910	G4024 .L3A3 1910 .H3	Joslyn; J. P. Hathaway			6½ × 13½
715.1	Oklahoma City 1890	G4024 .O6A3 1890 .F6	T. M. Fowler, Morrisville, Pa.	T. M. Fowler, Morrisville, Pa.	A. E. Downs, Lith., Boston	8 × 10 Photograph
715.2	Oklahoma City 1890	G4024 .O6A3 1890 .F6 1974	T. M. Fowler, Morrisville, Pa.	T. M. Fowler, Morrisville, Pa. Reproduced in 1974 by Historic Urban Plans, Ithaca, New York	A. E. Downs, Lith., Boston	20 × 27½ Facsimile
716	Tulsa 1918	G4024 .T8A3 1918 .F6 Fow 23	[T. M. Fowler] (T. M. Fowler Map Coll. 23)	Fowler & Kelly	[Meriden Gravure Co., Meriden, Conn.]	15½ × 35 Photo-engraved
716.1	Tulsa 1918	G4024 .T8A3 1918 .F6 1972		Fowler & Kelly, Pasaic, N.J. Reproduced in 1972 by Historic Urban Plans, Ithaca, New York		16½ × 35 Facsimile

Oregon

Entry No.	City and Date	LC Call No.	Artist	Publisher	Lithographer	Map Size (inches)
717	Jacksonville & the Rogue River Valley 1883	G4294 .J2A3 1883 .W3	Fred A. Walpole	Fred A. Walpole	Beck & Pauli, Lith., Milwaukee, Wisconsin	17 × 22
718	Oregon City [185-?]	G4294 .O6A35 185- .R5	J. H. Richardson, N.Y.			6 × 7½
719	Oregon City 1858	G4294 .O6A35 1858 .C6		Charman & Warner, Oregon City		16 × 22 Positive photostat
719.1	Oregon City 1858	G4294 .O6A35 1858 .K8 1973	Kuchel & Dressel	Charman & Warner, Oregon City. Reproduced in 1973 by Historic Urban Plans, Ithaca, New York	Kuchel & Dressel, Lithographers, S. F.	21 × 26½ Facsimile
720	Pendleton 1884	G4294 .P4A3 1884 .W4	H. Wellge	J. J. Stoner, Madison, Wisconsin	Beck & Pauli, Lith., Milwaukee, Wisconsin	14 × 22
721	Pendleton [189-?]	G4294 .P4A3 189- .E3		East Oregonian Publishing Co., Pendleton, Oregon	Dakin Publishing Co., San Francisco	21 × 28
721.1	Portland 1858	G4294 .P6A35 1858 .K8 1973	Kuchel & Dressel	Reproduced in 1973 by Historic Urban Plans, Ithaca, New York	Kuchel & Dressel, Lithographers, San Francisco, Cal.	23 × 34½ Facsimile

Oklahoma City, Indian Territory, 1890.

Tulsa, Oklahoma, 1918. Published by Fowler & Kelly.

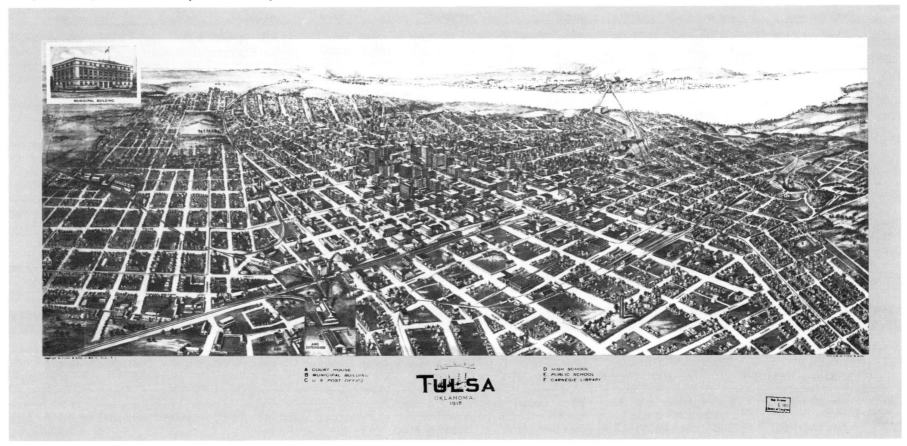

A COURT HOUSE   D HIGH SCHOOL
B MUNICIPAL BUILDING E PUBLIC SCHOOL
C U S POST OFFICE   F CARNEGIE LIBRARY

TULSA
OKLAHOMA.
1918

Canonsburg, Pennsylvania, 1897. Drawn by T. M.
Fowler.

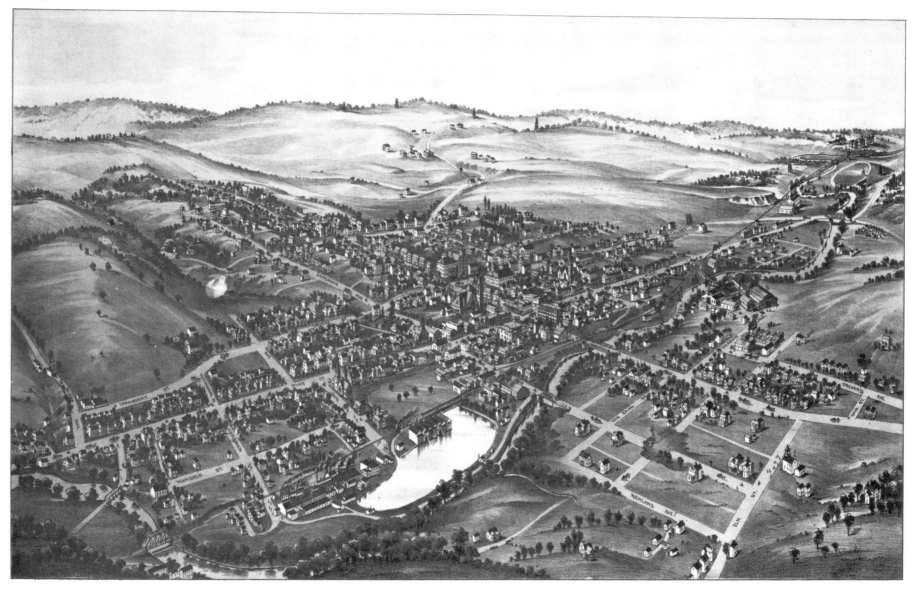

Entry No.	City and Date	LC Call No.	Artist	Publisher	Lithographer	Map Size (Inches)
757	Connellsville 1897	G3824 .C8A3 1897 .F6 Fow 73	T. M. Fowler, Morrisville, Pa. (T. M. Fowler Map Coll. 73)	T. M. Fowler & James B. Moyer		20 × 30½
757.1	Connellsville 1897	G3824 .C8A3 1897 .F6 1976	T. M. Fowler, Morrisville, Pa.	T. M. Fowler and James B. Moyer		15½ × 23 Facsimile
757.2	Connellsville 1897	G3824 .C8A3 1897 .F6 1978		[T. M. Fowler and James B. Moyer] Reprinted in [1978?] by the Print Shop, Mt. Pleasant, Pa.		15 × 21½ Facsimile
758	Corry 1870	G3824 .C87A3 1870 .R8 Rug 171	[Albert Ruger] (Ruger Map Coll. 171)	Ruger & Stoner, Madison, Wisconsin	Chicago Lithographing Co., Chicago	23 × 26
759	Corry 1895	G3824 .C87A3 1895 .F6 Fow 74	T. M. Fowler, Morrisville, Pa. (T. M. Fowler Map Coll. 74)	T. M. Fowler & James B. Moyer		19 × 30
760	Curwensville 1895	G3824 .C99A3 1895 .F6	T. M. Fowler, Morrisville, Pa.	T. M. Fowler & James B. Moyer		17 × 26
761	Dawson 1902	G3824 .D36A3 1902 .F6 Fow 34	T. M. Fowler, Morrisville, Pa. (T. M. Fowler Map Coll. 34)	T. M. Fowler, Morrisville, Pa.		15½ × 19
761.1	Derry Station 1900	G3824 .D38A3 1900 .F6	T. M. Fowler, Morrisville, Pa.	T. M. Fowler & James B. Moyer		15 × 22½
761.2	Donora 1901	G3824 .D5A3 1901 .F6	T. M. Fowler, Morrisville, Pa.	T. M. Fowler & James B. Moyer		6½ × 9½ Positive photostat
761.3[3]	Donora 1901	G3824 .D5A3 1901 .F61	T. M. Fowler, Morrisville, Pa.	T. M. Fowler and James B. Moyer		12½ × 18½ Positive photostat
762	Downingtown 1893	G3824 .D62A3 1893 .F6	T. M. Fowler, Morrisville, Pa.	James B. Moyer, Myerstown, Pennsylvania		19 × 26½
763	DuBois 1895	G3824 .D7A3 1895 .F6	T. M. Fowler, Morrisville, Pa.	T. M. Fowler & James B. Moyer		18½ × 34

[3]Reproduced from the original in the Pennsylvania Historical and Museum Commission, Division of Archives and Manuscripts, Harrisburg.

Entry No.	City and Date	LC Call No.	Artist	Publisher	Lithographer	Map Size (inches)
834	Point Marion 1902	G3824 .P72A3 1902 .F6	T. M. Fowler, Morrisville, Pa.	T. M. Fowler, Morrisville, Pa.		15 × 20½
834.1[3]	Pottstown 1893	G3824 .P8A3 1893 .F6	T. M. Fowler, Morrisville, Pa.	James B. Moyer, Myerstown, Pa.		Positive photostat in 2 parts, each 23 × 17½
834.2	Pottsville [1833?]	Prints & Photographs Division	J. R. Smith, Junr.		J. R. Smith, Senr.	13½ × 18
835	Pottsville 1889	G3824 .P9A3 1889 .F6	T. M. Fowler, Morrisville, Pa.	T. M. Fowler & James B. Moyer	A. E. Downs, Lith., Boston	20 × 34½
836	Providence 1892	G3824 .P974A3 1892 .D6 Fow 43	A. E. Downs, Boston (T. M. Fowler Map Coll. 43)			22 × 35 Manuscript
837	Reading 1881	G3824 .R3A3 1881 .K4	J. Hanold Kendall			25 × 32
837.1	Reading 1898	G3824 .R3A3 1898 .B3		Bailey & Moyer, Publishers, Boston, Mass.		20 × 30½
838	Ridgway 1895	G3824 .R52A3 1895 .F6	T. M. Fowler, Morrisville, Pa.	T. M. Fowler & James B. Moyer		19 × 29½
838.1	Rochester 1886	G3824 .R7A3 1886 .R8 1977		Ruger & Stoner, Madison, Wis. Reproduced in 1977 by the Rochester Historical Society, Pennsylvania	Beck & Pauli, Litho., Milwaukee, Wis.	16½ × 20½ Facsimile
839	Rochester 1900	G3824 .R7A3 1900 .F6	T. M. Fowler, Morrisville, Pa.	T. M. Fowler & James B. Moyer		19 × 30½
840	Roscoe 1902	G3824 .R76A3 1902 .F6	T. M. Fowler, Morrisville, Pa.	T. M. Fowler & James B. Moyer		12 × 19
840.1	Royersford 1893	G3824 .R88A3 1893 .F6	T. M. Fowler, Morrisville, Pa.	James B. Moyer, Myerstown, Pa.		16 × 23½
841	St. Mary's 1895	G3824 .S13A3 1895 .F6	T. M. Fowler, Morrisville, Pa.	T. M. Fowler & James B. Moyer		19 × 26
841.1	Saxton 1906	G3824 .S155A3 1906 .F6		Fowler & Kelly, Morrisville, Pa.		16 × 23½ Positive photostat

[3]Reproduced from the original in the Pennsylvania Historical and Museum Commission, Division of Archives and Manuscripts, Harrisburg.

Entry No.	City and Date	LC Call No.	Artist	Publisher	Lithographer	Map Size (inches)
842	Schwenksville 1894	G3824 .S185A3 1894 .F6	T. M. Fowler	T. M. Fowler & James B. Moyer		15 × 21
843	Scottdale & Everson 1890	G3824 .S19A3 1890 .S3		[Scottdale & Everson Land Co.]		6 × 9
843.1	Scottdale 1900	G3824 .S19A3 1900 .F6	T. M. Fowler, Morrisville, Pa.	T. M. Fowler & James B. Moyer		8 × 11½ Positive photostat
844	Scranton 1890	G3824 .S2A3 1890 .F6	T. M. Fowler & A. E. Downs	T. M. Fowler & James B. Moyer	A. E. Downs, Lith., Boston	24 × 40½
845	Sellersville 1894	G3824 .S24A3 1894 .F6	T. M. Fowler, Morrisville, Pa.	T. M. Fowler & James B. Moyer		16 × 25
846	Sharon 1901	G3824 .S3A3 1901 .F6	T. M. Fowler, Morrisville, Pa.	T. M. Fowler & James B. Moyer		18½ × 30½
847	Sharpsville 1901	G3824 .S34A3 1901 .F6	T. M. Fowler, Morrisville, Pa.	T. M. Fowler & James B. Moyer		15 × 24
848	Sheffield 1895	G3824 .S36A3 1895 .F6	T. M. Fowler, Morrisville, Pa.	T. M. Fowler & James B. Moyer		17 × 25
849	Shenandoah 1889	G3824 .S4A3 1889 .F6	T. M. Fowler, Morrisville, Pa.	T. M. Fowler & J. B. Moyer		21 × 29
850	Shippensburg 1894	G3824 .S43A3 1894 .F6	T. M. Fowler, Morrisville, Pa.	T. M. Fowler & James B. Moyer. Reproduced from the original belonging to Burkhart's Restaurant, Shippensburg, Pa.		8 × 10 Photograph
850.1	Sinking Spring 1898	G3824 .S47A3 1898 .F6 Vault	T. M. Fowler, Morrisville, Pa.			12 × 17 Manuscript
851	Somerset 1900	G3824 .S52A3 1900 .F6	T. M. Fowler, Morrisville, Pa.	T. M. Fowler & James B. Moyer		19½ × 24
851.1	Somerset 1900	G3824 .S52A3 1900 .F6 1978	[T. M. Fowler]	Reprinted [in 1978?] by the Print Shop, Mt. Pleasant, Pa.		17½ × 20½ Facsimile
852	Souderton 1894	G3824 .S53A3 1894 .F6	T. M. Fowler, Morrisville, Pa.	T. M. Fowler & James B. Moyer		16 × 20
853	South Fork 1900	G3824 .S58A3 1900 .F6	T. M. Fowler, Morrisville, Pa.	T. M. Fowler & James B. Moyer		16 × 23

Entry No.	City and Date	LC Call No.	Artist	Publisher	Lithographer	Map Size (Inches)
853.1[3]	Spring City 1893	G3824 .S735A3 1893 .F6	T. M. Fowler, Morrisville, Pa.	James B. Moyer, Myerstown, Pa.		17 × 23 Positive photostat
854	Strasburg 1903	G3824 .S861A3 1903 .F6 Fow 44	T. M. Fowler, Morrisville, Pa. (T. M. Fowler Map Coll. 44)	T. M. Fowler, Morrisville, Pa.		13 × 18
854.1	Stroudsburg 1884	G3824 .S87A3 1884 .B3 1974		O. H. Bailey & Co., Boston	O. H. Bailey & Co., Boston	15 × 22½ Positive photostat
854.2	Sunbury 1873	G3824 .S9A3 1873 .B3	O. H. Bailey	Reproduced in 1980 from the original held in the Historical Society of Pennsylvania, Philadelphia	J. H. Touvy & Co., Philadelphia	8 × 10 Photograph
854.3[3]	Tacony 1898	G3824 .P5:2T3A3 1898 .F6	T. M. Fowler, Morrisville, Pa.	T. M. Fowler, Morrisville, Pa.		Positive photostat in 2 parts, each 20 × 17½
855	Tarentum 1901	G3824 .T24A3 1901 .F6	T. M. Fowler, Morrisville, Pa.	T. M. Fowler & James B. Moyer		17 × 29½
855.1	Tarentum 1901	G3824 .T24A3 1901 .T3	T. M. Fowler of Morrisville, Pennsylvania	Reprinted in 1973 by the Tarentum History & Landmarks Foundation		16 × 29 Reprint
856	Telford 1894	G3824 .T32A3 1894 .F6 Fow 61	T. M. Fowler, Morrisville, Pa. (T. M. Fowler Map Coll. 61)	T. M. Fowler & James B. Moyer		14 × 20
856.1	Telford 1894	G3824 .T32A3 1894 .F6	T. M. Fowler, Morrisville, Pa.	T. M. Fowler & James B. Moyer		12 × 19½
857	Terre Hill 1894	G3824 .T35A3 1894 .F6 Fow 45	T. M. Fowler, Morrisville, Pa. (T. M. Fowler Map Coll. 45)	T. M. Fowler & James B. Moyer		15½ × 21½
858	Tidioute 1896	G3824 .T42A3 1896 .F6 Fow 46	T. M. Fowler, Morrisville, Pa. (T. M. Fowler Map Coll. 46)	T. M. Fowler & James B. Moyer		17 × 24½

[3]Reproduced from the original in the Pennsylvania Historical and Museum Commission, Division of Archives and Manuscripts, Harrisburg.

Entry No.	City and Date	LC Call No.	Artist	Publisher	Lithographer	Map Size (inches)
859	Tionesta 1896	G3824 .T46A3 1896 .F6 Fow 47	T. M. Fowler, Morrisville, Pa. (T. M. Fowler Map Coll. 47)	T. M. Fowler & James B. Moyer		13½ × 18
859.1	Tionesta 1896	G3824 .T46A3 1896 .F6	T. M. Fowler, Morrisville, Pa.	T. M. Fowler & James B. Moyer		13 × 17½
860	Titusville 1871	G3824 .T5A3 1871 .R8 Rug 173	A. Ruger (Ruger Map Coll. 173)		Chicago Lithographing Co., Chicago	23 × 26½
861	Titusville 1896	G3824 .T5A3 1896 .F6	T. M. Fowler, Morrisville, Pa.	T. M. Fowler & James B. Moyer		21 × 34
862	Topton 1893	G3824 .T53A3 1893 .F6 Fow 48	T. M. Fowler, Morrisville, Pa. (T. M. Fowler Map Coll. 48)	T. M. Fowler & James B. Moyer		13 × 20
862.1	Towanda 1880	G3824 .T55A35 1880 .P5		Philada. Publishing House; C. J. Corbin, Field Manager		16½ × 28½
863	Tullytown 1887	G3824 .T77A3 1887 .F6 Fow 49	T. M. Fowler (T. M. Fowler Map Coll. 49)			12 × 17½
864	Turtle Creek 1897	G3824 .T8A3 1897 .F6 Fow 50	T. M. Fowler, Morrisville, Pa. (T. M. Fowler Map Coll. 50)	T. M. Fowler & James B. Moyer		16 × 22½
864.1	Tyrone 1895	G3824 .T9A3 1895 .F6 Fow 68	T. M. Fowler, Morrisville, Pa. (T. M. Fowler Map Coll. 68)	T. M. Fowler & James B. Moyer		17 × 24½
865	Union City 1895	G3824 .U4A3 1895 .F6	T. M. Fowler, Morrisville, Pa.	T. M. Fowler & James B. Moyer		19 × 26½
865.1	Uniontown 1879	G3824 .U5A3 1879 .C6		C. J. Corbin	Thos. Hunter, Lith., Phila.	8 × 10 Positive photostat
866	Uniontown 1897	G3824 .U5A3 1897 .F6	T. M. Fowler, Morrisville, Pa.	T. M. Fowler & James B. Moyer		20½ × 27
866.1	Uniontown 1897	G3824 .U5A3 1897 .F6 1978		Reprinted [in 1978?] by the Print Shop, Mt. Pleasant, Pa.		16½ × 21½ Facsimile

Entry No.	City and Date	LC Call No.	Artist	Publisher	Lithographer	Map Size (inches)
867	Valley Forge 1890	G3824 .V18A3 1890 .D6 Fow 51	[T. M. Fowler] (T. M. Fowler Map Coll. 51)	James B. Moyer, Myerstown, Pa.	A. E. Downs, Lith., Boston	19 × 26
868	Verona & Oakmont 1896	G3824 .V4A3 1896 .F6	T. M. Fowler, Morrisville, Pa.	T. M. Fowler & James B. Moyer		20 × 28½
868.1[3]	Warren 1895	G3824 .W18A3 1895 .F6	T. M. Fowler, Morrisville, Pa.	T. M. Fowler & James B. Moyer		Positive photostat in 2 parts, each 20 × 18
869	Washington 1897	G3824 .W2A3 1897 .F6	T. M. Fowler, Morrisville, Pa.	T. M. Fowler & James B. Moyer		21 × 38
869.1[3]	Waynesboro 1894	G3824 .W24A3 1894 .F6	T. M. Fowler, Morrisville, Pa.	T. M. Fowler & James B. Moyer		16 × 22½ Positive photostat
870	Waynesburg 1897	G3824 .W25A3 1897 .F6	T. M. Fowler, Morrisville, Pa.	T. M. Fowler & James B. Moyer		17½ × 23
870.1	Webster 1904	G3824 .W265A3 1904 .F6	T. M. Fowler, Morrisville, Pennsylvania	T. M. Fowler, Morrisville, Pennsylvania		12 × 17 Positive photostat
870.2	West Bethlehem 1894	G3824 .W282A3 1894 .F6	T. M. Fowler, Morrisville, Pa.	T. M. Fowler & James B. Moyer		16 × 22
871	West Newton 1900	G3824 .W42A3 1900 .F6	T. M. Fowler, Morrisville, Pa.	T. M. Fowler & James B. Moyer		17 × 24
872	Wilkes-Barre 1889	G3824 .W6A3 1889 .F6	Fowler, Downs & Moyer	Fowler, Downs & Moyer	A. E. Downs, Lith., Boston	26 × 42½
873	Williamsburg 1906	G3824 .W66A3 1906 .F6	T. M. Fowler, Morrisville, Pa.	Fowler & Kelly, Morrisville, Pa.		22 × 24½
873.1	Williamsport 1872	G3824 .W7A3 1872 .B2 1970	H. H. Bailey	Reproduced in 1973 by Lycoming County Historical Society and Museum, Williamsport, Pa.	Strobridge & Co., Lith., Cin.	21 × 32½ Facsimile
874	Wilmerding 1897	G3824 .W74A3 1897 .F6	T. M. Fowler, Morrisville, Pa.	T. M. Fowler & James B. Moyer		17½ × 23½

[3]Reproduced from the original in the Pennsylvania Historical and Museum Commission, Division of Archives and Manuscripts, Harrisburg.

Entry No.	City and Date	LC Call No.	Artist	Publisher	Lithographer	Map Size (inches)
875	Wilson & Mendelssohn 1902	G3824 .W76A3 1902 .F6	T. M. Fowler, Morrisville, Pa.	T. M. Fowler & James B. Moyer		10 × 13
875.1	Windber 1900 (with Scalp Level)	G3824 .W8A3 1900 .F6	T. M. Fowler, Morrisville, Pa.	T. M. Fowler & James B. Moyer		18 × 28½
876	Wrightsville 1894	G3824 .W88A3 1894 .F6	T. M. Fowler, Morrisville, Pa.	T. M. Fowler & James B. Moyer		16 × 22
876.1	Wyoming 1885	G3824 .W92A3 1885 .R6 1977	H. H. Rowley, Utica, N.Y.	H. H. Rowley, Utica, N.Y.	C. H. Vogt & Son, Lith., Cleveland	17½ × 29½ Facsimile
876.2	York 1852	G3824 .Y6A35 1852 .W5		J. Thomas Williams	E. Sachse & Co., Balt.	22 × 27½
877	York 1879	G3824 .Y6A35 1879 .K4	Davoust Kern	Davoust Kern	A. Hoen & Co., Lith., Baltimore, Maryland	24 × 37½
878	Zelienople 1901	G3824 .Z3A3 1901 .F6	T. M. Fowler, Morrisville, Pa.	T. M. Fowler & James B. Moyer		14 × 21½

Rhode Island

Entry No.	City and Date	LC Call No.	Artist	Publisher	Lithographer	Map Size (inches)
878.1	Bristol 1891	G3774 .B7A3 1891 .B3		O. H. Bailey & Co., Boston	O. H. Bailey & Co., Boston	22½ × 31
879	Newport 1878	G3774 .N4A3 1878 .G3	Galt & Hoy, New York	Galt & Hoy, New York		25 × 27½
879.1[4]	Pascoag 1895	G3774 .P25A3 1895 .B3		O. H. Bailey & Co., Boston	O. H. Bailey & Co., Boston	8 × 10 Positive photostat
880	Pawtucket & Central Falls 1877	G3774 .P3A3 1877 .B3	O. H. Bailey & J. C. Hazen, Boston	O. H. Bailey & J. C. Hazen, Boston	C. H. Vogt, Lith., Milwaukee; J. Knauber & Co.	25 × 32½
881	Providence 1896	G3774 .P9A35 1896 .M3	M. D. Mason			16 × 20
881.1	Westerly 1877	G3774 .W8A3 1877 .B3	O. H. Bailey & J. C. Hazen, Boston	O. H. Bailey & J. C. Hazen, Boston		20 × 25½
882	Westerly 1911	G3774 .W8A3 1911 .H8		Hughes & Bailey, New York		29½ × 36

[4]Map may not be reproduced without written permission from the Merrimac Valley Textile Museum, North Andover, Massachusetts 01845.

South Carolina

Entry No.	City and Date	LC Call No.	Artist	Publisher	Lithographer	Map Size (inches)
882.1	Charles Town [1762]	G3914 .C3A35 1762 .E9 1977		Reproduced in 1977 by Historic Urban Plans, Ithaca, New York		10½ × 21 Facsimile
882.2	Charles Town [1768]	G3914 .C3A35 1768 .C3 1970	[P.] C. Canot	Reproduced in 1970 by Historic Urban Plans, Ithaca, New York		16 × 20½ Facsimile
883	Charleston 1872	G3914 .C3A3 1872 .D7	C. Drie	C. Drie	C. Drie	22½ × 33½
883.1	Charleston 1872	G3914 .C3A3 1872 .D7 1976	C. Drie	C. Drie. Reproduced in 1976 by Historic Urban Plans, Ithaca, New York	C. Drie, Lithographer	21½ × 27½ Facsimile
884	Columbia 1872	G3914 .C7A3 1872 .D7	C. Drie	C. Drie		22½ × 28
884.1	Columbia 1872	G3914 .C7A3 1872 .D7 1975	C. Drie	C. Drie. Reproduced in 1975 by Historic Urban Plans, Ithaca, New York		23½ × 27½ Facsimile

South Dakota

Entry No.	City and Date	LC Call No.	Artist	Publisher	Lithographer	Map Size (inches)
885	Aberdeen 1883	G4184 .A2A3 1883 .W4	H. Wellge	F. H. Hagerty & H. M. Marple, Aberdeen, Dakota Territory		15 × 25
886	Clark 1883	G4184 .C6A3 1883 .S7		J. J. Stoner, Madison, Wisconsin	Beck & Pauli, Lith., Milwaukee, Wisconsin	12 × 18
887	Deadwood 1884	G4184 .D3A3 1884 .H4 1969	W. V. Herancourt	Reproduced in 1969 by Historic Urban Plans, Ithaca, New York		13 × 20½ Facsimile
888	Flandreau 1883	G4184 .F5A3 1883 .B7	H. Brosius	J. J. Stoner, Madison, Wisconsin	Beck & Pauli, Milwaukee, Wisconsin	13 × 21
889	Frederick 1883	G4184 .F8A3 1883 .C3		C. F. Campau		12 × 16
889.1	Huron [1883]	G4184 .H9A3 1883 .H4	Wm. Valentine Herancourt	Reproduced from original in collection of the State Historical Society of Wisconsin, Madison		15½ × 23 Positive and negative photostats
890	Madison 1883	G4184 .M2A3 1883 .B7	H. Brosius	J. J. Stoner, Madison, Wisconsin	Beck & Pauli, Milwaukee, Wisconsin	13 × 20
890.1	Rapid City [1883]	G4184 .R3A3 1883 .H4	W. V. Herancourt			14 × 21½ Positive and negative photostats

Aberdeen, Dakota Territory, 1883. Drawn by H. Wellge. This view of Aberdeen [South Dakota] clearly shows the importance of the railroad needed to accommodate immigrants and speculators heading for the Black Hills. The town was laid out under the direction of Charles Prior, agent for the Chicago, Milwaukee and St. Paul Railway.

Entry No.	City and Date	LC Call No.	Artist	Publisher	Lithographer	Map Size (inches)
891	Redfield 1883	G4184 .R4A3 1883 .W4	H. Wellge	The Dakota Sun & Job Printing House, H. G. Rising, prop.		12 × 15½
891.1	Spearfish [1884]	G4184 .S8A3 1884 .H4	Wm. Valentine Herancourt	Reproduced from original in Grace Balloch Public Library, Spearfish, S.D.		8 × 10 Photograph
892	Watertown 1883	G4184 W3A3 1883 .S7		J. J. Stoner, Madison, Wisconsin	Beck & Pauli, Milwaukee, Wisconsin	13½ × 21

Tennessee

Entry No.	City and Date	LC Call No.	Artist	Publisher	Lithographer	Map Size (inches)
893	Chattanooga 1871	G3964 .C3A3 1871 .R8 Rug 174	A. Ruger, St. Louis, Mo. (Ruger Map Coll. 174)	A. Ruger, St. Louis, Mo.		23 × 31
894	Chattanooga 1886	G3964 .C3A3 1886 .W4	H. Wellge	Norris, Wellge & Co., Milwaukee, Wisconsin	Beck & Pauli, Lith., Milwaukee, Wisconsin	21 × 28½
894.1	Chattanooga 1886	G3964 .C3A3 1886 .W4 1975	H. Wellge	Norris, Wellge & Co., Milwaukee, Wis. Reproduced [in 1975?] by the Tennessee Valley Authority, Knoxville	Beck & Pauli, Litho., Milwaukee, Wis.	22½ × 28½ Facsimile
895	Chattanooga 1887	G3964 .C3A35 1887 .C5				20 × 25
896	Clarksville 1870	G3964 .C4A3 1870 .R8 Rug 175	[Albert Ruger] (Ruger Map Coll. 175)	Stoner & Ruger	Merchant Lith. Co., Chicago	23 × 26
897	Harriman 1892	G3964 .H3A3 1892 .N6	Geo. E. Norris, Brockton, Mass.	Geo. E. Norris, Brockton, Mass.	The Burleigh Lith. Co., Troy, New York	21 × 29½
898	Jackson 1870	G3964 .J2A3 1870 .R8 Rug 176	A. Ruger (Ruger Map Coll. 176)		Chicago Litho. Co., Chicago, Illinois	22½ × 26½
899	Knoxville 1871	G3964 .K7A3 1871 .R8 Rug 177	[Albert Ruger] (Ruger Map Coll. 177)		Merchants Lith. Co., Chicago	23 × 26½
900	Knoxville 1886	G3964 .K7A3 1886 .W4	H. Wellge	Norris, Wellge & Co., Milwaukee, Wisconsin	Beck & Pauli, Litho., Milwaukee, Wisconsin	21 × 28½
900.1	Knoxville 1886	G3964 .K7A3 1886 .W4 1975	H. Wellge	Norris, Wellge & Co., Milwaukee, Wis. Reproduced in 1975 by Historic Urban Plans, Ithaca, New York	Beck & Pauli, Litho., Milwaukee, Wis.	22 × 28 Facsimile

Entry No.	City and Date	LC Call No.	Artist	Publisher	Lithographer	Map Size (inches)
900.2	Knoxville 1886	G3964 .K7A3 1888 .W4 1975	[Henry Wellge]	Norris, Wellge & Co., Milwaukee, Wis. Reproduced [in 1975?] by the Tennessee Valley Authority, Knoxville	Beck & Pauli, Litho., Milwaukee, Wis.	21 × 28 Facsimile
901	Memphis 1870	G3964 .M5A3 1870 .R8 Rug 178	[Albert Ruger] (Ruger Map Coll. 178)			20 × 34
901.1	Memphis 1870	G3964 .M5A3 1870 .R8 1975	[Albert Ruger]	Reproduced in 1975 by Historic Urban Plans, Ithaca, New York		15½ × 19 Facsimile
902	Memphis 1887	G3964 .M5A3 1887 .H4		Henry Wellge & Co., Milwaukee, Wisconsin		28 × 41

Texas

Entry No.	City and Date	LC Call No.	Artist	Publisher	Lithographer	Map Size (inches)
902.1	Alvord 1890	G4034 .A49A3 1890 .F6	T. M. Fowler, Morrisville, Pa.	T. M. Fowler & James B. Moyer		12 × 17½
903	Amarillo (Business District) 1912	G4034 .A5A3 1912 .M6	E. E. Motter	G. C. Sturdivant	Panhandle Printing Co., Amarillo	17 × 19½
904	Brenham 1881	G4034 .B7A3 1881 .K6	Augustus Koch			8 × 10 Photograph
905	Childress 1890	G4034 .C4A3 1890 .F6 Fow 52	T. M. Fowler, Morrisville, Pa. (T. M. Fowler Map Coll. 52)	T. M. Fowler & James B. Moyer		10 × 16½
906	Clarendon 1890	G4034 .C47A3 1890 .F6 Fow 53	T. M. Fowler, Morrisville, Pa. (T. M. Fowler Map Coll. 53)	T. M. Fowler & James B. Moyer		14½ × 25
907	Dallas 1892	G4034 .D2A3 1892 .G5	Paul Giraud	Paul Giraud	Dallas Lith. Co.	21 × 29
908	Denison 1886	G4034 .D4A3 1886 .N6		Norris, Wellge & Co., Milwaukee, Wisconsin	Beck & Pauli, Lith., Milwaukee, Wisconsin	20 × 27
908.1	Denison 1891	G4034 .D4A3 1891 .F6	T. M. Fowler, Morrisville, Pa.	T. M. Fowler & James B. Moyer		21½ × 33½
909	Fort Griffin [184-?]	G4034 .F63A35 184- .F6				11 × 20 Negative photostat

Entry No.	City and Date	LC Call No.	Artist	Publisher	Lithographer	Map Size (inches)
910	Fort Worth 1886	G4034 .F7A3 1886 .W4	H. Wellge	Norris, Wellge & Co., Milwaukee, Wisconsin	Beck & Pauli, Litho., Milwaukee, Wisconsin	26½ × 34
911	Fort Worth 1891	G4034 .F7A3 1891 .W4	H. Wellge	American Publishing Co., Milwaukee, Wisconsin		20 × 33½
911.1	Fort Worth 1891	G4034 .F7A3 1891 .W41	H. Wellge	American Publishing Co., Milwaukee, Wis.		20 × 33½
911.2	Fort Worth 1891	G4034 .F7A3 1891 .W4 1971	[H. Wellge]	American Publishing Co., Milwaukee, Wis. Reproduced in 1971 by Historic Urban Plans, Ithaca, New York		15 × 22 Facsimile
912	Fort Worth 1913 [i.e. 1914]	G4034 .F7A3 1914 .H3	A. S. Harris			4 × 9½ Photograph
912.1	Galveston 1871	G4034 .G3A3 1871 .D7	C. Drie		Chicago Lithographing Co.	13½ × 18 Positive photostat
913	Greenville 1886	G4034 .G8A3 1886 .W4	H. Wellge	Norris, Wellge & Co., Milwaukee, Wisconsin	Beck & Pauli, Litho., Milwaukee, Wisconsin	18 × 25
914	Honey Grove 1886	G4034 .H77A3 1886 .W4	H. Wellge	Norris, Wellge & Co., Milwaukee, Wisconsin	Beck & Pauli, Litho., Milwaukee, Wisconsin	17 × 21½
915	Houston 1891	G4034 .H8A3 1891 .H6	[A. L. Westyard]	D. W. Ensign, Jr., Chicago		28 × 43
915.1	Houston 1891	G4034 .H8A3 1891 .H6 1977		Reproduced [in 1977?] by Historic Urban Plans, Ithaca, New York		14 × 18 Facsimile
916	Houston 1912	G4034 .H8A3 1912 .H6	Hopkins & Motter	Hopkins & Motter		16½ × 21
917	Jefferson 1872	G4034 .J6A3 1872 .B7 1937	H. Brosius	Reproduced in 1937 by A. Paul Brooks, United Gas Corporation		20 × 27½ Facsimile
917.1	Ladonia 1891	G4034 .L14A3 1891 .F6	T. M. Fowler, Morrisville, Pa.	T. M. Fowler & James B. Moyer		11½ × 20½
918	Laredo 1892	G4034 .L4A3 1892 .A6	[H. Wellge]	American Publishing Co., Milwaukee, Wisconsin		22½ × 33½
919	Paris 1885	G4034 .P4A3 1885 .N6	[H. Wellge]	Norris, Wellge & Co., Milwaukee, Wisconsin	Beck & Pauli, Milwaukee, Wisconsin	19½ × 25½
919.1	Plano 1891	G4034 .P72A3 1891 .F6	T. M. Fowler, Morrisville, Pa.	T. M. Fowler & James B. Moyer	A. E. Downs, Lith., Boston	8 × 10 Positive photostat

Entry No.	City and Date	LC Call No.	Artist	Publisher	Lithographer	Map Size (inches)
920	Port Arthur 1912	G4034 .P8A3 1912 .G6	E. S. Glover	Port Arthur Board of Trade		16 × 36½
920.1	Quanah 1890	G4034 .Q2A3 1890 .F6	T. M. Fowler, Morrisville, Pa.	T. M. Fowler & James B. Moyer. Reproduced from the original in the Barker Library, University of Texas at Austin		11 × 14 Photograph
920.2	Seymour 1890	G4034 .S44A3 1890 .F6	T. M. Fowler, Morrisville, Pa.			8 × 10 Photograph
920.3	Sunset 1890	G4034 .S854A3 1890 .F6	T. M. Fowler, Morrisville, Pa.	T. M. Fowler & J. B. Moyer		10½ × 15
921	Waco 1886	G4034 .W2A3 1886 .N6	[H. Wellge]	Norris, Wellge & Co., Milwaukee, Wisconsin	Beck & Pauli, Milwaukee, Wisconsin	22½ × 31
922	Waco 1892	G4034 .W2A3 1892 .W4	A. L. Westyard	D. W. Ensign & Co.	Shober & Carqueville Lith., Chicago	25 × 43
922.1	Wolfe City 1891	G4034 .W8A3 1891 .F6	T. M. Fowler, Morrisville, Pa.	T. M. Fowler & James B. Moyer		15 × 21

Utah

Entry No.	City and Date	LC Call No.	Artist	Publisher	Lithographer	Map Size (inches)
923	Brigham City & Great Salt Lake 1875	G4344 .B8A3 1875 .G6	E. S. Glover, Salt Lake City	E. S. Glover, Salt Lake City	Strobridge & Co., Cincinnati, Ohio	16 × 22½
924	Ogden City 1875	G4344 .O3A3 1875 .G6	E. S. Glover	E. S. Glover	Strobridge & Co., Cincinnati, Ohio	17 × 22½
924.1	Ogden City 1875	G4344 .O3A3 1875 .G6 1975	E. S. Glover, Salt Lake City, Utah Ty.	E. S. Glover, Salt Lake City, Utah Ty. Reproduced in 1975 by Historic Urban Plans, Ithaca, New York	Strobridge & Co. Lith., Cincinnati, O.	17 × 21½ Facsimile
925	Ogden City 1889	G4344 .O3A35 1889 .D3	Eugene F. Darling	Eugene F. Darling		22 × 37
926	Ogden 1890	G4344 .O3A3 1890 .A6	[H. Wellge]	American Publishing Co., Milwaukee, Wisconsin		20 × 35½
927	Salt Lake City 1867	G4344 .S3A35 1867 .R5 1969	C. Inger	Philip Ritz, Walla Walla, W. T. Reproduced in 1969 by Historic Urban Plans, Ithaca, New York	H. J. Toudy, Phila.	14 × 26 Facsimile
928	Salt Lake City 1870	G4344 .S3A3 1870 .K6	Augustus Koch	Augustus Koch	Chicago Litho. Co.	29 × 35

Salt Lake City, Utah Territory, 1870. Drawn by
Augustus Koch. This view of the eventual capital of
Utah, with its orderly design and planned development,
stands as the quintessential testimony to Mormon
enterprise and religious piety.

Entry No.	City and Date	LC Call No.	Artist	Publisher	Lithographer	Map Size (inches)
928.1	Salt Lake City 1870	G4344 .S3A3 1870 .K6 1967	Augustus Koch	Reproduced in 1967 by Historic Urban Plans, Ithaca, New York	Chicago Lithographing Co., Chicago, Ill.	20½ × 24½ Facsimile
928.2	Salt Lake City 1870	G4344 .S3A3 1870 .K6 1974	Augustus Koch	Reproduced [in 1974?] by Historic Urban Plans, Ithaca, New York	Chicago Lithographing Co., Chicago, Ill.	16½ × 19½ Facsimile
929	Salt Lake City 1875	G4344 .S3A3 1875 .G6	E. S. Glover	E. S. Glover	Strobridge & Co., Cincinnati, Ohio	24½ × 32½
929.1	Salt Lake City 1875	G4344 .S3A3 1875 .G61	E. S. Glover, Salt Lake City	E. S. Glover, Salt Lake City	Strobridge & Co. Lith., Cincinnati, O.	24½ × 32½
930	Salt Lake City 1891	G4344 .S3A3 1891 .W4	H. Wellge	American Publishing Co., Milwaukee, Wisconsin		24 × 44½

Vermont

Entry No.	City and Date	LC Call No.	Artist	Publisher	Lithographer	Map Size (inches)
931	Barre 1891	G3754 .B3A3 1891 .N6	Geo. E. Norris, Brockton, Mass.	Geo. E. Norris, Brockton, Mass.		19 × 30½
931.1	Bellows Falls [188-?]	G3754 .B4A35 188- .H8	S. W. Hull		L. H. Bradford & Co.'s Lith.	8 × 10 Photograph
932	Bellows Falls 1886	G3754 .B4A3 1886 .B8		L. R. Burleigh	The Burleigh Lith. Est., Troy, New York	17 × 26½
932.1[5]	Bennington & Bennington Centre 1877	G3754 .B5A3 1877 .S8	[A. Ruger]	J. J. Stoner, Madison, Wis.	Shober & Carqueville, Litho., Chicago	8 × 10 Photograph
933	Bennington 1887	G3754 .B5A3 1887 .B8	L. R. Burleigh	L. R. Burleigh	Burleigh Litho., Troy, New York	19 × 31½
934	Bethel 1886	G3754 .B55A3 1886 .B8		L. R. Burleigh, Troy, New York	The Burleigh Lith. Est., Troy, New York	14 × 21
934.1[5]	Brandon 1890	G3754 .B68A3 1890 .B8	L. R. Burleigh, Troy, N.Y.	L. R. Burleigh, Troy, N.Y.		8 × 10 Photograph
934.2[5]	Brattleboro 1876	G3754 .B7A3 1876 .B3	H. H. Bailey & J. C. Hazen	H. H. Bailey & J. C. Hazen	C. H. Vogt, Lith., Milwaukee, Wisconsin	8 × 10 Photograph
934.3[5]	Brattleboro [188-?]	G3754 .B7A35 188- .B8	[Bufford's Lithography]		J. H. Bufford's Lith.	8 × 10 Photograph
935	Brattleboro 1886	G3754 .B7A3 1886 .B8	L. R. Burleigh		The Burleigh Lith. Est., Troy, New York	14 × 27½

[5]Reproduced from the original in the collections of the Vermont Historical Society, Montpelier.

Entry No.	City and Date	LC Call No.	Artist	Publisher	Lithographer	Map Size (Inches)
953	Buena Vista 1891	G3884 .B9A3 1891 .A6	[H. Wellge]	American Publishing Co., Milwaukee, Wisconsin		21 × 33½
953.1	[Charlottesville 1856]	G3884 .C4A35 1856 .C4 1973		Reproduced in 1973 by Historic Urban Plans, Ithaca, New York		20½ × 27 Facsimile
954	Emporia 1907	G3884 .E5A3 1907 .F6	T. M. Fowler, Morrisville, Pa.	T. M. Fowler, Morrisville, Pa.		24 × 28
955	Franklin 1907	G3884 .F6A3 1907 .F6	T. M. Fowler, Morrisville, Pa.	T. M. Fowler, Morrisville, Pa.		18½ × 24
956	Fredericksburg 1862	G3884 .F7A3 1862 .S3		E. Sachse & Co., Baltimore	E. Sachse & Co., Baltimore	10½ × 17
957	Newport News 1891	G3884 .N4A3 1891 .A5	[H. Wellge]	American Publishing Co., Milwaukee, Wisconsin		22 × 34
957.1	Newport News 1891	G3884 .N4A3 1891 .A5 1974		American Publishing Co., Milwaukee, Wis. Reproduced in 1974 by Historic Urban Plans, Ithaca, New York		20½ × 27½ Facsimile
958	Norfolk & Portsmouth 1873	G3884 .N6A3 1873 .D7	C. N. Drie	C. N. Drie		23 × 34
959	Norfolk, Portsmouth, & Berkley 1891	G3884 .N6A3 1891 .K6	Augustus Koch	Augustus Koch	Morning News Lith., Savannah, Ga.	31½ × 41
960	Norfolk & Surroundings 1892	G3884 .N6A3 1892 .W4	H. Wellge	American Publishing Co., Milwaukee, Wisconsin; Hume & Bilisoly, Pub. Agt's Norfolk		24 × 40½
961	Pocahontas 1911	G3884 .P66A3 1911 .F6 Fow 54	T. M. Fowler, Flemington, N.J. (T. M. Fowler Map Coll. 54)	T. M. Fowler, Flemington, N.J.		16½ × 25½
961.1	Richmond 1863	G3884 .R5A35 1863 .W4	J. Wells; R. Hinshelwood	Virtue, Yorston & Co.		9 × 11½
962	Roanoke 1891	G3884 .R6A3 1891 .A6	[H. Wellge]	American Publishing Co., Milwaukee, Wisconsin		23½ × 39
962.1	Staunton 1857	Prints & Photographs Division	Ed Beyer			17½ × 29
963	Staunton 1891	G3884 .S8A3 1891 .A6	[H. Wellge]	American Publishing Co., Milwaukee, Wisconsin		21½ × 32½

Entry No.	City and Date	LC Call No.	Artist	Publisher	Lithographer	Map Size (inches)
964	Suffolk 1907	G3884 .S9A3 1907 .F6	T. M. Fowler, Morrisville, Pa.	Fowler & Kelly, Morrisville, Pa.		24 × 35½
965	Waynesboro 1891	G3884 .W4A3 1891 .A6	[H. Wellge]	American Publishing Co., Milwaukee, Wisconsin		22 × 32½
966	Winchester 1926	G3884 .W6A3 1926 .W6	Woods	W. A. Ryan		15 × 20

Washington

Entry No.	City and Date	LC Call No.	Artist	Publisher	Lithographer	Map Size (inches)
967	Cheney 1884	G4284 .C44A3 1884 .W4	H. Wellge	J. J. Stoner, Madison, Wisconsin	Beck & Pauli, Lith., Milwaukee, Wisconsin	14 × 20
968	Dayton 1884	G4284 .D3A3 1884 .W4	H. Wellge	J. J. Stoner, Madison, Wisconsin	Beck & Pauli, Lith., Milwaukee, Wisconsin	15 × 25
968.1	Fairhaven 1891 [Bellingham]	G4284 .F18A3 1891 .P5	B. W. Pierce		Elliott Pub. Co., S. F.	15½ × 22½ Positive and negative photostats
969	North Yakima 1889	G4284 .N75A3 1889 .A7	The Spike & Arnold Map Publishing Co.; W. Arnold	The Spike & Arnold Map Publishing Co.		24 × 31½
970	Olympia, East Olympia & Tumwater 1879	G4284 .O5A3 1879 .G6	E. S. Glover, Portland, Oregon	E. S. Glover, Portland, Oregon	A. L. Bancroft & Co., San Francisco	20 × 30
970.1	Olympia, East Olympia and Tumwater 1879	G4284 .O5A3 1879 .G6 1974	E. S. Glover, Portland, Oregon	E. S. Glover. Reproduced in 1974 by Historic Urban Plans, Ithaca, New York	A. L. Bancroft & Co., Lithographers, San Francisco	18 × 27½ Reduced facsimile
971	Olympia 1903	G4284 .O5A35 1903 .L3	Edw. Lange, Olympia, Wash.	Edw. Lange, Olympia, Wash.	Franklin Engraving & Electrotyping Co., Chicago, Illinois	17½ × 20½
972	Port Townsend 1878	G4284 .P6A3 1878 .G6	E. S. Glover, Portland, Oregon	E. S. Glover, Portland, Oregon	A. L. Bancroft, San Francisco, California	17 × 25
973	Seattle 1878	G4284 .S4A3 1878 .G6	E. S. Glover, Portland	E. S. Glover, Portland	A. L. Bancroft & Co., San Francisco	19½ × 30½
973.1	Seattle 1878	G4284 .S4A3 1878 .G6 1977	E. S. Glover, Portland, Oregon	E. S. Glover. Reproduced in 1977 by Historic Urban Plans, Ithaca, New York	A. L. Bancroft & Co., Lithography, San Francisco	15½ × 21½ Facsimile

Entry No.	City and Date	LC Call No.	Artist	Publisher	Lithographer	Map Size (Inches)
974	Seattle 1884	G4284 .S4A3 1884 .W4	H. Wellge	J. J. Stoner, Madison, Wisconsin	Beck & Pauli, Lith., Milwaukee, Wisconsin	17 × 32½
974.1	Seattle 1884	G4284 .S4A3 1884 .W4 1967	H. Wellge	J. J. Stoner, Madison, Wis. Reproduced in 1967 by Historic Urban Plans, Ithaca, New York	Beck & Pauli, Litho., Milwaukee, Wis.	18½ × 32½ Facsimile
975	Seattle & Environs 1891	G4284 .S4A3 1891 .K6	Augustus Koch	Augustus Koch	Hughes Litho. Co., Chicago	34 × 50½
976	Seattle (Main Business District) 1903	G4284 .S4A3 1903 .T8	Ross M. Tulloch	Periscopic Map Co., W. P. C. Adams, Mgr.		20 × 21
977	Seattle 1925	G4284 .S4A3 1925 .P6	Edwin C. Poland	Kroll Map Co.		32 × 55½ Blue line print
978	Spokane 1905 (Inset of Fort Wright)	G4284 .S7A3 1905 .J62		John W. Graham & Co., Spokane, Wash.		39 × 60
978.1	Spokane Falls [1890]	G4284 .S7A3 1890 .G5		Reproduced from original in the University of California at Berkeley Bancroft Library	Gies & Co., Buffalo, N.Y.	8 × 10 Photograph
979	Tacoma, New Tacoma & Mount Rainier 1878	G4284 .T2A3 1878 .G6	E. S. Glover, Portland	E. S. Glover, Portland	A. L. Bancroft & Co., San Francisco	17 × 25
980	Tacoma 1884	G4284 .T2A3 1884 .W4	H. Wellge	J. J. Stoner, Madison, Wisconsin	Beck & Pauli, Lith., Milwaukee, Wisconsin	16 × 33
980.1	Tacoma 1884	G4284 .T2A3 1884 .W4 1971	H. Wellge	J. J. Stoner, Madison, Wis. Reproduced in 1971 by Historic Urban Plans, Ithaca, New York	Beck & Pauli, Litho., Milwaukee, Wis.	16½ × 32½ Facsimile
981	Tacoma 1885	G4284 .T2A3 1885 .C5				17 × 34
982	Tacoma 1890	G4284 .T2A3 1890 .C3	Will Carson			32 × 43½
982.1	Tacoma 1890	G4284 .T2A35 1890 .T7		Geo. W. Traver. Reproduced from the original in the National Map Collection, Ottawa, Canada		Positive photostat in 2 parts, each 19 × 17½
983	Walla Walla 1876	G4284 .W2A3 1876 .G6	E. S. Glover	Everts & Able, Walla Walla	A. L. Bancroft & Co., San Francisco	19 × 28½

Entry No.	City and Date	LC Call No.	Artist	Publisher	Lithographer	Map Size (inches)
984	Walla-Walla W.T. 1884 (on verso of Fairport, New York 1885)	G3804 .F2A3 1885 .B8	H. Wellge	J. J. Stoner, Madison, Wis.	Beck & Pauli, Litho., Milwaukee, Wis.	18 × 27

West Virginia

Entry No.	City and Date	LC Call No.	Artist	Publisher	Lithographer	Map Size (inches)
985	Bayard 1898	G3894 .B31A3 1898 .F6	T. M. Fowler, Morrisville, Pa.	T. M. Fowler, Morrisville, Pa. Reproduced from the original belonging to Harold Shaffer, Bayard, W. Va. and Edwin Shaffer, Titusville, Florida		8 × 10 Photograph
986	Berkeley Springs 1889	G3894 .B53A35 1889 .M6		John Moray	A. Hoen & Co., Lith., Baltimore, Maryland	20 × 23½
987	Bluefield 1911	G3894 .B6A3 1911 .F6 Fow 55	T. M. Fowler (T. M. Fowler Map Coll. 55)	Fowler & Basham, Flemington, New Jersey		18½ × 38½
988	Buckhannon 1900	G3894 .B9A3 1900 .F6	T. M. Fowler, Morrisville, Pa.	T. M. Fowler & James B. Moyer		15 × 23½
988.1	Cairo 1899	G3894 .C12A3 1899 .F6	T. M. Fowler, Morrisville, Pa.	T. M. Fowler & James B. Moyer		18 × 22½
989	Cairo 1899	G3894 .C12A3 1899 .F6 Fow 76	T. M. Fowler, Morrisville, Pa. (T. M. Fowler Map Coll. 76)	T. M. Fowler & James B. Moyer		18 × 22½
989.1	Cameron 1899	G3894 .C15A3 1899 .F6	T. M. Fowler, Morrisville, Pa.	T. M. Fowler, Morrisville, Pa.	Wheeling News Lith.	17½ × 22½
990	Cameron 1899	G3894 .C15A3 1899 .F6 Fow. 64	T. M. Fowler, Morrisville, Pa. (T. M. Fowler Map Coll. 64)	T. M. Fowler, Morrisville, Pa.	Wheeling News Lith., Wheeling, West Virginia	17½ × 22½
990.1	Clarksburg 1898	G3894 .C6A3 1898 .F6	T. M. Fowler, Morrisville, Pa.	T. M. Fowler & James B. Moyer		20½ × 27½
991	Clarksburg 1898	G3894 .C6A3 1898 .F6 Fow 71	T. M. Fowler, Morrisville, Pa. (T. M. Fowler Map Coll. 71)	T. M. Fowler & James B. Moyer		20½ × 28

Entry No.	City and Date	LC Call No.	Artist	Publisher	Lithographer	Map Size (inches)
992	Davis 1898	G3894 .D3A3 1898 .F6	T. M. Fowler, Morrisville, Pa.	T. M. Fowler, Morrisville, Pa.		17 × 24
993	Elkins 1897	G3894 .E6A3 1897 .F6	T. M. Fowler, Morrisville, Pa.	T. M. Fowler & James B. Moyer		18 × 24½
993.1	Fairmont and Palatine 1897	G3894 .F2A3 1897 .F6	T. M. Fowler, Morrisville, Pa.	T. M. Fowler & James B. Moyer		20 × 29
994	Fairmont & Palatine 1897	G3894 .F2A3 1897 .F6 Fow 77	T. M. Fowler, Morrisville, Pa. (T. M. Fowler Map Coll. 77)	T. M. Fowler & James B. Moyer		20½ × 29
995	Grafton 1898	G3894 .G8A3 1898 .D6	A. E. Downs, Boston, Mass.	Fowler & Downs, Boston, Mass.		23 × 26½
996	Harrisville 1899	G3894 .H3A3 1899 .F6	T. M. Fowler, Morrisville, Pa.	T. M. Fowler & James B. Moyer		13 × 20
997	Keyser 1905	G3894 .K4A3 1905 .F6	T. M. Fowler, Morrisville, Pa.	Fowler & Kelly		8 × 10 Photograph
998	Keystone 1911	G3894 .K5A3 1911 .F6 Fow 56	[T. M. Fowler] (T. M. Fowler Map Coll. 56)	T. M. Fowler, Flemington, New Jersey		9½ × 20
999	Mannington 1897	G3894 .M3A3 1897 .F6	T. M. Fowler, Morrisville, Pa.	T. M. Fowler & James B. Moyer		17½ × 22½
1000	Morgantown 1897	G3894 .M7A3 1897 .F6	T. M. Fowler, Morrisville, Pa.	T. M. Fowler & James B. Moyer		19 × 28
1000.1	Moundsville 1899	G3894 .M8A3 1899 .D6	A. E. Downs, Boston, Mass.	James B. Moyer, Myerstown, Pa.		20 × 25½
1001	Moundsville 1899	G3894 .M8A3 1899 .F6 Fow 75	A. E. Downs, Boston, Mass. (T. M. Fowler Map Coll. 75)	James B. Moyer, Myerstown, Pennsylvania		20 × 25½
1002	New Martinsville 1899	G3894 .N4A3 1899 .F6	T. M. Fowler, Morrisville, Pa.	T. M. Fowler & James B. Moyer		18½ × 24½
1003	North Fork and Clark 1911	G3894 .N8A3 1911 .F6 Fow 57	[T. M. Fowler] (T. M. Fowler Map Coll. 57)	T. M. Fowler, Flemington, New Jersey		9 × 18
1004	Parkersburg [1861]	G3894 .P3A35 1861 .H6			A. Hoen & Co., Baltimore	20 × 31

Entry No.	City and Date	LC Call No.	Artist	Publisher	Lithographer	Map Size (inches)
1005	Parkersburg 1899	G3894 .P3A3 1899 .F6	T. M. Fowler, Morrisville, Pa.	T. M. Fowler & James B. Moyer		20 × 32½
1006	Parsons 1905	G3894 .P33A3 1905 .F6	Fowler & Kelly, Morrisville, Pa.	Fowler & Kelly, Morrisville, Pa.		20 × 22
1006.1	Pennsboro 1899	G3894 .P4A3 1899 .F6	T. M. Fowler, Morrisville, Pa.	T. M. Fowler & James B. Moyer		13½ × 20½
1007	Pennsboro 1899	G3894 .P4A3 1899 .F6 Fow 63	T. M. Fowler, Morrisville, Pa. (T. M. Fowler Map Coll. 63)	T. M. Fowler & James B. Moyer		14 × 20½
1008	Philippi 1861	G3894 .P47A3 1861 .P6	Mrs. M. D. Pool, Virginia			21 × 30
1009	Philippi 1897	G3894 .P47A3 1897 .F6	T. M. Fowler, Morrisville, Pa.	T. M. Fowler & James B. Moyer		12 × 15½
1010	St. Mary's 1899	G3894 .S24A3 1899 .F6	T. M. Fowler, Morrisville, Pa.	T. M. Fowler & James B. Moyer		12½ × 20½
1011	Salem 1899	G3894 .S3A3 1899 .F6	T. M. Fowler, Morrisville, Pa.	T. M. Fowler & James B. Moyer		15 × 23
1011.1	Sistersville 1896	G3894 .S46A3 1896 .F6	T. M. Fowler, Morrisville, Pa.	T. M. Fowler & James B. Moyer		16 × 21½
1012	Sistersville 1896	G3894 .S46A3 1896 .F6 Fow 67	T. M. Fowler, Morrisville, Pa. (T. M. Fowler Map Coll. 67)	T. M. Fowler & James B. Moyer		16 × 21½
1013	Wellsburg 1899	G3894 .W4A3 1899 .F6	T. M. Fowler, Morrisville, Pa.	T. M. Fowler, Morrisville, Pa.		8 × 10 Photograph
1014	Weston 1900	G3894 .W5A3 1900 .F6	T. M. Fowler, Morrisville, Pa.	T. M. Fowler & James B. Moyer		14 × 23½
1015	West Union 1899	G3894 .A95A3 1899 .F6	T. M. Fowler, Morrisville, Pa.	T. M. Fowler & James B. Moyer		8 × 10 Photograph
1016	Wheeling 1870	G3894 .W6A3 1870 .R8 Rug 180	[Albert Ruger] (Ruger Map Coll. 180)	Ruger & Stoner, Madison, Wisconsin	Chicago Lithographing Co., Chicago, Ill.	22½ × 34

		Wisconsin				
Entry No.	**City and Date**	**LC Call No.**	**Artist**	**Publisher**	**Lithographer**	**Map Size (inches)**
1016.1	Alma [1880]	G4124 .A35A3 1880 .B7	H. Brosius	Ruger & Stoner, Madison, Wis.	Beck & Pauli, Litho., Milwaukee, Wis.	13½ × 23 Positive and negative photostats
1017	Antigo 1886	G4124 .A5A3 1886 .N6		Norris, Wellge & Co., Milwaukee, Wisconsin	Beck & Pauli, Lith., Milwaukee, Wisconsin	17 × 23
1018	Appleton 1867	G4124 .A6A3 1867 .R8 Rug 181	A. Ruger, Chicago (Ruger Map Coll. 181)		Chicago Lith. Co.	22 × 28
1018.1[6]	Appleton [1881?]	G4124 .A6A3 1881 .R5	Marr Richards			8 × 10 Photograph
1019	Ashland 1886	G4124 .A8A3 1886 .W4	H. Welg [H. Wellge]	Norris, Wellge & Co., Milwaukee, Wisconsin	Beck & Pauli, Lith., Milwaukee, Wisconsin	20 × 35½
1020	Ashland 1890	G4124 .A8A3 1890 .P3	C. J. Pauli, Milwaukee, Wis.	The Ashland Daily Press	Marr & Richards Engraving, Milwaukee	23 × 41
1020.1	Baraboo 1870	G4124 .B2A3 1870 .R8		Ruger & Stoner, Madison, Wis.	Merchants Lithographing Co., Chicago	17½ × 21½ Positive and negative photostats
1021	Bayfield 1886	G4124 .B27A3 1886 .W4	H. Wellge	Norris, Wellge & Co., Milwaukee, Wisconsin	Beck & Pauli, Lith., Milwaukee, Wisconsin	17 × 20½
1022	Beaver Dam 1867	G4124 .B3A3 1867 .R8 Rug 182	A. Ruger (Ruger Map Coll. 182)		Chicago Lith. Co.	22½ × 24½
1023	Beloit 1890	G4124 .B4A3 1890 .A6	[H. Wellge]	American Publishing Co., Milwaukee, Wisconsin		22½ × 28
1024	Berlin 1867	G4124 .B5A3 1867 .R8 Rug 183	A. Ruger (Ruger Map Coll. 183)		Chicago Lith. Co.	20 × 24½
1024.1	Black Earth 1876	G4124 .B56A3 1876 .B7			D. Bremner & Co., Lith., Milwaukee	17 × 18½ Positive and negative photostats

[6]This map remains under copyright protection by the State Historical Society of Wisconsin, Madison, and may not be reproduced or republished without written permission from the society.

Entry No.	City and Date	LC Call No.	Artist	Publisher	Lithographer	Map Size (inches)
1024.2	Black River Falls [1875]	G4124 .B6A3 1875 .B7	H. Brosius	J. J. Stoner, Madison, Wis.		17½ × 22½ Positive and negative photostats
1025	Boscobel 1869	G4124 .B7A3 1869 .R8 Rug 184	[Albert Ruger] (Ruger Map Coll. 184)	Ruger & Stoner, Madison, Wisconsin	Chicago Lith. Co.	21 × 22½
1025.1	Brodhead 1871	G4124 .B79A3 1871 .B3	H. H. Bailey		Doniat & Zastrow, Milwaukee	17½ × 22½ Positive and negative photostats
1025.2	Burlington 1871	G4124 .B9A3 1871 .B3	H. H. Bailey	T. M. Fowler & Co., Madison, Wis. Reproduced from the original in the Burlington Historical Society	Chicago Lithographing Co.	12½ × 19 Negative photostat
1025.3	Burlington 1896	G4124 .B9A3 1896 .P3	[C. J. Pauli]	[C. J. Pauli] Reproduced from original held in the collections of the Burlington Historical Society		13 × 19½ Negative photostat
1026	Chippewa-Falls 1886	G4124 .C5A3 1886 .W4	H. W. [H. Wellge]	Norris, Wellge & Co., Milwaukee, Wisconsin	Beck & Pauli, Lith., Milwaukee, Wisconsin	22 × 26½
1027	Chippewa-Falls 1907	G4124 .C5A3 1907 .W4	H. W. [H. Wellge]	H. Wellge, Milwaukee, Wis.		20 × 30½
1027.1[6]	Clinton 1871	G4124 .C58A3 1871 .B3	H. H. Bailey	Reproduced from the original in the Chicago Historical Society	Doniat & Zastrow, Milwaukee	8 × 10 Photograph
1028	Columbus 1868	G4124 .C7A3 1868 .R8 Rug 185	A. Ruger (Ruger Map Coll. 185)		Chicago Lith. Co.	20 × 24
1028.1	Darlington 1871	G4124 .D3A3 1871 .B7	H. Brosius			16 × 20 Positive and negative photostats
1028.2	Darlington 1881	G4124 .D3A3 1881 .S7		J. J. Stoner, Madison, Wis.	Beck & Pauli, Lith., Milwaukee, Wis.	13½ × 20 Positive and negative photostats

[6]This map remains under copyright protection by the State Historical Society of Wisconsin, Madison, and may not be reproduced or republished without written permission from the society.

Entry No.	City and Date	LC Call No.	Artist	Publisher	Lithographer	Map Size (inches)
1028.3	Darlington 1896	G4124 .D3A3 1896 .P3	C. J. Pauli, Milwaukee, Wis.	C. J. Pauli, Milwaukee, Wis.		17½ × 17½ Positive and negative photostats
1029	Delavan 1884	G4124 .D4A3 1884 .B7	H. Brosius	J. J. Stoner, Madison, Wisconsin	Beck & Pauli, Milwaukee, Wisconsin	17½ × 27½
1029.1[6]	De Pere 1871	G4124 .D6A3 1871 .B3	H. H. Bailey		Chicago Lithographing Co.	8 × 10 Photograph
1029.2[6]	De Pere 1893	G4124 .D6A3 1893 .P3	C. J. Pauli, Milwaukee, Wis.	C. J. Pauli, Milwaukee, Wis.		8 × 10 Photograph
1029.3	Dodgeville [1875]	G4124 .D7A3 1875 .B7	H. Brosius			16½ × 20 Positive and negative photostats
1029.4	Eau Claire 1872	G4124 .E4A3 1872 .B7	H. Brosius	Reproduced [in 1975?] from copy in the State Historical Society of Wisconsin, Madison		17 × 22 Positive and negative photostats
1029.5	Eau Claire 1880	G4124 .E4A3 1880 .S7		J. J. Stoner, Madison, Wis. Reproduced [in 1975?] from the original in the State Historical Society of Wisconsin, Madison	Beck & Pauli, Milwaukee, Wis.	16½ × 22½ Positive and negative photostats
1029.6	Eau Claire 1891	G4124 .E4A3 1891 .P3	C. J. Pauli, Milwaukee	C. J. Pauli, Milwaukee. Reproduced from original in Chippewa Valley Museum, Eau Claire		11 × 14 Photograph
1029.7	Florence 1881	G4124 .F4A3 1881 .S7		J. J. Stoner, Madison, Wis.		14½ × 22 Positive and negative photostats
1030	Fond du Lac 1867	G4124 .F5A3 1867 .R8 Rug 186	A. Ruger (Ruger Map Coll. 186)		Chicago Lith. Co.	22 × 28½
1030.1	Fond du Lac 1867	G4124 .F5A3 1867 .R8 1974	A[lbert] Ruger	Reproduced by the Fond du Lac County Historical Society	Chicago Lithographing Co., Chicago	16½ × 21½ Facsimile

[6]This map remains under copyright protection by the State Historical Society of Wisconsin, Madison, and may not be reproduced or republished without written permission from the society.

Entry No.	City and Date	LC Call No.	Artist	Publisher	Lithographer	Map Size (inches)
1030.2	Fond du Lac 1896	G4124 .F5A3 1896 .P3	C. J. Pauli, Milwaukee, Wis.	C. J. Pauli, Milwaukee, Wis.		13 × 21 Positive and negative photostats
1030.3	Fond du Lac 1896	G4124 .F5A3 1896 .P3 1974	C. J. Pauli, Milwaukee, Wis.	C. J. Pauli, Milwaukee, Wis. Reproduced in 1974 from the original in the Fond du Lac Public Library		14 × 21½ Facsimile
1031	Fort Atkinson 1870	G4124 .F6A3 1870 .R8 Rug 187	[Albert Ruger] (Ruger Map Coll. 187)	Ruger & Stoner, Madison, Wisconsin	Merchant's Lith. Co., Chicago	17½ × 20½
1031.1	Grand Rapids 1874	G4124 .G625A3 1874 .C5	A. J. Cleveland	A. J. Cleveland	A. M. Oleograph Co., Mil.	17 × 22½
1032	Green Bay & Fort Howard 1867	G4124 .G7A3 1867 .R8 Rug 188	A. Ruger (Ruger Map Coll. 188)		Chicago Lith. Co.	22 × 28
1032.1[7]	Green Bay & Fort Howard 1893	G4124 .G7A3 1893 .P3	C. J. Pauli, Milwaukee, Wis.	C. J. Pauli, Milwaukee, Wis.		12½ × 19½ Positive photostat
1032.2	Hartford 1879	G4124 .H3A3 1879 .S7		J. J. Stoner, Madison, Wis.	Beck & Pauli, Lith., Milwaukee, Wis.	15½ × 22½ Positive and negative photostats
1033	Hudson 1870	G4124 .H8A3 1870 .R8 Rug 189	[Albert Ruger] (Ruger Map Coll. 189)	Ruger & Stoner, Madison, Wisconsin	Merchant's Lith. Co., Chicago	20½ × 23
1034	Hurley 1886	G4124 .H9A3 1886 .N6		Norris, Wellge & Co., Milwaukee, Wisconsin	Beck & Pauli, Lith., Milwaukee, Wisconsin	12½ × 19
1034.1	Janesville 1877	G4124 .J3A3 1877 .V6			C. H. Vogt & Co., Milwaukee, Wis.	17½ × 19½ Positive and negative photostats
1035	Jefferson 1870	G4124 .J4A3 1870 .R8 Rug 190	[Albert Ruger] (Ruger Map Coll. 190)	Ruger & Stoner, Madison, Wisconsin	Chicago Lith. Co.	20½ × 23

[7]Reproduction rights restricted. Contact Neville Public Museum, Green Bay, Wisconsin.

Entry No.	City and Date	LC Call No.	Artist	Publisher	Lithographer	Map Size (inches)
1035.1[8]	Kaukauna [1882?]	G4124 .K3A3 1882 .R5	[Marr Richards]			8 × 10 Photograph
1035.2	Kaukauna 1886	G4124 .K3A3 1886 .W4	H. Wellge	Norris, Wellge & Co., Milwaukee, Wis.	Beck & Pauli, Litho., Milwaukee, Wis.	16½ × 19½ Positive and negative photostats
1035.3	Kewaskum 1878	G4124 .K42A3 1878 .P3				17½ × 20½ Positive and negative photostats
1035.4	Kewaunee 1893	G4124 .K45A3 1893 .P3	C. J. Pauli, Milwaukee, Wis.	C. J. Pauli, Milwaukee, Wis.		16 × 16 Positive photostat
1035.5	Kilbourn City 1870	G4124 .W79A3 1870 .B3	H. H. Bailey		Doniat & Zastrow, Milwaukee	15½ × 18½ Positive and negative photostats
1036	La Crosse 1867	G4124 .L2A3 1867 .R8 Rug 191	A. Ruger (Ruger Map Coll. 191)		Chicago Lith. Co.	23 × 28½
1037	La Crosse 1873	G4124 .L2A35 1873 .E5	Geo. H. Ellsbury		Milwaukee Lith. & Eng. Co.	14 × 23½
1038	La Crosse 1887	G4124 .L2A3 1887 .W4		H. Wellge, Milwaukee, Wisconsin	Beck & Pauli, Lith., Milwaukee, Wisconsin	23 × 41
1038.1	[Lake] Geneva 1871	G4124 .L3A3 1871 .B3	H. H. Bailey		Chicago Lithographin[g] Co.	15½ × 20½
1038.2	Lake Geneva 1882	G4124 .L3A3 1882 .W4	[Henry] Wellge & [Albert] Poole	J. J. Stoner, Madison, Wis.	Beck & Pauli, Lithographers, Milwaukee, Wis.	20 × 32½
1038.3	Lancaster [1875]	G4124 .L4A3 1875 .B7	H. Brosius	J. J. Stoner, Madison, Wis.		17½ × 20 Positive and negative photostats
1038.4	Lone Rock 1879	G4124 .L75A3 1879 .B4				13 × 17½ Positive and negative photostats

[8]This map remains under copyright protection by the State Historical Society of Wisconsin, Madison, and may not be reproduced or republished without written permission from the society.

Entry No.	City and Date	LC Call No.	Artist	Publisher	Lithographer	Map Size (inches)
1038.5	Madison 1855	G4124 .M2A35 1855 .D6 1974	S. H. Donnel	Reproduced in 1974 by Historic Urban Plans, Ithaca, New York	C. Curriers, Lith., N.Y.	15½ × 19 Facsimile
1039	Madison 1867	G4124 .M2A3 1867 .R8 Rug 192	A. Ruger (Ruger Map Coll. 192)		Chicago Lith. Co., Chicago	21½ × 28½
1040	Madison 1885	G4124 .M2A3 1885 .N6		Norris, Wellge & Co., Milwaukee, Wisconsin	Beck & Pauli, Lith., Milwaukee, Wisconsin	22 × 31½
1041	Madison 1885	G4124 .M2A3 1885 .N61		Norris, Wellge & Co., Milwaukee		27½ × 41½
1041.1	Manitowoc 1883	G4124 .M3A3 1883 .S7		J. J. Stoner, Madison, Wis.	Beck & Pauli, Lithographers, Milwaukee, Wis.	12 × 21 Positive and negative photostats
1041.2	Manitowoc [1895]	G4124 .M3A3 1895 .P3	C. J. Pauli, Milwaukee, Wis.	C. J. Pauli, Milwaukee, Wis.		13½ × 20 Positive and negative photostats
1041.3	Marinette 1881	G4124 .M4A3 1881 .S7		J. J. Stoner, Madison, Wis.	Beck & Pauli, Lith., Milwaukee, Wis.	11 × 23 Positive and negative photostats
1041.4	Marshall 1879	G4124 .M48A3 1879 .S7		J. J. Stoner, Madison, Wis.	Beck & Pauli, Lith., Milwaukee, Wis.	14 × 19½ Positive and negative photostats
1041.5	Mauston 1870	G4124 .M55A3 1870 .B3	H. H. Bailey		Doniat & Zastrow, Milwaukee	15½ × 22 Positive and negative photostats
1041.6	Mazomanie [1875]	G4124 .M565A3 1875 .B7	H. Brosius	J. J. Stoner, Madison, Wis.	C. Shober & Co., Prop. Chicago Lith. Co.	14½ × 17
1042	Medford 1885	G4124 .M57A3 1885 .W4	H. Wellge	Norris, Wellge & Co., Milwaukee, Wisconsin	Beck & Pauli, Lith., Milwaukee, Wisconsin	15 × 18½
1042.1	Menasha 1870	G4124 .M6A3 1870 .B3	H. H. Bailey		Doniat & Zastrow, Milwaukee	17 × 19½ Positive and negative photostats

Madison, Wisconsin, 1867. Drawn by Albert Ruger.
During the 1860s and 1870s the major publishers and
lithographers of panoramic maps were concentrated in
the Chicago-Milwaukee area because of proximity to the
artists' center of Madison.

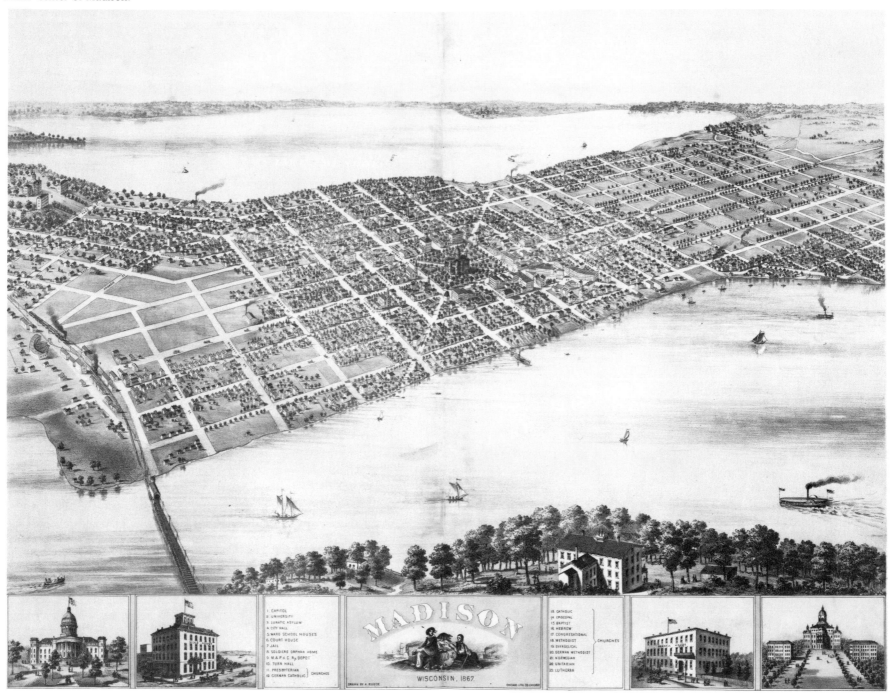

Entry No.	City and Date	LC Call No.	Artist	Publisher	Lithographer	Map Size (inches)
1042.2	Menomonee [sic] [1875]	G4124 .M62A3 1875 .B7	H. Brosius			16½ × 20 Positive and negative photostats
1043	Menomonee Falls 1886	G4124 .M613A3 1886 .N6		Norris, Wellge & Co., Milwaukee, Wisconsin	Beck & Pauli, Lith., Milwaukee, Wisconsin	12 × 18½
1044	Merrill 1883	G4124 .M63A3 1883 .W4	H. Wellge	J. J. Stoner, Madison, Wisconsin	Beck & Pauli, Lith., Milwaukee, Wisconsin	13½ × 31
1044.1	Middleton 1876	G4124 .M67A3 1876 .B4				16½ × 19½ Positive and negative photostats
1044.2	Milton Junction 1881	G4124 .M69A3 1881 .B4				13½ × 21 Positive and negative photostats
1044.3	Milwaukee [1854]	Prints & Photographs Division	Geo. J. Robertson	Smith Brothers & Co., New York	D. W. Moody, Lith.	27½ × 40½
1045	Milwaukee [ca. 1872]	G4124 .M7A3 1872 .B3	H. H. Bailey	Holzapfel & Eskuche, Milwaukee, Wisconsin	Milwaukee Lith. & Eng. Co.	27 × 39
1046	Milwaukee 1879	G4124 .M7A3 1879 .S7		J. J. Stoner & Co., Madison, Wisconsin	Beck & Pauli, Lith., Milwaukee, Wisconsin	26½ × 39
1047	Milwaukee 1882	G4124 .M7A35 1882 .B4		Beck & Pauli, Milwaukee, Wisconsin		16½ × 27
1047.1	Milwaukee 1882	G4124 .M7A35 1882 .B4 1978		Reproduced in 1978 by Historic Urban Plans, Ithaca, New York	Beck & Pauli, Milwaukee, Wis.	16 × 25½ Facsimile
1047.2	Milwaukee 1898	Prints & Photographs Division			The Gugler Lithographic Co., Milwaukee, Wis.	14½ × 47½
1047.3	Mineral Point 1872	G4124 .M74A3 1872 .B7	H. Brosius			16 × 19½ Positive and negative photostats
1047.4	Mineral Point 1872	G4124 .M74A3 1872 .B7 1971	H. Brosius	Reproduced in 1971 by the Mineral Point Historical Society		18 × 23½ Facsimile

Entry No.	City and Date	LC Call No.	Artist	Publisher	Lithographer	Map Size (inches)
1047.5	Monroe 1871	G4124 .M8A3 1871 .B3	H. H. Bailey		Doniat & Zastrow, Milwaukee	17 × 20½ Positive and negative photostats
1047.6	Muscoda 1879	G4124 .M94A3 1879 .M8				15 × 20½ Positive and negative photostats
1047.7	Neenah 1870	G4124 .N2A3 1870 .B3	H. H. Bailey		Doniat & Zastrow, Milwaukee, Wis.	16 × 21 Positive and negative photostats
1047.8	Neillsville 1880	G4124 .N213A3 1880 .S7		J. J. Stoner, Madison, Wis.	Beck & Pauli, Lith., Milwaukee, Wis.	12 × 22½ Positive and negative photostats
1047.9	New-London 1871	G4124 .N4A3 1871 .B3	H. H. Bailey		Chicago Lithographing Co.	15½ × 23½ Positive and negative photostats
1047.95	Oconomowoc 1870	G4124 .O3A3 1870 .B3	H. H. Bailey	T. M. Fowler & Co., Madison, Wis.	Doniat & Zastrow, Milwaukee	17½ × 23 Positive and negative photostats
1047.96	Oconomowoc 1885	G4124 .O3A3 1885 .W4	H. Wellge	Norris, Wellge & Co., Milwaukee, Wis.	Beck & Pauli, Litho., Milwaukee, Wis.	19½ × 30½
1048	Oconomowoc [1890?]	G4124 .O3A3 1890 .M3		Marr & Richards Eng. Co., Milwaukee, Wis.	Marr & Richards Eng. Co., Milwaukee, Wis.	16½ × 34½
1048.1	Omro 1870	G4124 .O58A3 1870 .F6		Th. M. Fowler & Co., Madison, Wis.	Chicago Lithographing Co.	16½ × 22 Positive and negative photostats
1048.2	Oshkosh [185-?]	Prints & Photographs Division	L. Kurz	Kurz & Seifert, Milwaukee, Wis.	Kurz & Seifert, Milwaukee, Wis.	16½ × 22½
1049	Oshkosh 1867	G4124 .O8A3 1867 .R8 Rug 193	A. Ruger (Ruger Map Coll. 193)		Chicago Lith. Co.	22½ × 28½

Entry No.	City and Date	LC Call No.	Artist	Publisher	Lithographer	Map Size (inches)
1049.1	Peshtigo 1871	G4124 .P3A3 1871 .F6		T. M. Fowler & Co., Madison, Wis.	Chars. Shober & Co., Props. Chicago Lith. Co.	16½ × 20 Positive and negative photostats
1049.2	Peshtigo 1881	G4124 .P3A3 1881 .S7		J. J. Stoner, Madison, Wis.	Beck & Pauli, Lith., Milwaukee, Wis.	16 × 22½ Positive and negative photostats
1049.3	Platteville [1875]	G4124 .P4A3 1875 .B7	H. Brosius			17 × 20½ Positive and negative photostats
1049.4	Plymouth 1870	G4124 .P5A3 1870 .B3	H. H. Bailey		Doniat & Zastrow, Milwaukee	15½ × 22 Positive and negative photostats
1050	Portage 1868	G4124 .P7A3 1868 .R8 Rug 194	A. Ruger (Ruger Map Coll. 194)		Chicago Lith. Co.	22½ × 28
1051	Prairie du Chien 1870	G4124 .P8A3 1870 .R8 Rug 195	[Albert Ruger] (Ruger Map Coll. 195)	Ruger & Stoner, Madison, Wisconsin	Chicago Lith. Co.	21 × 23½
1052	Prairie du Sac 1870	G4124 .P82A3 1870 .R8 Rug 196	[Albert Ruger] (Ruger Map Coll. 196)	Ruger & Stoner, Madison, Wisconsin	Chicago Lith. Co.	16 × 17
1052.1	Racine 1874	G4124 .R2A3 1874 .B7	H. Brosius	J. J. Stoner, Madison, Wis.	Chas. Shober & Co. Prop., Chicago Lith. Co.	15 × 21½ Positive and negative photostats
1053	Racine 1883 (Inset Racine 1841)	G4124 .R2A3 1883 .S7		J. J. Stoner, Madison, Wisconsin		23 × 34
1054	Reedsburg 1874	G4124 .R3A3 1874 .R8 Rug 197	[Albert Ruger] (Ruger Map Coll. 197)	J. J. Stoner, Madison, Wisconsin	J. Knauber & Co., Milwaukee, Wisconsin	15 × 16½
1054.1	Richland Center [1875]	G4124 .R6A3 1875 .B7	H. Brosius	J. J. Stoner, Madison, Wis.		16 × 21 Positive and negative photostats

Entry No.	City and Date	LC Call No.	Artist	Publisher	Lithographer	Map Size (inches)
1055	Ripon 1867	G4124 .R7A3 1867 .R8 Rug 198	A. Ruger (Ruger Map Coll. 198)		Chicago Lith. Co.	21 × 24
1056	Sauk City 1870	G4124 .S3A3 1870 .R8 Rug 199	[Albert Ruger] (Ruger Map Coll. 199)	Ruger & Stoner, Madison, Wisconsin	Chicago Lith. Co.	15 × 18½
1057	Sheboygan 1885	G4124 .S4A3 1885 .W4	H. Wellge	Norris, Wellge & Co., Milwaukee, Wisconsin	Beck & Pauli, Lith., Milwaukee, Wisconsin	22½ × 31
1057.1	Sheboygan 1885 (on verso of Oconomowoc 1885)	G4124 .O3A3 1885 .W4		Norris, Wellge & Co., Milwaukee, Wis.	Beck & Pauli, Litho., Milwaukee, Wis.	22½ × 31
1057.2[8]	Sheboygan Falls 1871	G4124 .S42A3 1871 .B3	H. H. Bailey	Th. M. Fowler & Co., Madison, Wis.	Calvert Lith. Co., Detroit	8 × 10 Photograph
1057.3	Stoughton 1871	G4124 .S77A3 1871 .B3	H. H. Bailey		Chicago Lithographing Co.	15½ × 21 Positive and negative photostats
1057.4	Stoughton 1883	G4124 .S77A3 1883 .S7		J. J. Stoner, Madison, Wis.	Beck & Pauli, Lithographers, Milwaukee, Wis.	12 × 21 Positive and negative photostats
1057.5	Sun Prairie [1875]	G4124 .S87A3 1875 .B7	H. Brosius	J. J. Stoner, Madison, Wis		16½ × 19 Positive and negative photostats
1058	Superior 1883	G4124 .S9A3 1883 .W4	H. Wellge	J. J. Stoner, Madison, Wisconsin	Beck & Pauli, Lith., Milwaukee, Wisconsin	13 × 31½
1058.1	Superior 1893	G4124 .S9A3 1893 .L3	Charles Lagro	Charles Lagro		15½ × 20½ Positive and negative photostats
1059	Superior 1913	G4124 .S9A3 1913 .B7		Bradley-Brink Co.	Bureau of Engraving, Minneapolis	21 × 27½
1060	Superior, Wisconsin & Duluth, Minnesota 1915	G4124 .S9A3 1915 .W4	H. Wellge; Russell		Freeman Eng. Co., Minneapolis	16½ × 35½

Entry No.	City and Date	LC Call No.	Artist	Publisher	Lithographer	Map Size (inches)
1060.1	Tomah 1870	G4124 .T6A3 1870 .B3	H. H. Bailey		Doniat & Zastrow, Milwaukee	15 × 20½ Positive and negative photostats
1060.2	Viroqua 1879	G4124 .V8A3 1879 .S7		J. J. Stoner, Madison, Wis.	Beck & Pauli, Lith., Milwaukee, Wis.	15 × 21 Positive and negative photostats
1061	Washburn 1886	G4124 .W16A3 1886 .N6		Norris, Wellge & Co., Milwaukee, Wisconsin	Beck & Pauli, Milwaukee, Wisconsin	16 × 20½
1061.1	Waterloo [1875]	G4124 .W19A3 1875 .B7	H. Brosius	J. J. Stoner, Madison, Wis.		15 × 20½ Positive and negative photostats
1062	Watertown 1867	G4124 .W2A3 1867 .R8 Rug 200	A. Ruger (Ruger Map Coll. 200)		Chicago Lith. Co.	22½ × 28½
1063	Watertown 1885	G4124 .W2A3 1885 .W4	H. Wellge	Norris, Wellge & Co., Milwaukee, Wisconsin	Beck & Pauli, Milwaukee, Wisconsin	23 × 31½
1063.1	Waukesha [185-?]	Prints & Photographs Division	L. Kurz	Kurz & Seifert, Milwaukee	Kurz & Seifert, Milwaukee	16½ × 22½
1063.2	Waukesha 1874	G4124 .W3A3 1874 .S7		J. J. Stoner, Madison, Wis.		16½ × 19½ Positive and negative photostats
1064	Waukesha 1880	G4124 .W3A3 1880 .W4	H. Wellge	J. J. Stoner, Madison, Wisconsin	Beck & Pauli, Lith., Milwaukee, Wisconsin	20 × 26
1064.1[8]	Waupaca 1871	G4124 .W34A3 1871 .B3	H. H. Bailey	Th. M. Fowler & Co., Madison, Wis.	Chicago Lithographing Co.	8 × 10 Photograph
1064.2	Waupun 1870	G4124 .W38A3 1870 .B3	H. H. Bailey		Chicago Lithographing Co.	15 × 21 Positive and negative photostats
1064.3	Waupun 1885	G4124 .W38A3 1885 .W4	H. Wellge	Norris, Wellge & Co., Milwaukee, Wis.	Beck & Pauli, Litho., Milwaukee, Wis.	17 × 24½

[8]This map remains under copyright protection by the State Historical Society of Wisconsin, Madison, and may not be reproduced or republished without written permission from the society.

Entry No.	City and Date	LC Call No.	Artist	Publisher	Lithographer	Map Size (inches)
1064.4	Wausau 1891	G4124 .W4A3 1891 .P3	C. J. Pauli, Milwaukee, Wis.	C. J. Pauli, Milwaukee, Wis.		14½ × 22 Positive and negative photostats
1065	Wauwatosa & Western Suburbs of Milwaukee 1892	G4124 .W5A3 1892 .M3		Marr & Richard Engraving Co., Milwaukee		20 × 29
1065.1	West Bend 1878	G4124 .W62A3 1878 .W4				15½ × 23 Positive and negative photostats
1066	West Superior 1887	G4124 .S9: 2W4A3 1887 .H4	Henry Wellge & Co., Milwaukee, Wis.	A. L. Langellier		18 × 21½
1066.1	Weyauwega 1870	G4124 .W68A3 1870 .B3	H. H. Bailey		Doniat & Zastrow, Milwaukee	16 × 16½ Positive and negative photostats
1066.2	Whitewater 1870	G4124 .W73A3 1870 .R8		Ruger & Stoner	Merchants Lith. Co., Chicago	17½ × 19 Positive and negative photostats
1067	Whitewater 1885	G4124 .W73A3 1885 .N6		Norris, Wellge & Co., Milwaukee, Wisconsin	Beck & Pauli, Lith., Milwaukee, Wisconsin	19½ × 31

Wyoming

Entry No.	City and Date	LC Call No.	Artist	Publisher	Lithographer	Map Size (inches)
1067.1	Cheyenne 1870	G4264 .C5A3 1870 .K6	Augustus Koch	Reproduced from original in the Wyoming State Archives, Museums and Historical Department, Cheyenne	Chicago Lithographing Co.	8 × 10 Photograph
1068	Cheyenne 1882	G4264 .C5A3 1882 .S7	J. J. Stoner	J. J. Stoner, Madison, Wisconsin	Beck & Pauli, Lith., Milwaukee, Wisconsin	18 × 23½
1068.1	Cheyenne 1882	G4264 .C5A3 1882 .S7 1974		J. J. Stoner, Madison, Wis. Reproduced in 1974 by Historic Urban Plans, Ithaca, New York	Beck & Pauli, Lithographers, Milwaukee, Wis.	16 × 20½ Facsimile

Canada

Entry No.	City and Date	LC Call No.	Artist	Publisher	Lithographer	Map Size (inches)
1069	Brantford, Ontario 1875	G3464 .B7A3 1875 .B7	H. Brosius		Chas. Shober & Co., Prop's Chicago Lith. Co.	23 × 32½
1069.1[9]	Brockville, Ontario 1874	G3464 .B8A3 1874 .B7	H. Brosius		Chas. Shober & Co., Props. Chicago Lith. Co.	Positive photostat in 2 parts, each 21 × 17
1069.2[9]	Charlottetown, Prince Edward Island 1878	G3444 .C5A3 1878 .R8	[A.] Ruger			14½ × 16 Positive photostat
1070	Chatham, Ontario [1870-1880?]	G3464 .C4A3 1880 .B5				29 × 39
1070.1[9]	Dawson, Yukon Territory 1903	G3524 .D3A3 1903 .E6	H. Epting		B. C. Print & Engr. Corp. Ltd., Vancouver, B. C.	Positive photostat in 2 parts, each 16 × 13
1070.2	Frederickton, New Brunswick 1882	G3434 .F7A3 1882 .H8 1979	Alexander M. Hubly	Reproduced from the original held in the collections of the Provincial Archives, Frederickton	O. H. Bailey & Co., Lith.	22 × 27 Facsimile
1071	Halifax, Nova Scotia 1879	G3424 .H2A3 1879 .R8 Rug 1	A. Ruger (Ruger Map Coll. 1)			20 × 35½
1071.1	Halifax, Nova Scotia 1890	G3424 .H2A3 1890 .C8 1973		D. D. Currie, Moncton, N. B. Reproduced in 1973 by Mr. Laurie LaViolette, Scotia Sales and Marketing, Halifax		18½ × 28 Facsimile
1071.2	Hamilton, Ontario 1859	Prints & Photographs Division	G. S. Rice	Rice & Duncan	Lith. of Endicott & Co., N.Y.	25½ × 36
1071.3[9]	Kentville, Nova Scotia 1879	G3424 .K4A3 1879 .F6	T. M. Fowler		Kentville Publishing Company Limited	16 × 22 Positive photostat
1071.4	Kingston, Ontario 1875	G3464 .K5A3 1875 .B7 1970	H. Brosius	J. J. Stoner, Madison, Wis.	Chas. Shober & Co., Chicago Lith. Co.	18 × 22½ Facsimile
1072	London, Ontario 1872	G3464 .L6A3 1872 .G6 1932	E. S. Glover	Reproduced in 1932 for Smallman & Ingram, Ltd.		15 × 25½ Reprint

[9]*Reproduced from the original in the National Map Collections, Public Archives of Canada, Ottawa.*

Brantford, Ontario, Canada, 1875. Drawn by Herman Brosius. Published by Charles Shober & Co., Chicago, Illinois. This is one of the most sophisticated urban designs of the thirty-six Canadian views in the Geography and Map Division.

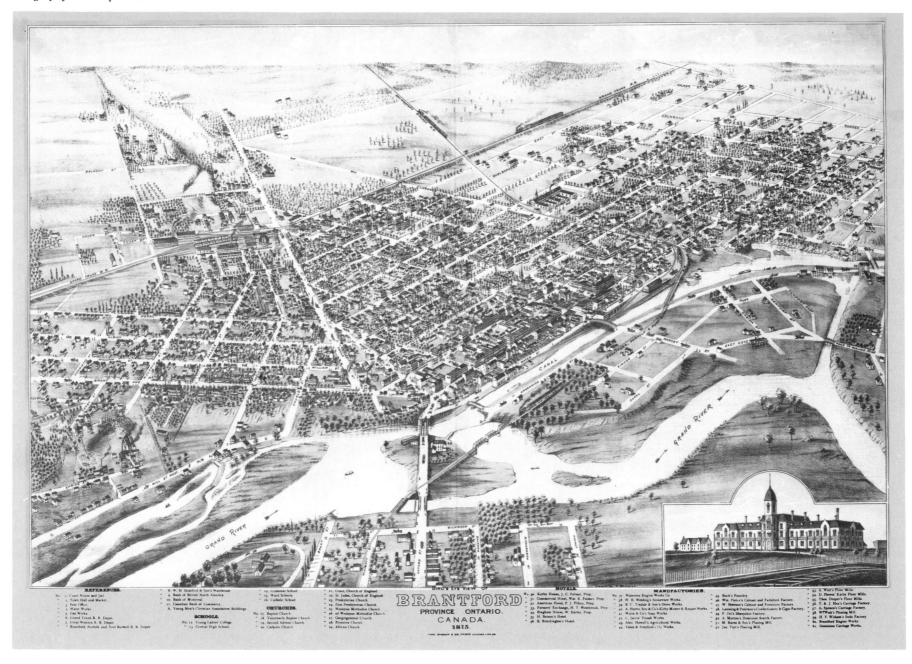

Entry No.	City and Date	LC Call No.	Artist	Publisher	Lithographer	Map Size (inches)
1072.1	Louisburg, Nova Scotia 1758	G3424 .L6A3 1758 .I6 1970	Capt. Ince	Reproduced in 1970 by Historic Urban Plans, Ithaca, New York		15½ × 20 Facsimile
1072.2[9]	Montreal, Quebec 1889	G3454 .M8A35 1889 .G4	George Bishop		George Bishop, Eng. & Print. Co.	12 × 17 Positive photostat
1072.3[9]	Norwich, Ontario 1881	G3464 .N8A3 1881 .F6	[T. M. Fowler]			8 × 10 Photograph
1072.4	Ottawa, Ontario 1876	G3464 .O8A3 1876 .B7 1969	Herm. Brosius	Reproduced in 1969 by Canada Department of Energy, Mines & Resources	Chas. Shober & Co., Chicago Lith. Co.	20½ × 26 Facsimile
1073	Ottawa, Ontario [1895?]	G3464 .O8A3 1895 .T6			Toronto Lithographing Co.	32½ × 41
1073.1[9]	Peterborough, Ontario 1875	G3464 .P5A3 1875 .B7	H. Brosius		Chas. Shober & Co., Pr. Chicago Lith. Co.	15½ × 22½ Positive photostat
1073.2[9]	Port Arthur, Ontario 1885	G3464 .P6A3 1885 .E3	R. J. Edwards, Architect, Port Arthur, Ontario	J. C. Young, Port Arthur, Ont.	Rolph Smith & Co., Toronto, Ont.	Positive photostat in 4 parts, each 17½ × 24
1073.3	Quebec, Quebec [1755]	G3454 .Q4A35 1755 .L4 Roch 4	[Georges Louis Le Rouge]			9½ × 12½
1073.4	Quebec, Quebec [1768]	G3454 .Q4A35 1768 .S6 1970	Captain Hervey Smyth; P. Benazech	Reproduced in 1970 by Historic Urban Plans, Ithaca, New York		12½ × 20 Facsimile
1073.5	St. Catharines, Province Ontario 1875	G3464 .S2A3 1875 .B7	H. Brosius	Reprinted by the St. Catharines Historical Museum 1981	Chas. Shober & Co. Prop's Chicago Lith. Co.	17½ × 23½ Reprint
1073.6[9]	St. John's, Newfoundland 1879	G3604 .S2A35 1879 .R8	A. Ruger			12 × 17 Positive photostat
1074	St. Thomas, Ontario [1896?]	G3464 .S28A3 1896 .B7	H. Brosius	J. J. Stoner, Madison, Wis.	C. H. Vogt, Lith.; J. Knauber & Co., Milwaukee	22½ × 32½
1074.1	Simcoe, Ontario 1881	G3464 .S5A3 1881 .F6	T. M. Fowler	Fowler & Coombs		17½ × 20½ Positive photostat

[9]Reproduced from the original in the National Map Collections, Public Archives of Canada, Ottawa.

Entry No.	City and Date	LC Call No.	Artist	Publisher	Lithographer	Map Size (inches)
1074.2[9]	Tilsonburg, Ontario [1881?]	G3464 .T5A3 1881 .F6	T. M. Fowler	Fowler & Rhines	Beck & Pauli, Lith., Milwaukee, Wis.	8 × 10 Photograph
1074.3[9]	Toronto, Ontario 1876	G3464 .T7A3 1876 .G7	P. A. Gross, Toronto, Ont.	P. A. Gross, Toronto, Ont.	P. A. Gross, Toronto, Ont.	Positive photostat in 8 parts, each part 22½ × 18
1074.4	Vancouver, British Columbia 1898	G3514 .V3A3 1898 .M3 1973	J. C. McLagan	Vancouver World Printing and Publishing Co., Ltd.; Repub. in 1973 by Gastown Galleries, Ltd.	Toronto Lithographing Co., Ltd.; Lithographed in 1973 by Smith Grant Mann, Ltd.	16½ × 23½ Facsimile
1075	Victoria, British Columbia 1860	G3514 .V5A35 1860 .T5	H. O. Tiedemann	Day & Son	T. Picken, Lith.	10 × 35
1076	Victoria, British Columbia 1878	G3514 .V5A3 1878 .G6	E. S. Glover	M. W. Waitt & Co., Victoria, B. C.	A. L. Bancroft & Co., Lithographers, San Francisco, Cal.	22 × 32½
1076.1	Victoria, British Columbia 1884	G3514 .V5A35 1884 .S3	L. Samuel	J. B. Ferguson & Co., Publisher & Proprietors, Victoria, B. C.	The West Shore, Portland, Or.	19 × 28
1077	Victoria, British Columbia 1889	G3514 .V5A3 1889 .E5	R. H.	Ellis & Co., Victoria, B.C.		27 × 40
1077.1[9]	Windsor, Nova Scotia 1878	G3424 .W5A3 1878 .F6	T. M. Fowler	[T. M. Fowler]		12½ × 16½ Positive photostat
1077.2	Windsor, Ontario 1878	G3464 .W7A3 1878 .F6	T. M. Fowler			11 × 16 Positive photostat
1078[9]	Winnipeg, Manitoba 1880	G3484 .W5A3 1880 .F6	T. M. Fowler	J. J. Stoner, Madison, Wisc.	Beck & Pauli, Lith., Milwaukee, Wis.	11 × 16½ Positive photostat
1079[9]	Winnipeg, Manitoba 1881	G3484 .W5A3 1881 .F6	[T. M. Fowler]		A. Mortimer Lith., Ottawa	11 × 16½ Positive photostat

[9]Reproduced from the original in the National Map Collections, Public Archives of Canada, Ottawa.

Index

Numbers refer to entries

A

A. E. D.,
    see Downs, Albert E.
Aberdeen, S. Dak., 885
Able, _____,
    see Everts & Able
Absecon, N.J., 500
Adams, W. P. C., 976
Adickes, W., 507
Adkins, R. M., 640
Adrian, Mich., 332
Akron, Ohio, 675–677
Alabama, 1–10
Albany, Ga., 120
Albany, N.Y., 533.2–534
Albert Lea, Minn., 380.1
Albion, Mich., 333
Albuquerque, N. Mex., 531.1
Alburtis, Pa., 728
Alexandria, Va., 950–950.4
Alexandria Drafting Co., 950.4
Allegheny, Pa., 832.1–832.3
Allentown, Pa., 728.1–731
Almyville, Conn., 85.2
Alsop, _____,
    see Landis & Alsop
Alton, Ill., 135
Alton, N.H., 469.2
Alton Bay, N.H., 469.2
Altoona, Pa., 731.1–731.2
Alvord, Tex., 902.1
Alvord, Kellogg & Campbell, 113
Alvord-Peters Co., 707
Amarillo, Tex., 903
Ambler, Pa., 731.3
American Oleograph Co., 77.3,
    325.1

American Publishing Co., 58.2,
    65, 74, 170, 185, 193, 207,
    210, 214–215, 454, 457–457.1,
    461–462, 464, 466, 911–911.2,
    918, 926, 930, 951, 953,
    957–957.1, 960, 962, 963, 965,
    1023
American West Publishing Co., 35.1
Amerine, C. H., 59.1
Amesbury, Mass., 263.3–265
Amesville, Ohio, 677.1
Amityville, N.Y., 535
Anaheim, Calif., 16.1
Andreas, Alfred T., *Illustrated
    Historical Atlas of the State of
    Iowa,* 205.1, 208.2,
    209.1–209.2, 212.1, 223.1,
    224.1
Andreas, Alfred T., *An Illustrated
    Historical Atlas of the State of
    Minnesota,* 382, 388, 399, 403
Ann Arbor, Mich., 334–334.1
Annapolis, Md., 252
Anniston, Ala., 1–3
Anoka, Minn., 381
Ansonia, Conn., 76.1–77
Antigo, Wis., 1017
Antrim, N.H., 469.3
Antwerp, N.Y., 536
Apollo, Pa., 732
Appleton, Minn., 382
Appleton, Wis., 1018–1018.1
Archbald, Pa., 733
Ardmore, Okla., 713.2
Arizona, 10.1–11.2
Arkansas, 12–16
Arlington, N.J., 501
Armstrong & Co., 277, 307
Arnold, _____,
    see Spike & Arnold Map
    Publishing Co.
Arnold, W., 969
Asbury Park, N.J., 501.1–504
Ashburnham, Mass., 267

Asheville, N.C., 658–659
Ashland, Mass., 268
Ashland, N.H., 470
Ashland, Wis., 1019–1020
Ashtabula Harbor, Ohio, 678
Aspen, Colo., 53.2
Aspen Times (Aspen, Colo.), 53.2
Asselineau, Charles, 826.6
Atchison, Kans., 226–226.1
Athol, Mass., 269
Atlanta, Ga., 121.1–123
Atlantic, Iowa, 205.1
Atlantic City, N.J., 504.1–509
Atlantic Highlands, N.J., 510
Attica, Ind., 191
Atwater, Lyman W.,
    see Parsons & Atwater
Atwill, _____,
    see Casilear & Atwill

Aurora, Ill., 136–137
Aurora, Mo., 417.1
Austen, Edward J., 468
Austin, Minn., 383
Avoca, Pa., 733.1
Ayer, Mass., 270
Azusa, Calif., 16.2

B

B.C. Print & Engr. Corp. Ltd.,
    1070.1
Bachman, John, 80.3, 240.1, 272.3,
    276–276.2, 594.3, 594.6,
    595.3–595.4, 827.1
Bailey, H. H., 191.1, 354.1, 367,
    873.1, 1025.1–1025.2, 1027.1,
    1029.1, 1035.5, 1038.1, 1041.5,
    1042.1, 1045, 1047.5, 1047.7,
    1047.9–1047.95, 1049.4,
    1057.2–1057.3, 1060.1,
    1064.1–1064.2, 1066.1
Bailey (H. H.) & Co., 106, 568
Bailey (H. H.) & Hazen (J. C.), 102.2,
    304.1–304.2, 305.1–305.2

Russell, _____, 1060
Russian River Valley, Calif., 21
Rutherford, N.J., 526
Rutland, Vt., 943
Ryan, W. A., 966

S

S & O Engraving Co., 124.1
Sachse, Adolphe, 254.1
Sachse (Adolphe) & Co., 109–110, 254.1
Sachse, Edward, 106.2, 253–253.1, 788
Sachse, (Edward) & Co., 106.2–106.3, 106.5, 253–254, 258.1, 638, 876.2, 956
Sacramento, Calif., 31.1–32
Saginaw, Mich., 373–374
Saint, Robert M., 411
St. Albans, Vt., 943.1
St. Anthony, Minn., 393–393.1
St. Catharines, Ont., Canada, 1073.5
St. Catharines Historical Museum (Ontario, Canada), 1073.5
St. Charles, Mo., 436
St. Clair, Mich., 375
St. Cloud, Minn., 406
St. Johns, Mich., 376
St. John's, Newfld., Canada, 1073.6
St. Johnsbury, Vt., 944
St. Johnsville, N.Y., 627
St. Joseph, Mo., 437
St. Louis, Mo., 438–448
St. Louis (Mo.) Globe-Democrat Job Printing Co., 439
St. Mary's, Pa., 841
St. Mary's, W. Va., 1010
St. Mary's City, Md., 263.1–263.2
St. Mary's City Commission, Md., 263.1–263.2
St. Paul, Minn., 406.1–411
St. Peter, Minn., 412
St. Thomas, Ont., Canada, 1074

Salem, Mass., 321.1
Salem, N.Y., 628
Salem, Oreg., 724.1, 726
Salem, W. Va., 1011
Salida, Colo., 75
Salisbury Mills, Mass., 263.3
Salmon Falls, N.H., 494
Salt Lake City, Utah, 927–930
Salzburg, Mich., 338
Samuel, Leo, 1076.1
Sandby, Paul, 737.2
San Bernardino, Calif., 32.1
San Buenaventura, Calif., 32.2
San Diego, Calif., 19.1, 32.3–33
San Diego Bay, Calif., 19.1, 208.2
Sandusky, Ohio, 705–707
Sandwich, Ill., 186
Sandy Hill, N.Y., 629
Sanford, Maine, 251
San Francisco, Calif., 33.1–38
San Gabriel, Calif., 39–39.1
San Jacinto, Calif., 39.2
San Jose, Calif., 40–42
San Luis Obispo, Calif., 42.1
San Mateo, Calif., 43
San Mateo Park, Calif., 44
San Pedro, Calif., 44.1
Santa Barbara, Calif., 45–47
Santa Fe, N. Mex., 533–533.1
Santa Monica, Calif., 26
Santa Rosa, Calif., 48–48.1
Saranac, Mich., 377
Saratoga Springs, N.Y., 630
Sarnia, Ont., Canada, 370
Sarony, Napoleon, 31.1
Sarony & Major, 34.1, 272.3
Sauk City, Wis., 1056
Saunders, H.G.,
    see Saunders & Kline
Saunders & Kline, 122
Saxton, Pa., 841.1

Scalp Level, Pa., 875.1
Schaghticoke, N.Y., 631
Schaus, W., 594.2
Schellhorn, E., 788.3
Scheu, F., 512
Schlegel, G., 595.2–595.4
Schmidt Label & Lithographing Co., 11–11.1, 22.1
Schneider & Kueppers, 33
Schofield, John, 258.1
Schuylerville, N.Y., 632
Schwartz & Weaver, 737.3
Schwenksville, Pa., 842
Scio, Ohio, 708–709
Scotia Sales and Marketing, 1071.1
Scottdale, Pa., 843–843.1
Scottdale & Everson Land Co., 843
Scranton, Pa., 844
Scranton Republican Lith., Pa., 794.2
Seattle, Wash., 973–977
Sedalia, Mo., 449
Seifert, _____,
    see Kurz & Seifert
Sellersville, Pa., 845
Selma, Ala., 9
Semi-Tropic Homestead Co., 28–28.1
Seymour, Conn., 94.3
Seymour, Tex., 920.2
Shaffer, Edwin, 985
Shaffer, Harold, 985
Shakopee, Minn., 413
Sharon, Pa., 846
Sharpsville, Pa., 847
Shasta, Calif., 48.2
Shaw, C. A., 307
Sheboygan, Wis., 1057–1057.1
Sheboygan Falls, Wis., 1057.2
Sheffield, Pa., 848
Shelbyville, Ill., 187
Shelton, Conn., 95
Shenandoah, Pa., 849
Sherburne, N.Y., 633

Sheridan, Pa., 817
Shippensburg, Pa., 850
Shober (Charles) & Co., 203, 205.1, 208.2, 209.1–209.2, 212.1, 223.1, 224.1, 236–236.1, 249, 349, 357, 365, 394.1, 414.1, 416, 461.2, 467.2, 710, 1041.6, 1049.1, 1052.1, 1069–1069.1, 1071.4, 1072.4, 1073.1, 1073.5
Shober & Carqueville Lithographing Co., 2, 159, 167.1, 366, 472, 687–687.2, 922, 932.1, 936.1
    see also Chicago Lithographing Co.
Shreveport, La., 242
Shushan, N.Y., 633.1
Siasconset, Mass., 312
Sidney, N.Y., 634
Simcoe, Ont., Canada, 1074.1
Simpson, _____, 594.1
Sinking Spring, Pa., 850.1
Sinz & Fausel, 696
Sioux City, Iowa, 225
Sistersville, W. Va., 1011.1–1012
Skaneateles, N.Y., 635
Smallman & Ingram, 1072
Smith, A. M., 397–398
Smith, A. C.,
    see Bennett, L. G., and A. C. Smith, *Map of Winona County, Minnesota 1867*
Smith, F. A., 725
Smith, J. R., Jr., 834.2
Smith, J. R., Sr., 834.2
Smith, J. W., 167.1
Smith, P. H., 613
Smith & Buckingham, 697
Smith Brothers & Co., 533.2, 609.1, 624.1, 1044.3
Smith, Cremens & Co., 826.3
Smith Grant Mann, Ltd., 1074.4
Smith (Rolph) & Co., 1073.2

Smyth, Hervey, 1073.4
Snow & May, 35, 37
Snow & Roos, 35.2
Soderberg, F. & H., 30
Somerset, Pa., 851–851.1
Somers-Point, N.J., 527
Somerville, N.J., 527.1
Sonne, Charles, 146
    see also Braunhold & Sonne
Sonora, Calif., 49
Souderton, Pa., 852
South Acton, Mass., 322
South Bend, Ind., 202–204
South Bethlehem, Pa., 737.3
South Carolina, 882.1–884.1
South Coventry, Conn., 95.1
South Dakota, 885–892
South Fork, Pa., 853
South Hadley Falls, Mass., 301
South Hingham, Mass., 299
South Manchester, Conn., 97
South New Market, N.H., 495
South Norwalk, Conn., 90
South Orange, N.J., 527.2
South Peterboro, N.H., 490
South Rocky Mount, N.C., 668
Southeast Pennsylvania
    Genealogical Services, 797.1
South Weymouth, Mass., 323
South Wolfboro, N.H., 499
Southern California Land Co., 27
Southington, Conn., 96
Spearfish, S. Dak., 891.1
Spencer, Mass., 324
Spike & Arnold Map Publishing
    Co., 969
Spofford, Edward W., 255, 831.2
Spokane, Wash., 978
Spokane Falls, Wash., 978.1
Spooner, W. R., 271.2
    see also Barton & Spooner Co.
Spring City, Pa., 853.1
Springfield, Ill., 188
Springfield, Mass., 325

Springfield, Vt., 945
Stafford Springs, Conn., 97.1
Stamford, Conn., 97.2
Stamford, N.Y., 636
Stankovits & Co., 516, 614
Statesville, N.C., 669
Staunton, Va., 962.1–963
Stein, Ky., 17.1
Stewart, Ohio, 709.1
Stewart, D. J., *Combination Atlas
    Map of Logan County, Ohio,*
    680.1, 691.1
Stillwater, Minn., 414
Stillwater, N.Y., 637
Stockton, Calif., 49.1–53
Stone, N.J., 17
Stone, (N.J.) Co., 42
Stoner, Joseph J.
    Colo., 54–56, 58–58.1, 68–70,
        72–73, 75–76
    Fla., 111.5–111.7, 116.1
    Ill., 137, 173, 181
    Ind., 203
    Kans., 226.2
    Maine, 244–244.2, 246.3, 249
    Mass., 282, 301, 312–312.1,
        315
    Mich., 334–334.1, 340.1, 341.2,
        344, 349–349.3,
        356–358.1, 359.1, 360.1,
        363, 371.1, 378.1
    Minn., 380.1, 385, 391, 395,
        409.1
    Mont., 453–453.1, 456,
        458–460
    N.H., 479, 492–492.2
    N. Mex., 532–533.1
    N.Y., 554.1, 575, 608–609, 616
    N. Dak., 672–674
    Ohio, 680, 686–687.1, 691.2,
        710, 712.1
    Oreg., 720, 727

    Pa., 740.1
    S. Dak., 886, 888, 890, 892
    Vt., 932.2, 936.1, 936.3
    Wash., 967–968, 974–974.1,
        980–980.1, 984
    Wis., 1024.2, 1028.2, 1029,
        1029.5, 1029.7, 1032.1,
        1038.2–1038.3, 1041.1,
        1041.3–1041.4, 1041.6,
        1044, 1047.8, 1049.2,
        1052.1–1054.1,
        1057.4–1057.5, 1058,
        1060.2, 1061.1,
        1063.2–1064
    Wyo., 1068–1068.1
    Canada, 1071.4, 1074, 1078
    see also Ruger & Stoner,
    Stoner (J. J.) & Co., Stoner &
    Ruger
Stoner (J. J.) & Co., 1046
Stoner & Ruger, 896
Stonington, Conn., 97.3
Stoughton, Wis., 1057.3–1057.4
Strasburg, Pa., 854
Strengele, _____,
    see Clohessy & Strengele
Strickland, William, 140.1
Stringer & Townsend, 31.2
Strobel, _____, 406.1
Strobridge & Co., 56.1, 61–62, 67.1,
    199.2, 873.1, 923–924.1, 929–
    929.1
Stroudsburg, Pa., 854.1
Studley, H. W., 944
Sturdivant, G. C., 903
Suffolk, Va., 964
Sulman, T., 274, 597.2
Sunbury, Pa., 854.2
Sun Prairie, Wis., 1057.5
Sunset, Tex., 920.3
Superior, Wis., 1058–1060
Swasey, William F., 33.2–34
Syme (W. H.) & Co., 32.1
Syracuse, N.Y., 638

T

TMF, 677.1, 693.1, 709.1
Tacoma, Wash., 979–982.1
Tacony, Pa., 854.3
Tallahassee, Fla., 118–119
Tallapoosa, Ga., 131
Tamsen & Dethlefs, 595.4
Tarentum, Pa., 855–855.1
Tarentum History & Landmarks
    Foundation (Pennsylvania),
    855.1
Taunton, Mass., 325.1
Tavern Restaurant, 731.1
Taylor, Howard P., 605
Taylor, Will L., 599
Tecumseh, Kans., 230.1
Tecumseh, Mich., 378
Telford, Pa., 856–856.1
Tennessee, 893–902
Tennessee Valley Authority,
    894.1–900.2
Terre Haute, Ind., 205
Terre Hill, Pa., 857
Teufel, Robert, 404
Texarkana, Ark., 15
Texarkana, Tex., 15
Texas, 902.1–922.1
The Dalles, Oreg., 727
Thomaston, Conn., 97.4
Thomasville, Ga., 132–133
Tice, W. G., 613
Ticonderoga, N.Y., 639–640
Tidioute, Pa., 858
Tiedemann, H. O., 1075
Tilsonburg, Ont., Canada, 1074.2
Tilton, N.H., 496
Tinker, _____,
    see Root & Tinker
Tionesta, Pa., 859–859.1
Titusville, Pa., 860–861
Toledo, Ohio, 710

☆ U. S. GOVERNMENT PRINTING OFFICE: 1984 0-387-995: QL2